Neglected Links in Economics and Society

Dieter Bögenhold

Neglected Links in Economics and Society

Inequality, Organization, Work and Economic Methodology

palgrave
macmillan

Dieter Bögenhold
Faculty of Economics and Management
Department of Sociology
University of Klagenfurt
Klagenfurt, Austria

ISBN 978-3-030-79192-6 ISBN 978-3-030-79193-3 (eBook)
https://doi.org/10.1007/978-3-030-79193-3

This Palgrave Macmillan imprint is published by the registered company Springer Nature Switzerland AG.
The registered company address is: Gewerbestrasse 11, 6330 Cham, Switzerland

Preface

In March 2021 the Suez Canal evolved to become a firm address in world's top news in all media. The container cargo ship "Ever Given" was in such a position that it blocked all traffic through the channel. The ship could no longer be navigated and no other ship could pass the Suez. Hundreds of ships were in a waiting position on both ends of the channel and many further ships decided not to wait but to take the much longer way around the Cape of Good Hope on their route from Asia to Europe or vice versa. This singular event in the world of international cargo traffic may have looked like a mere maritime accident with simple international effects but it was much more: The blocking of ship traffic through the Suez Canal was unexpected and it has shown several unintended consequences. International routes of trade and exchange have been revealed as being extremely weak and vulnerable in view of the system of the world economy. Production, trade, and transport are parts of international cooperation and working relations which are designed as just-in-time processes where everything is a little cog in a big wheel. And, if one element is not working properly anymore, the whole system of economic and social interaction comes crashing to a halt. The stranding of the "Ever Given" led to serious problems in international supply chains and to problems in production processes of many small, medium, large, and multinational biggest companies in Asia and in Europe. Even car factories were in danger of not being able to deliver newly manufactured cars since single supply elements were missing, harbors in central Western economies could not work effectively anymore, and customers and households had to wait for various goods which they were used to receiving on a daily basis. These surprising and non-intended consequences of particular events and calamities give a wonderful example of the dynamic interrelations of the modern world economy where all parts of the world are related to each other, and one element can affect many others and vice versa. The world society and the world economy must be viewed as complex systems of reciprocal interactions.

Having received such broad attention in the daily media, the "Ever Given" event is rapidly becoming a teaching case in the history of learning effects in civil societies, showing complexities and underlining the need for thinking in interdisciplinary relations and trying to link causes and effects in relations that continuously form anew. What is more, the case serves to illustrate the need to think in terms of interlaced spheres, and highlights the necessity to identify and understand the limits of mono-disciplinary approaches. If everything affects everything, no single academic take in the classic nature of the division of specific academic domains and their limited competencies can satisfy anymore. On the contrary, contemporaries must increasingly acknowledge "Neglected Links" in economy, society, and in social sciences, especially in economics, sociology and history, to demonstrate complexities of the social and physical world, the link to interdependencies of international cooperation and the fragility and vulnerability of global supply chains and, of course, the limitations of our intellectual order of thought often ignores the need for thinking out of the box.

The topic of this book continues a line of thought which the author has recently provided together with Farah Naz in our book "*Unheard Voices*" (Naz & Bögenhold, 2020). In this book, the authors have shown how production processes in a developing country in a specific region are related to Western companies and daily-life consumption processes of customers who care little about the production processes of goods being produced in distant regions of different continents. In a wider sense, the authors follow a much more general question by taking the local observations and evaluations as an example of general mechanisms of one and the same global world system of capitalism. In fact, one has to take the singularity of cases to show universal principles of global divisions of work. Having this in mind, the book delivers a portrait of modern capitalism by focusing an intensive spotlight on the particular phenomena of recent economic societies in order to highlight very general mechanisms behind those phenomena. As a consequence, the study tells a fascinating story about the political economy of the world society and offers a critique of the political economy simultaneously.

The linkage between economy and society is a well-known slogan which we have learned to use at least since the writings of Max Weber at the beginning of the twentieth century. However, as convincing as it is that economy and society are interwoven and despite the permanent credo for interdisciplinarity, academic practices of everyday life are organized in a quasi-autistic way, where differentiation and separation dominate over cooperation and exchange processes. Links are almost entirely neglected although it is a matter of fact that the global world society can only be thought of and conceptualized with the multidimensional and reciprocal relations and interactions, especially in the digital age.

"Neglected Links", however, is at a different level with another focus. Here, discussion centers on the academic bonds of arguments and inner principles of thought which govern political economy, sociology, economics and social sciences in general. One must always ask about the inner bonds of different academic domains and relate their different fragments to each other in order to arrive at a more adequate picture and understanding of the complex world system with its world society and inherent world economy. Processes of globalization can only be seen and analysed through multiple lenses which combine approaches of different disciplines. To give an example, business administration or mainstream economics usually acknowledge only work, capital, and finance. What is neglected is the fact that those issues hardly work well or at all, if we do not take further soft dimensions into account, such as social networks and forms of trust and distrust, family systems which are effective even across national borders, communication patterns including media structures, systems of religious belief and patterns of life-styles in general. The book tries to include and combine such seemingly different topics as inequality, organization, work, and economic methodology to discuss common elements as one and the same story which are told in the different chapters.

No book should go without the acknowledgement of the support of, at the very least, a few persons who helped to bring it to its current form. Karen Meehan and Helen Heaney endeavored to polish the English of a first version to arrive at a more elaborated version, while Kornelia Maria Kanyo took on the proper production of figures. Finally, Wyndham Hacket

Pain (Palgrave Macmillan Publishers) invested trust and hope into the project, without which the book would hardly have come to print. Additionally, anonymous reviewers gave helpful comments on an initial book draft. Last but not least, two chapters in this book were produced jointly with co-authors and I am very grateful for having worked with these colleagues.

Klagenfurt, Austria
April 2021

Dieter Bögenhold

Reference

Naz, F., & Bögenhold, D. (2020). *Unheard Voices. Women, Work and Political Economy of Global Production*. London: Palgrave Macmillan Publishers.

Contents

List of Figures

CHAPTER 1

Neglected Links and the Idea of an Inner Bond of Different Academic Domains

Introduction

This book deals with *Neglected Links* in economics, sociology, and society. Those neglected links are the inner bonds and lines that keep the spheres of society and economy together and that are interconnected, although they are very often treated and discussed separately in different discourses. Contemporary discussion has forgotten to think universally and to integrate items into one common field of observation. Instead, too often, particular items are studied and discussed as being independent of each other without acknowledging a broader context. The book gives exemplary instructions on how to treat reciprocal links and how to work in an interdisciplinary way, which tackles history, sociology, and economics at the very least. By doing this, the book can also serve as educational instruction for doing integrative and interdisciplinary science instead of recapitulating monodisciplinary approaches.

The book assembles essays from a variety of domains, all under the shared umbrella of 'neglected links', covering social and economic inequality research, limits of rationality, and orthodoxies and heterodoxies of economic research, as well as a discussion of the heroes of interdisciplinary thought. The 'Big Three in Economics', namely, Adam Smith, Karl Marx, and John Maynard Keynes, to echo with Mark Skousen (2015), always practiced a decidedly universal approach when doing economics, which included, besides economics, also moral, social, and political lenses and

D. Bögenhold, *Neglected Links in Economics and Society*,
https://doi.org/10.1007/978-3-030-79193-3_1

issues. Economics has lost history (Hodgson, 2001) but also links to sociology and psychology with which it was originally closely connected at the beginning of the twentieth century. Much of discussion in the twentieth century became rather silent with regard to forging and maintaining links between different academic domains. The explicit acknowledgment and pointing out of links between individual academic domains and their subjects has been forgotten. This was the general and true case that we have come to know during extended periods of the twentieth century and up until the contemporary discussion. Too often, particular items are studied and discussed as being independent of each other without acknowledging the existence of a broader context.

Instead, we should take up the challenge to investigate the reciprocal links, asking how to work in interdisciplinary settings that address the relationship between history, sociology, and economics. Due to increasing specialization and differentiation, economics, sociology, psychology, and history started to evolve together with their own research profiles and clear borders of reciprocal demarcation (Cedrini & Fontana, 2017). Yet, leading representatives of economics (Akerlof, 2007, 2020) have realized that topics must be included that are in the core competency of sociology but of mutual interest for the other disciplines, such as social norms and their evolution, the formation of preferences and social priorities, social networks and (dis)trust, family and kinship patterns, clan behavior, power of religions, happiness, well-being and capabilities, or social and economic inequalities.

The question of academic convergences within scientific development, on the one side, and separate tracks and differentiations, on the other side, shall be discussed systematically. Those items refer to a need for interdisciplinary cooperation to arrive at a satisfying and more adequate take. It is evident that economics has changed gradually by embracing an increased social-scientification (Bögenhold, 2018) during the last 25 years, but many questions are still unresolved and the true direction of the academic future remains in darkness. Social science is always related to a study of societies (Hunt & Colander, 2011). In order to understand the working of economies, one has to start by studying societies, because economies never take place in a vacuum, but rather they are always embedded in a societal context.

The process of growing academic fragmentation, which we can observe continuously, generates new islands of academic activity and knowledge, while bridges between these islands often remain nonexistent or invisible.

Ultimately, academic development in the twentieth century may be classified as a process of ongoing vulcanization within the landscape of economic and social sciences. The aim of the research at hand is to indicate new bridges in order to (re-)open the social sciences (Wallerstein et al., 1996).

Thus, the questions on the agenda do not merely involve a science-related discussion on the nature of academic fields with no real evidence in the material world, for this world in which we are living is full of practical examples of things that are interdependent and linked to each other. Our modern world has become highly digitalized and 'just-in-time' in terms of its design, with one cogwheel meshing so tightly with the next that problems in logistics ultimately affect completely different spheres in the economy and society, or the evolution of new viruses leads to new diseases that can bring the world economy to a standstill. One cause may have consequences in more than one other field, which mirrors the complexity of the world economy as a world society. We are living in a dynamic world including different dimensions of uncertainty that make up different degrees of uncertainty, constantly leading to effects that defy prediction. The sociologist Robert Merton (1936) spoke about the issue of unintended consequences and the economist Friedrich Hayek (1969) used the term of spontaneous order, which is "the result of human actions, not of human design" (Hayek, 1969, p. 97) and which leads in consequence to evermore new forms of organizations, market processes, and market structures (see Vanberg, 1986). In other words, we have to search for the inner bonds between different academic knowledge domains in order to arrive at a more holistic and comprehensive understanding of diverse phenomena in business and society.

In practice, the economy and economic processes never take place in a void and thus they do not only recognize the analytical categories of labor, capital, and technology, but they also acknowledge institutional arrangements in defined times and spaces. Economic processes invariably take place in an economic space *in concreto*, which, unlike economic spaces *in abstracto*, is always bound by specific coordinates of time and space. With their respective specificities, these shape the concrete economic conditions. This coincides with the notion that economic activity is always shaped by a particular culture, which exhibits socio-spatial-temporal characteristics and conveys a set of norms and global value orientations. These values are correlated with certain patterns of social institutions (language, religion, family and kinship systems, educational systems, training regulations, systems of trust and distrust).

If Culture Matters, then Sociology Matters

Taken together, all of these determine the conjunction of economy and society, as was made especially clear in the works of Max Weber and Werner Sombart, when they spoke of economic attitudes and economic mentalities. This involves the task of communicating economic phenomena and the associated dynamics of change with the question of culturally mediated dispositions of action. The institutional integration of economic realities corresponds with the level of recognition of the impact of culture within the process of economic development and the acceptance of its relative autonomy. Accordingly, when we hear the question *Does Culture Matter?* (Harrison & Huntington, 2000), then at least two different aspects are being addressed: First, can and should we recognize in an analytical sense that cultural factors play a role in the measurement and explanation of economic events and in the practice of economics in a global context? Second, if we concede that culture should be regarded, at least in part, as an influencing variable, then we must subsequently examine how and to what extent this happens. In other words, the issue at hand is *How does Culture Matter?* (Sen, 2004).

If we start by affirming the question 'Does Culture Matter?', then this immediately constitutes a counter-program to a materialistic approach, which is represented by neoclassical and Marxist views in equal measure. For it is at this point that the supposition comes into play that economic activity does not take place in a vacuum, that is, devoid of history and spatial coordinates, but instead always occurs in specific social contexts.

The acceptance of the efficacy of culture as a complex of standards, values, and social institutions implies that there are no autonomous economies and economic cycles, but, rather, in reality they are always integrated into society. This suggests the relevance of a 'social system of production'. If 'culture matters', the immediate conclusion to be drawn from this is that 'sociology matters'.

This yields a rule of three, according to which the economy cannot be adequately measured in analytical terms in the absence of society, and thus social dimensions must inevitably be included as explanatory variables. If indeed culture interacts with economic development in such a way, it follows that the concert of academic disciplines must also embrace domains that fall beyond the narrow canon of economics along with their core competencies. These include, for example, economic and social history, sociology, (economic) psychology, organizational and administrative sciences, religious studies, communication and media studies, and corresponding interdisciplinary fields such as network and family research, to name just a few among the areas of application. What emerges is the inevitable necessity to study subject areas that are seemingly not directly related to the subject of economics, but which are nevertheless highly relevant to the topic.

Thus, in order to arrive at a better understanding of the social elements integrated into the social system of production, it is necessary to (additionally) examine and analyze noneconomic phenomena, which at first appear fairly distant and thematically separate from the economic question itself. The 'great' economists of the twentieth century already practiced this kind of approach as a matter of course (Bögenhold, 2009): Keynes, for instance, explained that the reader "feels that this general, philosophical disquisition on the behavior of mankind is somewhat remote from the economic theory under discussion" (Keynes, 1937, p. 209). In common with sociologists Max Weber and Werner Sombart, Keynes attributed the development of economic trends in either one direction or another to prevailing moods and economic attitudes in society. The partly instinctive 'feeling about money' is the mainspring of many economic processes, "it operates, so to speak, at a deeper level of our motivation" (Keynes, 1937, p. 216). In fact, Keynes makes mention of 'animal spirits' (instinctive behavior) that economic agents may display.

The term 'animal spirits' refers to behavior that cannot be predicted *a priori* or represented in models, and that is not measured against classical ideas of familiar rationality. The degree to which people (do not) spend money serves as a barometer of confidence and mistrust with regard to economic development, and is based on assessments that are inevitably accompanied by varying levels of uncertainty and represent different degrees of pessimism or optimism about the future. In this respect, theories of supply and demand always depend on a "psychology of society" (Keynes, 1937, p. 214), in which factors such as (in)security play a dominant role.

Like Keynes, Schumpeter also worked in an interdisciplinary manner, not only reflecting explicitly on methodology (Bögenhold, 2014), but also by exemplary application of interdisciplinarity in his studies on entrepreneurship. Entrepreneurial behavior is classified by Schumpeter as "irrational or of a different kind of rationalism". Hence, entrepreneurial conduct—in the Schumpeterian conceptualization—has much in common with certain components of the eroticism of success and of athletic competition (Schumpeter, 1963 [1934], pp. 93–94). Schumpeter introduces elements of motivation in business life, which are "the impulse to fight and to prove oneself superior to others" (Schumpeter, 1963 [1934], p. 93).

It is one of the *principal theses* of this book that this kind of academic view, as practiced vicariously by Schumpeter and Keynes, is becoming increasingly expedient in our modern world, given the backdrop of ever-increasing expressions of interconnectedness and complexity, including those associated with globalization. Two contradictory lines of development can be observed at this time: In the first instance, the practical arrangement of academic subjects and the organization of university teaching remain largely in the majority ownership of the disciplines as we are familiar with them from recent decades. As such, they are traditionally oriented to subject boundaries once drawn and to the definitions of responsibilities and competences that are thereby enforced, and whose narrow confines allow little room for cross-border academic synergies. *On the other hand,* we also have a number of globally distinguished experts who, often decorated with the Nobel Prize in Economic Sciences, are engaged in an innovative revitalization and reinterpretation of economics. They do this, sometimes approaching it from the vantage point of historical theory, at other times from psychology, law, or other specializations. These latter positions and their authors represent modern developments and reformulations of the economic theme; they have much in common with the elaborations of an integrative-holistic view of economic life, but without diffusing appreciably into the teaching of the 'here and now' at universities. Elsewhere, this same development has been labeled as increasing the 'social-scientification of economics' (Bögenhold, 2018). While traditional content is faithfully reproduced in textbooks, insiders and committees are busily determining what is new and innovative and are bestowing awards accordingly.

If we take Keynes' analytical perspective of moods (animal spirits) or Schumpeter's perspective of motives of prestige and of succeeding "for the sake, not for the fruits of success, but of success itself" (Schumpeter, 1963 [1934], p. 93), we invariably see that explanations pertaining to the relative functioning or nonfunctioning of elements of economic life are located *outside* the traditionally defined purview of economics.

If that is true—and herein lies the first key point of the considerations so far—it is only logical to conclude that academic *non*-economists may occasionally offer key analytical potential for economic policy issues and concepts, a potential that is denied to economists with their classical repertoire of analytical tools. What sounds very simple admittedly has a powerful disruptive impact on the traditional understanding of the distribution of academic and political roles and reciprocal collaboration. In that case, to use an example, the idea that economic policy and its decision makers (must) seek professional expertise from the field of economics may not necessarily be consistent; instead, one might consider whether demographers, sociologists, economic psychologists, economic historians, and other professionals might not be better suited to assessing and resolving economic and economic policy questions when it comes to evaluating certain issues.

Werner Sombart, one of the leading economists in the German-speaking world during the first two decades of the twentieth century, thus conceptualized economics as though it were, to an extent, subordinate to sociology. He argued, for instance, that sociology is the science of human coexistence. Logically, he argued, it follows that economics is sociology. He did, however, exclude economic *empiricism*, since the concept of sociology had to be limited to the theory of human coexistence. Finally, he concluded that economic sociology was thus synonymous with economic theory (Sombart, [1931] 1982, p. 216).

In the twenty-first century, such a statement, together with the corresponding reasoning with regard to the real power distributions, certainly seems to have fallen out of fashion. In large swathes of the social and economic world, economics claims the interpretative authority and definitional power in the discussion and interpretation of economic facts in everyday academic life. For this reason, there is some talk of a kind of *imperialism of economics*, which is candidly proclaimed in Lazear (2000): "The ascension of economics results from the fact that our discipline has a rigorous language that allows complicated concepts to be written in relatively simple, abstract terms. The language permits economists to strip away complexity. Complexity may add to the richness of description, but it also prevents the analyst from seeing what is essential" (Lazear, 2000, pp. 99–100). A similar view is taken by G. Becker (2010), who sees economics as a monodisciplinary 'supreme science'.

Granovetter (2017) writes that different social sciences are either *over*-socialized or *under*socialized with regard to the issue of human behavior.

In the case of the undersocialized models, scarcely any relative autonomy of social action is assumed *a priori*, that is, behavior is construed more or less as a reflex to external economic conditions, irrespective of what empirical findings suggest either one way or another. Conversely, in the oversocialized models, people appear as exclusively driven by norms and as if they were fully socialized and, in that sense, should be regarded merely as reflexes of their environment. It very quickly becomes clear that, both theoretically and empirically, the key to approaching reality must lie somewhere between the two extremes: This means that people are socialized and controlled by their environment, but only to a certain extent. Accordingly, social action, social change, and progress can only be adequately comprehended if, notwithstanding any contingencies, we can allow scope for the openness of development paths that are not determined from the outset. It makes good sense, therefore, to speak of the relative autonomy of development trajectories. The discussion on path dependencies (David, 1985, 2007; Greener, 2002; Bergek & Onufrey, 2014) demonstrates compellingly that it is easy in retrospect to show previous periods of status quo, but it is difficult to forecast future developments with regard to their relative openness.

The question of the significance of culture in the context of economic development can be considered in an analogous way. Economics *in concreto* inevitably bears a proximity to culturalist considerations. Yet, this does not reveal anything about culture's degree of determination. "The acknowledgment of the importance of culture cannot be instantly translated into ready-made theories of cultural causation. It is evidently too easy to jump from the frying pan of neglecting culture into the fire of crude cultural determinism" (Sen, 2004, p. 55). Culture cannot be thought of as separated from a variety of other dimensions of social and economic life; therefore, culture serves as a kind of proxy for dimensions that are exogenous to the pure economic forces. "If culture is recognized to be nonhomogeneous, nonstatic, and interactive, and if the importance of culture is integrated with rival sources of influence, then culture can be a very positive and constructive part in our understanding of human behavior and of social and economic development" (Sen, 2004, p. 44). Sen, who received the Nobel Prize in Economic Sciences in 1998, observed: "Sociologists, anthropologists, and historians have often commented on the tendency of economists to pay inadequate attention to culture in investigating the operation of societies in general and the process of development in particular" (Sen, 2004, p. 37).

Economic activities can be analyzed at different levels, from local and household-centered levels over regional to national levels and finally to international or global dimensions. Economist and Nobel laureate (1987) Robert M. Solow has already pointed out what many graduate students of economics do not find in their textbooks: "All narrowly economic activity is embedded in a web of social institutions, customs, beliefs, and attitudes.... Few things should be more interesting to a civilized economic theorist than the opportunity to observe the interplay between social institutions and economic behavior over time and place" (Solow, 1985, pp. 328–329). This statement illustrates the need to think in an integrated perspective, combining different academic fields of knowledge.

There has been a heightened awareness, especially in the last two decades, of the progressive fragmentation and parceling of the scientific cosmos and the attendant problems. Increasingly, scholars are recognizing that the landscape of academic knowledge has become ever-more vulcanized and that bridges allowing mutual integration and communication are lacking. Of course, as social development has become more complex, the various units of society have become increasingly interdependent: Changes in one area trigger changes in others and *vice versa*. In its report, the *Gulbenkian Commission for the Restructuring of Social-Sciences* (Wallerstein et al., 1996) concluded almost 20 years ago that processes of mutual reintegration must be initiated to counteract a subject autism that ignores developments in neighboring subjects and excludes synergy effects. That is also why it is said that all relevant knowledge today should be translated from monodisciplinary knowledge silos into transdisciplinary contexts.

The term of heterodox economics has been around at the very least since the beginning of the twentieth century, but what was a practiced coexistence of approaches in earlier decades has come to be understood more as a deliberate academic counter-program in more recent years (Bögenhold, 2010). The same can be said for the *new* institutionalism in economics, which—by its choice of words alone—can certainly be viewed in the tradition of the *older* institutionalism of the final quarter of the nineteenth and the beginning of the twentieth centuries. Even today, the *Journal of Economic Literature* Code (JEL Code) lists the two abbreviations OIE and NIE as self-explanatory abbreviations for *Old* and *New Institutional Economics*. Institutionalist approaches—*nomen est omen*—focus heavily on the relevance of institutions such as the legal system, the cultural context, and the temporal and spatial specificities within which economic systems are embedded (North, 1990, 1991).

The simple juxtaposition of mainstream economics and heterodox economics (Komlos, 2014) seems in some ways too schematic and too crude, given that the substance, and thus the terrain, of mainstream economics is also constantly changing (Hodgson, 2007). In this respect, mutual diffusion exists in economics between these so-called two 'economics', which are constantly shifting and overlapping. Scientific progress in the social sciences is entirely different from, for example, that in physics, where groundbreaking inventions leading to new paradigms are much more likely to occur (Collins, 1994). In the social sciences, changes will always occur through protracted processes of mutual interactions, corrections, and shifting levels in the context of path dependencies, that is to say, in the context of what marks the state of thought and discussion at any given time. In this respect, scientific progress is most probably a change in the sense of the (partial) overwriting of traditional stocks of knowledge.

Admittedly, sociology also features various strands of reasoning that deliberately disregard the results of academic differentiation and segmentation. Luhmann's concept of the "economy of society" (Luhmann, 1988), in which the economy is conceptualized as a subsystem of society, is a programmatic representation of this. But similarly, the 'new economic sociology' in the North American style is less and less content with the status quo that has been achieved so far, and is pursuing new efforts in diverse disciplines such as social economics, network analysis, historical sociology, and research with inter- and intranational comparisons of social, economic, and employment structures embedded in different cultures (Bögenhold, 2010). Taken together, this serves to demonstrate that the structure of the specialist divisions is in a state of flux and, in some cases, is moving perceptibly toward partial reintegration.

The twenty-first century looks back on this scientific period of development, differentiation, and consolidation of the social sciences that took place over the course of the twentieth century. It seems, however, that we are now in a historical situation in which we can take stock of previous developments, reassess potentials, and discover and assess future paths with a view to innovation opportunities. When we discuss the relationship of society to the economy and vice versa, we necessarily also discuss the relationship of sociology to the economic sciences. When we do this, it instantly becomes apparent how difficult it is to even speak about the objects and their boundaries in their unified totality.

Not only sociology but also economics and other social sciences are remarkable because of the sheer breadth of content they have achieved so far. This entails that there is now a plurality of subject designations and specializations in each designated subject that act like specialized subjects within a subject. They are platforms upon which careers are built, publications and conferences are held, and communication in general takes place. Set against the manifold differentiations within the conventional subjects it can be noted, in turn, that the borders between subjects are becoming blurred, sometimes overlapping or coalescing (Fig. 1.1).

The troika of economics, sociology, and political sciences (Ostrom & Ahn, 2009), which should be extended to a quartet by the addition of history, at least illuminates the inner bond of social sciences. The reciprocal integration of economy, society, and culture (Granovetter, 2017) and the increasingly visible overlapping of psychology, history, sociology, and economics must be better acknowledged in academic reflections of a science of science so that disciplinary authorities will be defined accordingly.

The punch line here is that today's economics graduates are more likely to demonstrate excellence in the application of mathematical procedures, the use of statistics, and sophisticated computer simulations than in the history of the development of their own discipline. While in mathematics the mastery of simple multiplication is the basis for the mastery of compound multiplication, it seems that in contemporary economics the elementary developmental stages of the history of economic ideas can be skipped: When one asks today's modern economists how many texts they have read by authors like Menger, Marshall, Keynes, Schumpeter, or Hayek, they will come up with a number that rarely exceeds zero.

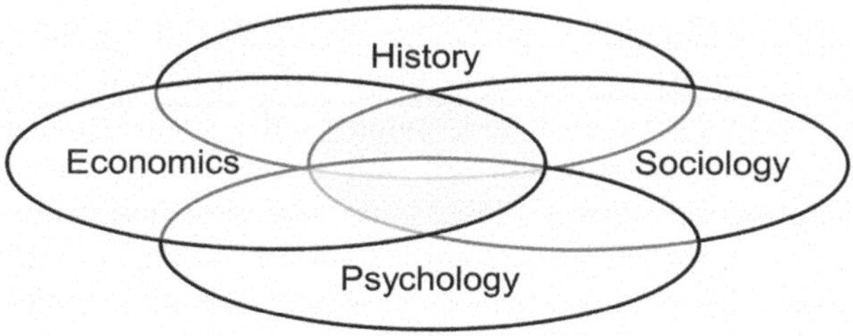

Fig. 1.1 Fields of tension and cooperation between economics, sociology, history, and psychology. (Author's own representation)

To put it another way: “Recruitment and professional advancement are generally on the basis of technical competence, rather than knowledge of the real economy or of the evolution of economics as a discipline. This bias towards formalism has become deeply ingrained and institutionalized in the academy. It is compounded by the fragmentation of the profession into technical specialisms, often lacking the generalist background that enables communication and synthetic advance” (Hodgson, 2007, p. 19). It must be emphasized that statistics and mathematical procedures—a trend Romer (2015) called ‘mathiness’—are certainly valuable and indispensable for modern economics at the present elaborated level (McCloskey, 1987; Weintraub, 2002; Morgan, 2012; Hodgson, 2012). Yet instruments must not become ends in themselves, and data generation and analysis must (be able to) be related back to sophisticated theoretical questions.

The trend sketched above, which moved toward abstract formalism (Lachmann, 1950, 1975), served as the traction engine of the development period in the twentieth century. Neoclassicism in particular was based on three core assumptions, which were then subject to various forms of criticism and further development during the twentieth century: Firstly, there was the reduction of human activity to an ideal type of agent, which became widely known as *homo oeconomicus.* This agent is not differentiated by age, gender, country of birth, religious affiliation, etc., so that it appears unreal. Secondly, there was the premise that economic societies are characterized by information symmetries. In fact, the opposite is more likely to be the case, since people differ not only in terms of education through differentiated qualification profiles, but also because varying cognitive properties and information corridors form the very basis for entrepreneurial opportunities. Finally, the third premise of neoclassicism held that the economy is in a state of equilibrium. As a matter of fact, we have known ever since the work of Schumpeter, if not before, that capitalist economies are permanently in a dynamic process of disequilibrium. “The essential point to grasp is that in dealing with capitalism we are dealing with an evolutionary process. […] Capitalism, then, is by nature a form or method of economic change and not only never is but never can be stationary” (Schumpeter, 2003 [1942], p. 82). For example, Douglass North, recipient of the Nobel Prize in Economic Sciences in 1993 for his achievements in institutional economics, articulated the imperative on the part of economics to open up to neighboring disciplines, not only in the direction of sociology, but also in the direction of psychology and other cognitive sciences. In other words, one has to ask why people really do what they do rather than operating with assumptions.

Motivation and Cognition

Previously, we considered whether and how the 'culture factor' is responsible, both inter- and intranationally, for the fact that economic systems and the implementation of the economy differ in specific ways and, respectively, that the 'culture factor' is virtually the mirror image of these differences. This inevitably results in variations in the way people act, how they interact in economic life and—vice versa—what meaning they attach to life. In other words, this is a question about the rationality of action, about the degree to which action is reasonable, and about the standards that indicate the degree of reasonableness in the first place.

When economics conspicuously raises the question of motives, then this coincides perfectly with the subject matter that was first dealt with in detail in sociology by Max Weber in his theory of categories on the 'meaning' of social action (Weber, 1972, part I, chapter 1). Later on, it was addressed above all in phenomenology and the sociology of knowledge, with questions focusing explicitly on the structures of relevance of human action (Schutz, 1970; Berger & Luckmann, 1966). A comparison of natural with social sciences shows some principal differences: "It is up to the natural scientists to determine which sector of the universe of nature, which facts and events therein, and which aspects of such facts and events are topically and interpretationally relevant to their specific purpose. These facts and events are neither preselected nor preinterpreted; they do not reveal intrinsic relevance structures. Relevance is not inherent in nature as such, it is the result of the selective and interpretative activity of man within nature or observing nature. The facts, data, and events with which the natural scientist has to deal are just facts, data, and events within his observational field but this field does not 'mean' anything to the molecules, atoms, and electrons therein" (Schutz, 1962, p. 5).

Expressions of reason may differ according to diverse social logics within a society and between different societies, both in contemporary and historical societies. Philosophy has also dealt with this issue, and it was Karl Popper, most notably, who discussed the relativity of reason in great breadth and depth in the context of his critical rationalism (Popper, 1959).

In sociology, Max Weber was among the first authors to conceptualize different bases of influence that imbue social action with meaning. Cultural factors including religion and related dispositions are factors that, according to Max Weber, influence the rationality of social behavior. Thus, he developed a typology of social action based on different reasons for the legitimacy of action. These included traditional action (actions performed on the basis of tradition and cultural norms), affective social action (actions based directly on emotions), instrumental and purposeful social action ('purposive rationality'), and value-rational action ('value rationality'), where the ends determine the means. According to this typology, there is no single ideal type of rationality.

Thinking of rationality as a driver of social action, however, by no means implies that people can always decipher the individual elements of the forces by which they are governed and guided. "In the great majority of instances, real action proceeds in dull semi-conscious awareness of its 'intended meaning'. The agent 'senses' it vaguely rather than knowing it or 'achieving clarity about it'; in most cases, the agent acts instinctively or habitually. [...] In reality, truly effective, i.e. fully conscious and clear, meaningful action is only ever a borderline case" (Weber, 1972, p. 10). Sociology is well acquainted with the term 'habitus', which refers to deeply internalized routines of action that help to manage everyday life. In a sense, habitus is a savings measure, allowing us to carry out actions without the need to constantly establish and query a context of justification (Berger & Luckmann, 1966). Unlike the practice in sociology, psychology refers to the sphere of the subconscious that influences people's behavior without the actors being fully aware of it and without having full control over the decisions, as Sigmund Freud (Freud, 2014) first explained. In looking at preferences in combination with lifestyles, needs, and behaviors, it was the social psychologist Maslow (1954) who developed a diagram of different tiers that set specific goals for human behavior, which he ranked into the shape of a pyramid.

The famous formulation of bounded rationality goes back to Herbert Simon, who received the Nobel Prize in Economic Sciences in 1978, and whose work has contributed decisively to decision theory. The term has evolved to become a kind of program for diverse arguments against the neoclassical conception of a *homo oeconomicus*. Simon conducted theoretical studies as well as producing empirical works and he was one of the first to use large datasets with the aid of computer simulations (Bögenhold, 2016). He is regarded as an important author from the academic angles of philosophy, psychology, organization theory, and economics. His principal matter of investigation may be described by the following question:

"How do human beings reason when the conditions for rationality postulated by neoclassical economics are not met?" (Simon, 1989, p. 377). The term of bounded rationality takes into account that (1) agents often act in ways that could be characterized as nonrational behavior driven by emotions; (2) the use of bounded rationality emphasizes that the access to information is limited, since people do not share the same bits of information necessary for deciding among the alternatives in order to achieve the optimal result; (3) even in a situation of equally shared information, human beings are characterized by cognitively diverse and also limited skills in evaluating the single best solution in any given situation with the information provided.

Discussing Simon and his famous formulation of a bounded rationality establishes Simon as an important milestone within the context of the history of economic theory. Since then, several authors have taken up ideas by Simon in order to modify or generalize them. In economics, it was especially the psychologist Daniel Kahneman (2003, 2012), recipient of the Nobel Prize in Economic Sciences in 2002, who conducted further pioneering work on bounded rationality. According to Kahneman, social action must be interpreted as a kind of choice between alternatives and, therefore, social action is difficult to forecast since human beings often act intuitively and are driven by emotions: "The central characteristic of agents is not that they reason poorly but that they act intuitively. And the behavior of these agents is not guided by what they are able to compute but by what they happen to see at a given moment" (Kahneman 2003, p. 1469). In sociology, specifically, the work of Jon Elster (1983, 1999) focuses on emotions and issues of rationality. Though the word 'rational' stands for the adjective 'reasonable' in the vernacular, it has a different connotation for economists and decision theorists (Kahneman, 2012, p. 411).

The point Kahneman seeks to emphasize here, namely, that it is the consistency of systems of interpretation that matters and that employing terms of irrationality can be problematic, had long before been highlighted by Ludwig von Mises (1933). In his praxeology, the latter criticized Max Weber's typification of social action, with Mises arguing that the types postulated by Weber were highly diffuse in practice and that different ferments of social action overlapped one another. Furthermore, Mises objected to the term 'rational action', which he understands as an instrument of value judgment.

Nobel laureates Akerlof and Shiller (2009) subsequently also posited that economics is insufficiently active with respect to a pertinent emphasis on and consideration of questions of motivation of human action and the inherent analysis of these factors. It has been argued time and again that economics needs to be more interested in opening up toward behavioral and cognitive approaches (Akerlof, 2007; Akerlof & Kranton, 2000; Akerlof & Shiller, 2009) in order to drive the trend of economics from a world of ideas based on abstract modeling toward more realistic perceptions. These voices have turned into a ringing credo of the 'new economics'.

All of these shifts toward a stronger acknowledgment of motivation in macroeconomics are not only connected with an emphasis on behavioral aspects but also with the need to consider sociological competencies: "Sociology has a further concept that gives an easy and natural way to add those norms to the utility function. Sociologists say that people have an ideal for how they should or should not behave. Furthermore, that ideal is often conceptualized in terms of the behavior of someone they know, or some exemplar whom they do not know" (Akerlof, 2007, p. 10). It is especially the social context seen by Akerlof (2007) that gives a frame to social action and its learning processes. Last but not least, religion is also considered to be one of the tools to socialize individual's economic behavior: "Sociology is dense in examples of people's views as to how they and others should behave, their joy when they live up to those standards, and their discomfort and reactions when they fail to do so" (Akerlof, 2007, p. 10). Acknowledging sociology helps to understand consumption processes, including their inherent preferences for choices that are sometimes hidden but almost always in contrast to those abstract utility functions as used in economics. In other words, "[s]ociology gives motivations for consumption that are very different from the reasons for it in the life-cycle model" (Akerlof, 2007, p. 15). In the wording of Bowles (1998), consumption practices are based upon endogenous preferences that are socially learned and not part of the human DNA.

It is remarkable that Akerlof not only refers to the relevance of social norms but also to sociology as a pertinent academic discipline in general to deal adequately with social behavior. Here, in fact, we see the opposite of Nobel laureate Becker's imperialism, which tries to operationalize behavior and every form of social activity in categories of utility maximization. Akerlof (2007) discusses sociologists like Goffman and Bourdieu as if no border existed between economics and sociology. He clearly acknowledges that which sociologist DiMaggio (1994) had expressed earlier, namely, "the starting point of any discussion of life styles and consumption patterns must be the work of Thorstein Veblen and Pierre Bourdieu" (DiMaggio, 1994, p. 458).

Following Akerlof's (2020) argumentation, we should be much more liberal and tolerant and much less apodictic toward the question as to the right way of doing economics: Too often those ways have changed, too random is that matter that is just at the forefront of truth and power of definition and too visible are the visible shortcomings and misconceptions in economics, which show time and again that economics is far from being a hard science like physics. Akerlof writes: "The norms regarding how economics should be done should call for flexibility of methodology—instead of insistence on methodological purity that might be perfect for some important problems, but leaves other problems and other approaches outside the domain of economic research. Historically, those paradigms—norms for how economic research should be done, and also for what constitutes 'economic research'—have developed out of an evolutionary process" (Akerlof, 2020, p. 416). The coronavirus pandemic and its unpredictable and disastrous effects on the world economy coupled with the obvious interdisciplinary and global interrelations have revealed our limited powers to forecast and explain developments when small unknown issues enter the stage because they were excluded from initial calculations. The same admission of failure happened with the global economic crisis in 2007–2008, which was, in itself, the same plea to open up social sciences in order to arrive at a discussion and theoretical orchestration that is more adequate.

The reciprocal integration of economy, society, and culture, and the increasingly visible overlapping of psychology, history, sociology, and economics must be better acknowledged in academic reflections of a science of science so that disciplinary authorities will be defined accordingly. Of course, there are also immanent consequences for public funding and political decisions regarding the use of research money, which are always shifting and in a continuous and historically changing battle over public funding (Solovey, 2020). Social-scienciation is an ongoing process that we can acknowledge in diverse examples in economics and that has serious implications for a new division of the academic landscape.

Neglected Links: A Plea for Cross-disciplinary Settings and References to Complexities

Akerlof also referred to cultural contexts that entail different cultural norms (Akerlof, 2007, p. 10), which, in turn, broaden the discussion to include the issue of culture. Cultures along with their corresponding times and spaces—and this brings us full circle to the discussion introduced at the beginning—bring with them different considerations of individual rationality. Culture can be seen as an analytical variable that is indicative of different constellations of norms and corresponding behavior (North, 1990; Jones, 2006). Accordingly, culture operates as a framework of and for behavior and is a factor that represents real—as opposed to abstract—economies and societies. The historian David Landes succinctly summed up this kind of statement as follows: "Culture makes almost all the difference" (Landes, 2000, p. 2). Assuming this to be true, then one conclusion must be that not merely sociology but also historical science are vitally important for the adequate examination of socioeconomic processes. Economic historians consistently stress the tremendous importance of "cultural factors in economic growth" (Cochran, 1960) and, following on from this, conclude that the "really fundamental problems of economic growth are non-economic" (Buchanan & Ellis, 1955, p. 405).

Although, in the view of Sombart, theory is the prerequisite to any scientific writing of history. Postulating "no theory—no history!" (Sombart, 1929, p. 3), he warned, on the other hand, against doing theory without history: "The economic theorist moved in an unreal, abstract world. He concentrated his attention upon the exchange operations of 'economic men.' He failed to reap the abundant harvest offered by the manifold variety of actual life, and thus deprived the economic historian of indispensable material" (Sombart, 1929, p. 8).

The Covid-19 virus pandemic, which arose in early 2020 and which started in the city of Wuhan in the People's Republic of China, demonstrates very well how fragile and interdependent the global world system is. The virus rapidly spread over the whole globe, ignoring national borders and leading to a tremendous number of infected people of whom several hundred thousand have died. The virus brought the entire world society and economy to a lock-down, a standstill, which has never happened in this way before. No single country proved to be immune against the evolution of the disease, and no country was successfully prepared and armed against the upcoming developments. People fell ill and died everywhere, and the whole traditional system of reasonable forecasting proved to be full of scientific flaws. The task of modeling economic, social, and environmental developments is always dependent upon the axiomatic input of model constructers. Complexity studies give us an idea about the manifold interrelations of actors and their different causes and effects so that one often does not really know where the beginning and the end of those processes of action and interaction are, since all too often the overall observation runs in systems of diverse individual elements of activity (Meyers, 2009).

A fuller consideration of the spatial and temporal coordinates (Ostrom, 2005) requires socioeconomic perceptions that are also reflected in discussions of path dependence (David, 2007). If we respect the topic of path dependence as an important research topic, then we must also respect the fact that real economies are shaped by concrete temporal and spatial coordinates (Ostrom, 2005; Acemoglu et al., 2005). One opportunity for sharpening the sociological profile lies in historicization. Concepts of path dependency must be read in this context of efforts toward dynamization. A further field of application in which such forms of historicity may be documented is that of historical network research. Network perspectives—no matter how finely calibrated—are capable of illustrating the continual 'in the making' of societies. This is one of the reasons why we can observe a growing attention to networks in historical research as well.

From the perspective of (economic) sociology, it is possible to address the criticism to the field of economics that the latter usually regards the institution of the market as a kind of black box in which supply and demand 'somehow' coincide and are negotiated. Sociology, meanwhile, has increasingly emphasized the fact that markets are also based on and represent highly social processes. Markets, in particular, are venues of social life and exchange with inherent social structures and sets of rules. To abstract from this implies an inadequate academic perception of the inner workings of one of the central institutions of economics. "Sociologists primarily view markets as institutions, while economists focus on the issue of price formation, mainly by constructing models. But even mainstream economics has not paid much attention to markets as institutions or as empirical phenomena [...]" (Swedberg, 2003, p. 130).

Taking into account the preambles of economic sociology provides a more appropriate way of examining the functioning of economies, in which structures appear as being permanently 'in the making'. Indeed, Granovetter's preambles delivered the inspiration for sociological work in various fields of application: (1) The pursuit of economic goals is usually accompanied by goals of a noneconomic nature, which include sociability, social recognition, status, and power. (2) Economic action (just like any other action) is socially situated and cannot be explained by individual motives alone; it is embedded in existing networks of personal relationships and is not carried out by atomized agents. Finally, (3) economic institutions (like all institutions) do not necessarily emerge in some automatic form due to external circumstances, but instead they are 'socially constructed' (Granovetter, 2017).

If we follow a consistent line of thought, this also means that the academic discussion must not be reduced to a narrow and sterile consideration of purely economic phenomena when gauging relevant economic and economic policy issues in the area of economic strengths. Rather, what is needed here is a focus on and inclusion of social soft factors, which have a significant influence on and contribute to economic activity and economic conditions in the real world. Economic research must inevitably encompass sociological institutional research, and that means it must perforce also engage with the academic field of sociology (still very relevant: Albert 1960). If we gather together these pointed remarks, a common denominator emerges to the effect that contemporary formulations of 'social embeddedness' (Granovetter, 1985) encompass the shared intersection of various academic disciplines. The concept of social embeddedness—which can be traced back to Polanyi (see Bögenhold, 2007)—is so popular that it was already described as 'economic sociology's most celebrated metaphor' as far back as 20 years ago (Guillén et al., 2002, p. 4). Recent works on the sociology of markets (Preda, 2009; Wherry, 2012; Aspers, 2013) must ultimately be seen on this tour of thought and argumentation.

Markets are in constant state of flux; they emerge, they disappear, they change. These markets and their potential are shaped and sustained by agents who, in turn, relate to specific constellations of people whom they trust or distrust. Thus, the 'social matter' of economic life is arranged along categories of trust, according to which those people who are denoted as friends stand over here and others are regarded as hostile competitors. Whatever shape concrete markets take, in each instance they exhibit highly social characteristics, and economics would fall short, if it ignored these issues. Processes of competition must be analyzed and interpreted as ongoing social processes that are embedded in social structures and that are engaged in a permanent process of (re)organization (White, 1988; Burt, 1995).

We may summarize here: (1) Times change, and with them the organization and the state of science. (2) That, which in the course of the twentieth century constituted the prolonged trend of differentiation of the individual sciences and the establishment of new academic branches of knowledge, is now beginning to move in another direction once again; we recognize imperatives of reintegration. (3) In contrast to an image that occasionally appears rather weak, sociology today holds hitherto unimagined potential, and it must properly acknowledge this potential itself, if it is to convince its contemporaries. (4) Increasingly, recent developments and proponents in economics are appropriating important insights from the fields of sociology and psychology, so that domains must be defended and reclaimed here as well. (5) In order to explain issues in the field of economics, social soft factors (communication, trust, social networks, and more general issues of culture and institutions) are gaining more and more importance, and these fall mainly into the domain of sociology.

This volume draws together previously published articles and unpublished papers on the wider topic of ***neglected links***. These were written by the author alone or in collaboration with coauthors, primarily over the space of the past two decades. Each of these essays can be read 'by itself', but all serve as exemplary contributions to the idea of an inner bond of different academic domains.

References

Acemoglu, D., Johnson, S., & Robinson, J. A. (2005). Institutions as a Fundamental Cause of Long-run Growth. In P. Agihon & S. N. Durlauf (Eds.), *Handbook of Economic Growth* (pp. 385–472). Elsevier.

Akerlof, G. A. (2007). The Missing Motivation in Macroeconomics. *The American Economic Review, 97*(1), 5–36.

Akerlof, G. A. (2020). Sins of Omission and the Practice of Economics. *Journal of Economic Literature, 58*(2), 405–418.

Akerlof, G. A., & Kranton, R. E. (2000). Economics and Identity. *The Quarterly Journal of Economics, 115*, 715–753.

Akerlof, G. A., & Shiller, R. J. (2009). *Animal Spirits: How Human Psychology Drives the Economy, and Why it Matters for Global Capitalism.* Princeton University Press.

Albert, H. (1960). Nationalökonomie als Soziologie. Zur sozialwissenschaftlichen Integrationsproblematik. *Kyklos, 13*(1), 1–43.

Aspers, P. (2013). *Markets.* Polity Press.

Becker, G. S. (2010). Economic Imperialism. *Religion & Liberty, 3*(2) https://www.acton.org/events
Bergek, A., & Onufrey, K. (2014). Is One Path Enough? Multiple Paths and Path Interaction as an Extension of Path Dependency Theory. *Industrial and Corporate Change, 23*(5), 1261–1297.
Berger, P. L., & Luckmann, T. (1966). *The Social Construction of Reality*. Doubleday.
Bögenhold, D. (2007). Polanyi. In R. E. Weir (Ed.), *Encyclopedia of American Social Class* (pp. 620–621). Greenwood Press.
Bögenhold, D. (2009). Die Psychologie im Wirtschaftsleben. Keynes und Schumpeter als Pioniere. In G., Raab & A. Unger (Eds.), *Der Mensch im Mittelpunkt wirtschaftlichen Handelns* (pp. 522–537). Pabst Science Publishers.
Bögenhold, D. (2010). From Heterodoxy to Orthodoxy and Vice Versa: Economics and Social Sciences in the Division of Academic Work. *American Journal of Economics and Sociology, 69*(5), 1566–1590.
Bögenhold, D. (2014). Schumpeter as a Universal Social Theorist. *The Atlantic Economic Journal, 42*, 205–215.
Bögenhold, D. (2016). Bounded Rationality. In G. Ritzer & C. Rojek (Eds.), *Encyclopedia of Sociology*. Blackwell. https://doi.org/10.1002/9781405165518.wbeos0787
Bögenhold, D. (2018). Economics between Insulation and Social-Scienciation: Observations by a Sociology of Economics. *Journal of Economic Issues, 52*(4), 1125–1142.
Bowles, S. (1998). Endogenous Preferences: The Cultural Consequences of Markets and other Economic Institutions. *Journal of Economic Literature, 36*(1), 75–111.
Buchanan, N. S., & Ellis, H. S. (1955). *Approaches to Economic Development*. Twentieth Century Fund.
Burt, R. S. (1995). *Structural Holes: The Social Structure of Competition*. Harvard University Press.
Cedrini, M., & Fontana, M. (2017). Just Another Niche in the Wall? How Specialization is Changing the Face of Economics. *Cambridge Journal of Economics, 42*(2), 427–451.
Cochran, T. C. (1960). Cultural Factors in Economic Growth. *Journal of Business History., 20*(4), 515–530.
Collins, R. (1994). Why the Social Sciences Won't become High-consensus, Rapid-discovery Science. *Sociological Forum, 9*, 155–177.
David, P. A. (1985). Clio and the Economics of QWERTY. *The American Economic Review, 75*(2), 332–337.
David, P. A. (2007). Path Dependence: A Foundational Concept for Historical Social Science. *Cliometrica, 1*(2), 91–114.

DiMaggio, P. (1994). Social Stratification, Life-style, and Social cognition. In D. B. Grusky (Ed.), *Social Stratification in Sociological Perspective. Race and Gender* (pp. 458–468). Westview Press.
Elster, J. (1983). *Sour Grapes*. Cambridge University Press.
Elster, J. (1999). *Alchemies of the Human Mind: Rationality and the Emotions*. Cambridge University Press.
Freud, S. (2014). *Abriß der Psychoanalyse*. Frankfurt a. M.: Fischer.
Granovetter, M. S. (1985). Economic Action and Social Structure: The Problem of Embeddedness. *The American Journal of Sociology, 91*, 481–510.
Granovetter, M. S. (2017). *Society and Economy: Framework and Principles*. The Belknap Press of Harvard University Press.
Greener, I. (2002). Theorising Path-dependency: How Does History Come to Matter in Organisations? *Management Decision, 40*(6), 614–619.
Guillén, M. F., Collins, R., England, P., & Meyer, M. (Eds.). (2002). *The New Economic Sociology. Developments in an Emerging Field*. Russell Sage Foundation.
Harrison, L. E., & Huntington, S. P. (Eds.). (2000). *Culture Matters. How Values Shape Human Progress*. Basic Books.
Hayek, F. A. (1969). *Studies in Philosophy, Politics and Economics*. Touchstone.
Hodgson, G. (2001). *How Economics Forget History*. Routledge.
Hodgson, G. (2007). Evolutionary and Institutional Economics as the New Mainstream? *Evolutionary and Institutional Economics Review, 4*(1), 7–25.
Hodgson, G. M. (2012). *Mathematics and Modern Economics*. Edward Elgar.
Hunt, E. F., & Colander, D. C. (2011). *Social Science. An Introduction to the Study of Society*. Allyn & Bacon.
Jones, E. L. (2006). *Cultures Merging. A Historical and Economic Critique of Culture*. Princeton University Press.
Kahneman, D. (2003). A Perspective on Judgment and Choice: Mapping Bounded Rationality. *American Psychologist, 58*(9), 697–720.
Kahneman, D. (2012). *Thinking, Fast and Slow*. Penguin.
Keynes, J. M. (1937). The General Theory of Employment. *The Quarterly Journal of Economics, 51*(2), 209–223.
Komlos, J. (2014). *What Every Economics Student Needs to Know and Doesn't Get in the Usual Principles Text*. M.E. Sharpe.
Lachmann, L. M. (1950). Economics as Social Science. *South African Journal of Economics, 18*, 233–241.
Lachmann, L. M. (1975). *Makroökonomischer Formalismus und die Marktwirtschaft*. J.C.B. Mohr.
Landes, D. (2000). Culture Makes almost all the Difference. In L. E. Harrison & S. P. Huntington (Eds.), *Culture Matters. How Values Shape Human Progress* (pp. 2–13). Basic Books.
Lazear, E. P. (2000). Economic Imperialism. *The Quarterly Journal of Economics, 115*(1), 99–14.

Luhmann, N. (1988). *Die Wirtschaft der Gesellschaft*. Suhrkamp.
Maslow, A. H. (1954). *Motivation and Personality*. Harper & Row.
McCloskey, D. (1987). *Econometric History*. Macmillan.
Merton, R. K. (1936). The Unanticipated Consequences of Purposive Social Action. *American Sociological Review, 1*(6), 894–904.
Meyers, R. A. (Ed.). (2009). *Encyclopedia of Complexity and Systems Science*. Springer.
Mises, L. v. (1933). *Grundprobleme der Nationalökonomie. Untersuchungen über Verfahren, Aufgaben und Inhalt der Wirtschafts- und Gesellschaftslehre*. Gustav Fischer.
Morgan, M. (2012). *The World in the Model: How Economists Work and Think*. Cambridge University Press.
North, D. C. (1990). *Institutions, Institutional Change and Economic Performance*. Cambridge University Press.
North, D. C. (1991). Institutions. *The Journal of Economic Perspectives, 5*(1), 97–112.
Ostrom, E. (2005). *Understanding Institutional Diversity*. Princeton University Press.
Ostrom, E., & Ahn, T.-K. (Eds.). (2009). *Handbook of Social Capital: The Troika of Sociology, Political Science and Economics*. Edward Elgar.
Popper, K. (1959). *The Logic of Scientific Discovery*. Routledge.
Preda, A. (2009). *Knowledge, Information, and Economic Life. An Introduction to the Sociology of Markets*. University Press.
Romer, P. M. (2015). Mathiness in the Theory of Economic Growth. *American Economic Review, 105*(5), 89–93.
Schumpeter, J. A. (1963 [1934]). *The Theory of Economic Development*. Oxford University Press.
Schumpeter, J. A. (2003 [1942]). *Capitalism, Socialism and Democracy*. Routledge.
Schutz, A. (1962, 1964, 1970). *Collected Papers, I, II, III*. The Hague, Boston, London: Nijhoff.
Sen, A. (2004). How Does Culture Matter? In V. Rao & M. Walton (Eds.), *Culture and Public Action* (pp. 37–58). Stanford University Press.
Simon, H. A. (1989). The Scientist as a Problem Solver. In D. Klahr & K. Kotowsky (Eds.), *Complex Information Processing. How do Human Beings Reason* (pp. 375–398). Erlbaum.
Skousen, M. (2015). *The Big Three in Economics. Adam Smith, Karl Marx, and John Maynard Keynes*. Taylor and Francis.
Solovey, M. (2020). *Social Science for What? Battles Over Public Funding for the Other Sciences at the National Science Foundation*. MIT Press.
Solow, R. M. (1985). Economic History and Economics. *Americam Economic Review, 75*(2), 328–331.

Sombart, W. (1929). Economic Theory and Economic History. *The Economic History Review, 2*(1), 1–19.
Sombart, W. (1982 [1931]). Wirtschaft. In A. Vierkandt (Ed.), *Handwörterbuch der Soziologie* (pp. 209–216). Enke.
Swedberg, R. (2003). Economic and Sociological Approaches to Markets. In R. Swedberg (Ed.), *Principles of Economic Sociology* (pp. 104–131). Princeton University Press.
Vanberg, V. (1986). Spontaneous Market Order and Social Rules: A Critical Examination of FA Hayek's Theory of Cultural Evolution. *Economics & Philosophy, 2*(1), 75–100.
Wallerstein, I., et al. (1996). *Open the Social Sciences. Report of the Gulbenkian Commission on the Restructuring of the Social Sciences.* Stanford University Press.
Weber, M. (1972). *Wirtschaft und Gesellschaft* [orig. 1921]. J.C.B. Mohr.
Weintraub, R. E. (2002). *How Economics Became a Mathematical Science.* Duke University Press.
Wherry, F. (2012). *The Culture of Markets.* Polity Press.
White, H. C. (1988). Varieties of Markets. In B. Wellman & S. D. Berkowitz (Eds.), *Social Structures: A Network Approach* (pp. 226–260). Cambridge University Press.

PART I

Social Inequality and Social Stratification

CHAPTER 2

Social Inequality and the Plurality of Lifestyles: Material and Cultural Aspects of Social Stratification

Introduction

Many people have argued that the semantics of class has lost its earlier attractiveness. The rising importance of dimensions such as age, gender, nationality, race, political attitudes, and the multitude of choices in organizing one's life course has rendered the debate about the concept of class obsolete. Some argue that the semantics of class no longer seems appropriate for analyzing and interpreting society. This perception is closely connected to the emergence of entirely new topics such as individualization and the plurality of lifestyles. My main thesis is that the currently expanding discussion on lifestyle is not necessarily a substitute but an important supplement to the tradition of social stratification research. What people "are" and what people "do" can no longer be conceptualized by a simple one-to-one-fit. The concept of lifestyle can provide a link between social rank and social practice. The logic of how people organize their leisure time and how they spend their income is not a simple mirror of income level but must be regarded as being embedded in social behavior.

Bögenhold, Dieter. Social Inequality and the Plurality of Life-Styles: Material and Cultural Aspects of Social Stratification, in: The American Journal of Economics and Sociology, Vol. 60, 2001, pp. 829–847.

D. Bögenhold, *Neglected Links in Economics and Society*,
https://doi.org/10.1007/978-3-030-79193-3_2

Social Stratification

The debate about the relevance of the concept of class is unresolved at the end of the twentieth century. The past 100 years have witnessed the establishment of a capitalist society that has, on balance, revealed a strong bond between creativity and destructiveness. This bond is a source of innovation and prosperity (Bögenhold, 1995). Average living standards within the population continuously improved during the twentieth century. Economic growth triumphed while average weekly working hours were reduced. One question about class concerned the social distribution of economic wealth among different population segments. The visibly increasing rise in disposable time that people won during this historical process and the rise in income that allowed them to develop new patterns of personal consumption and leisure activities, patterns of behavior that had already been revealed with a strange ambivalence by Riesman et al. (1950) during the middle of this century, are worth noting.

From a historical perspective, we see production and consumption constantly changing (Becher, 1980). This is reflected in a rapidly changing succession of topics in the history of economic and social thought (Stihler, 1998). Whereas Max Weber ([1905/1906] 1988) attributed the success of the industrial revolution to the Protestant ethic, our contemporary understanding of that success is different. Economy and society are increasingly dependent on the levels of effective consumer demand. A constant rise in the production of goods must find a market outlet (Camphell, 1987; Mason, 1998). If asceticism served as a foundation for the development of a capitalist economic system in Max Weber's world, then the connection between production and demand, that is the cycle of production, sale, and consumption, has in our understanding become the foundation for the modern economic society: No production without demand and vice versa.[1]

The enormous rise in productivity in European countries since the middle of the nineteenth century has led to changes in social and occupational structures as well. If more and more can be produced with less and less labor, then transport and trade will become more important. In Germany in 1882, for example, it was estimated that for every person in trade and transport there were nine laborers in the factories. By 1996, this ratio had been reduced to about 1 to 2.5 (Bögenhold, 1996: ch. V).

This development, among other things, makes the growing role of income distribution within economy even more important. In other words, the ratio between those who produce and those who transport and trade, administer and organize has changed. The reduction in working hours, along with a simultaneous rise in purchasing power in the long-term development, has supplied the social framework for new demands. We now speak about "entertainment" and "tourist" industries. Due to the rapid growth of social wealth, it is becoming ever-more interesting for sociologists to see how disposable time is used and how leisure practices relate to money income. The change in the context of economic and social structures has led to a continuous change in the ratio between blue collar workers and white collar workers. These changes have also influenced the expansion of the classical category of the working class (cf. Erikson & Goldthorpe, 1992 regarding their data for previous decades).

Max Weber described the Janus-faced nature of a formally "free" contract form of wage labor in his socio-legal observations: A contract that obeys the law of the most powerful on the labor market (Weber, 1972, Sec. VII). The process of continuing proletarianization and the accompanying development of an objectified world in an "iron cage" (Weber, 1988) must indeed be seen as one of the most important innovations of this century.[2]

In the history of social thought, many well-known positions on the issue of social stratification can be interpreted as a constant dialogue with the epochal Marxist theses. The works of authors such as Max Weber (1972), Emil Lederer (1912), Werner Sombart ([1927]1987), Theodor Geiger (1932, 1949), Ralf Dahrendorf (1959), Stanislaw Ossowski (1963), Goldthorpe et al. (1968), Anthony Giddens (1973), and Daniel Bell (1974) are cases in point. It was above all the dichotomous and bipolar division of society into blocks of uniform individuals (bourgeoisie and proletariat) that Götz Briefs described as "sweet simplicity" in his article "Proletariat" (Briefs, 1931, p. 458) at the beginning of the 1930s. This conception is too simplistic to characterize a society that is ever becoming more and more differentiated.

Regarding the analysis of social stratification in the twentieth century, it seems that the occupational and economic differentiations within society have become too complex to be able to reduce these distinctions to a single common denominator. Geiger referred to this problem in one of his later works, "Die Klassengesellschaft im Schmelztiegel" ("The Class Society in the Melting Pot") published in 1949. He expressed it as follows: "Everything seems to be gliding now, a clear definable structure is hardly to be found. However, certain tendencies toward a shift in class can be seen which lately seem to stretch right through the Marxist class ranks" (Geiger, 1949, p. 147). Geiger explicitly characterized this stratification that stretches straight through these Marxist class ranks as "horizontal stratification". This type of stratification is "first and foremost of the utmost socio-cultural importance" (p. 146).

Geiger's view of a "horizontal stratification" is the essence of the following considerations. My thesis is that Geiger's analysis was already conceptually drawn up by Georg Simmel ([1900] 1978), Thorstein Veblen (1899), and Max Weber ([1921] 1972). The present discussion on so-called individualization and pluralization that is popular in Germany has been built on this earlier literature and has not made reference to Geiger's work.[3]

The Analysis of Lifestyles

Contemporary discussion of the pluralization of lifestyles reflects the fact that the level of vertical differentiation in terms of financial resources has little to do with the level of cultural expression as a form of individual life practice. Ulrich Beck's (1992) book *Risk Society* holds the view that the evidence within life practice for bonding in a specific class constellation has disappeared. His opinion is that biographies are becoming even more "open". Societies that are becoming increasingly complex multiply the possible life courses of individuals and thus, due to institutional handicaps and handicaps in life-history, result in "kits for possible biographic combinations" (Beck, 1992, p. 217).

It is of utmost importance that the question of choice of lifestyles is connected to the diversification and individualization of life situation: The more distinct the autonomy becomes in reference to the use of time and money, the more open-ended does the question become in which concrete practice this use materializes. Benjamin Zablocki and Rosabeth Moss Kanter (1976) clearly pointed this out more than two decades ago. This is the perfect link to the discussion of lifestyles, which presently seems to be held with growing enthusiasm.

The concept of 'lifestyles' is often used in differing ways. In the Zapf et al. formulation (1987), for example, 'lifestyle' is a relatively stable pattern of organizing everyday life within the framework of a given life situation, taking account available resources. Different forms of organizing household work and employment, alternate patterns of consumption, varying living-patterns, how time is used, and even plans for the future with their specific planning contents and planning horizons are, on an empirical level, among the most important elements in constructing a life-style chart (Zapf et al., 1987, pp. 14–16).

Consequently, lifestyles reveal specific patterns with various components and a large range of influences that sociologists specializing in one thematic area and different academic disciplines have treated disparately. These studies include consumer research and market research, election polls, tourist polls, sociology of leisure-time and time itself, women's studies, household economics, urban and regional studies, education studies, biographic research studies, sociology of religion and family, to mention just a few. All of these research programs have their own empirical research traditions and have made contributions to the field of research known as 'lifestyle research'. Typologies for lifestyles already exist in each and every one of these fields of research (especially in the case of electoral poll research, market research, and research into leisure activities). However, for the most part these results tend to summarize a situation and are inadequate for sociological stratificationary research.

The central issue addressed by this chapter is what sociology of social structures can be linked to the topic of lifestyles. The central question may be phrased as follows: Is the analysis of lifestyles a useful 'extension' to the now largely accepted theory of individualization and does it offer an important contribution to a (better) understanding of social inequality? A principal benefit in lifestyle analysis (I shall anticipate the response in the form of a thesis) is that it appears to provide a cultural point of view that allows social heterogeneity to be linked to a cultural embedding in a historical life-form. Thus, a varied composition of differing patterns of life organization can be drawn in connection with vertical and horizontal disparities, adequately reflecting the complex network of distribution and relationships in contemporary structures of inequality.

Distribution and Status

The relationship between material 'possession' and its appropriate use in terms of a concrete cultural use of material resources was a topic in the sociological contemplations of the classic authors whose pioneering works do not always seem to gather the necessary attention today. The insights propounded by Georg Simmel, Max Weber, or even Thorstein Veblen, whose ideas developed in completely different contexts in styles of life, have not been systematically pursued and have been revived in connection with Bourdieu's sociocultural studies.

While Veblen pointed out the "conspicuous consumption" of the upper classes in his *Theory of the Leisure Class* (1899), Simmel was generally more interested in the outlines of the modern style of life in a time when society was not only experiencing cultural change but was also going through turbulent economic changes as well. For example, in Simmel's *The Philosophy of Money* (1978), he examined in detail this modern "style of life", which complicates human relationships. Complications are seen in the ever-increasing detachment in social circles and the replacement of traditional rhythms in social life by more complex forms as well as in an increase in the tempo in which society was changing. These distinctions in everyday culture can be seen in Simmel (1978) as a growing "multiplicity" of cultural styles that are forever changing. This led to Simmel's following definition of lifestyles:

> *Indeed, the mere existence of style is in itself one of the most significant instances of distancing. Style, as the manifestation of our inner feelings, indicates that these feelings no longer immediately gush out but take on a disguise the moment they are revealed. Style, as the general form of the particular, is a veil that imposes a barrier and a distance in relation to the recipient of the expression of these feelings.* (1978, p.473)

Weber also explored the concept of lifestyle. However, unlike Simmel, Weber did not pay any special attention to the term and it was not among the central definitions (Grunbegriffe) to be found in *Economy and Society* (Weber, 1972). Weber often used it synonymously with Lebensführung (life-conduct). The concept of lifestyle within the framework of his Protestant Ethics is mostly used as a caricature of the modern and "standardized free" way of living. References are to be found to class structures where "lifestyle" is expressed as being an expressively cultural moment in consumption and in social inclusion and exclusion of groups.[4]

Pierre Bourdieu's elaborations on the subject of "distinction" first appeared in France in 1979. It has had a lasting influence and inspiration on the current debate about lifestyles. Bourdieu's works can probably be described as being a sociology of culture based on Veblen and Simmel, influenced by Weber.[5]

Bourdieu sees the social world in terms of a metaphor: Consider a multidimensional social sphere in which different groups of actors reflect, on the one hand, the sphere of social position and, on the other hand, the sphere of lifestyles (see Swartz, 1997). Material distribution in the sense of different social positions is portrayed in one sphere, whereas in the other sphere the provisions of cultural resources are staked out and manifested in the form of varying lifestyles. He thereby places the "sphere of social positions" in analytical contrast to the "sphere of life styles." Of course, both of these spheres are virtually interlocked with one another.

However, Bourdieu did not leave it at that, but, what is more, used the concept of disposition as a central term. Life-requirements are strengthened by a process of institutionalization, which forms the actor's habitus. It is this disposition that is repeated by practice and reinforced by existing lifestyles. The connections between structure, habitus, and practice are to be seen as loose hinges. Differing forms of lifestyles are now rationalized by using the connection between disposition and practice. Finally, the effect of different lifestyles on a symbolic level is evaluated by means of "distinction."

Bourdieu's concept has an interesting effect when looking at social stratification and lifestyles, especially where Bourdieu has benefitted from Simmel's discussion. For example, directly linking his sociocultural analysis with a sociostructural dimension: If inequalities in a differentiated distribution struggle, or rather are no longer directly expressed by such struggle but are expressed or symbolized by distinctive practices, then Bourdieu's way of looking at this topic is a subject of current interest and relevance. Bourdieu (1979) has thus linked Weber's class observations with an empirical study in subtle representative areas such as holiday locations, house/flat furnishing, etc., studies that overall were based in France. Radically refined social inequalities can be portrayed as reflecting different styles of practice.

Of course, it does pose great difficulties to transpose this method onto another method of application without a lot of bother while also taking theoretical and empirical components into account. An oscillation between pure empiricism components, on the one hand, and grand theory, on the other hand, can be seen in the current discussion. We can reach an understanding for lifestyles on a general level by using Bourdieu's admittedly somewhat problematic concept of habitus. Correspondingly, lifestyles attain a sort of independent self-logic, so that in the end they are indeed a product of human action but do have their own objective independent existence as well—an independent existence that opposes other types of lifestyles designed by people themselves.

However, it is surprising that Bourdieu does not search for explicit links to establish academic forms of social network analysis (cf. Wellman, 1988; Zukin & DiMaggio, 1990; Burt, 1992; Scott, 1992; Wasserman & Faust, 1994), even though the relationship between Bourdieu's approach and social network analysis is a close one (Anheimer et al., 1995; Erickson, 1996). The cultural stratification analysis of society into forms of differing lifestyles is linked to communicative mechanisms of social closure. The ability of lifestyles to communicate is still treated symbolically. Style is stylized in order to present it to the public (Harris, 1996; Gronow, 1997; Bryson, 1996). Style is transformed by interpretative schemes and tastes into a construct of the social and object worlds and is, above all, defined by difference. With this in mind, communication and affiliation to certain social networks are based on the immediate level as sharing common signs.[6]

The current sociological discussion of lifestyles makes no reference to this classic sociologist. For this reason, I would now like to return to the central question treating the relationship between social stratification and lifestyles. The issue at question is whether the concept of lifestyles can become an addition to or a substitution for traditional research in social stratification. The debate between Clark and Lipset (1991), Hout et al. (1993), and Pakulski (1993) on the question of whether social classes are dying owes, above all, its origins to the fact that different concepts exist about what class or social class consists of. Ossowoski's old criticism (1963) of Marx, that in his work a gradual, functional, and dichotomic class scheme is found that is often practically jumbled up, is still the case today. Max Weber differentiates social classes in his class terminology by the terms *Erwerbsklassen* and *Besitzklassen*. However, one problem is that authors more often than not lean on one set definition of a particular author without being conscious of others' interpretations of the same definitions.

A basic question is: Is class just a descriptive category of distribution, or is it also part of a definite "class consciousness", no matter how defined; do we also require further information on forms of class mobility? Goldthorpe and Marshall, for example, supply a broadly interpreted concept:

> *Class analysis, in our sense, has as its central concern the study of relationships among class structures, class mobility, class-based inequalities and class-based action. More specifically, it explores the interconnections between positions defined by employment relations in labour markets and production units in*

> *different sectors of national economies; the processes through which individuals and families are distributed and redistributed among these positions over time; and the consequences thereof for their life-chances and for the social identities that they adopt and the social values and interest that they pursue.* (1992, p. 382)

However, such a far-reaching claim is in danger of not being realized in practical research. Aage Soerensen (1991) came to the conclusion in his discussion on the equally popular approach of John Goldthorpe and Erik Olin Wright that it is important to classify positions as a result of material processes of distribution within vertical stratification. However, both approaches, Goldthorpe's as well as Wright's, have missed the mark. Both remained on the level of descriptive analysis:

> *The two main uses of the concept of class in recent stratification research are Goldthorpe's analysis of mobility from a class formation perspective and Wright's analysis of income inequality generated in the labour market. The main problem with both efforts is that a satisfactory theory of how class generates inequality within the labour market is not available. In general, one does not need to identify positions as classes or in some other manner use class analysis to make use of the idea that positions are relevant.* (Soerensen, 1991, p. 83)

On balance, positions of social inequality can be differentiated and classified in the sense of social differences without having to rely on one of the various sociological connotations of class.[7] In one sense, class or rather class situation is just a result of the distribution processes in ongoing labor market processes. To use Luhmann's terms: class is the "distribution of division" (Luhmann, 1995, p. 129) and classes are heuristic classifications (see Rose & O'Reilly, 1997).

The degree to which contemporary societies are egalitarian is a question that must be researched empirically. Glancing at the differing empirical results within the German discussion, Mayer and Blossfeld (1990) claim that a trend toward a greater rigidity in social inequalities is evident and increasing. Blossfeld and Shavit (1993) showed in their evaluation of educational opportunities in 13 different countries that rapid educational expansion did not reduce inequalities of educational opportunities. They concluded:

> *As a consequence of educational expansion societies can produce a higher average level of educational attainment from one birth cohort to the next, without changing the educational opportunities of children from different social strata*

> *Thus, the modernization theorists' hypothesis that educational opportunities must be turned on its head: expansion actually facilitates to a large extent the persistence of inequalities in educational opportunity.* (1993, p. 22)

For more in the same direction, see most of the contributions in Shavit and Müller (1998).

If it is correct that the hierarchy of material inequality between people has remained relatively stable, then what is hiding behind the discussion of lifestyles? My argument is that this change in the discussion reflects the asymmetry between social situations that are conditioned by distribution, on the one hand, and by corresponding cognitive relevant structures among actors, on the other hand. This has not only resulted in a relative decoupling between locations on the vertical-material stratification scale and choice of behavior (Nieuwbeerta, 1995) but numerous patterns of consumption and leisure activities are also to be found that cannot be directly derived from positions on the stratification scale. A relative dissociation is to be found between social distribution structures. Increasing inequalities in industrial societies and growing unemployment in many contemporary societies do not necessarily lead to political action and unique class consciousness.

Clark and Lipset (1991) observed that "new forms of social stratification are emerging" (1991, p. 397). In fact, social reality seems to be becoming so increasingly diverse and complex that it has to be studied in a different way. There are new lines and topics of social conflict, new social movements have appeared, ethnic differences have become more obvious, as well as gender issues. If lifestyle research is the answer, what is the question? The question is to what extent should we take the cultural determination of life-forms beyond the material and/or structural survey of life-chances into account? It is a question of the relationship between life-chances and lifestyles.

Weber noticed this earlier noncongruence in distribution situations, cultural attitudes, and patterns of behavior when he distinguished "class" from "status." He wanted to convey that classification into classes represents one thing, and human social organizations and socialization represents something else. This early foundation for the discussion on lifestyles, which Simmel had formulated in broader terms, had already been integrated and taken into consideration by Weber. To quote Weber himself, "Classes can be divided according to their relationships to production how they acquire goods, 'status' according to the principle in which goods in the form of specific types of life styles are consumed" (Weber, 1972, p. 538, translated from the original German).

Lifestyle Research

Many features of lifestyle research still seem rather indefinite. The semantic delimitation of lifestyles compared with other categories such as mentalities, milieus or subcultures does not seem to exist. A greater part of the discussions on lifestyles is due to the discomfort with vertical stratification models. Since the forms of possession in vertical class situations are not inevitably transposed into the presumed corresponding sociological practice forms, the need for innovative sociological tools for theoretical and empirical surveys on the organization and articulation of life has now arisen. However, the latter forms will not necessarily become empty and obsolete due to the former; both can complement each other wisely.

The fact that these issues are only now gaining ground is connected with the internal logic in the development of new topics and theses in the academic discussion.[8] The mainstream discussion is now asking questions about the congruence between material 'possession' and cultural stylization—an issue that has already been mentioned by a series of authors many decades ago.[9,10] The more differentiated modern societies become, the greater is the possible scope for expressively staging social life. The better the material provisions, the broader the margins will become, from which one or the other form can be selected.

However, even among social positions that already are at the lower end of the stratification scale, the broadening of competing social expressions is obvious. Let us look at the category of unemployed persons. No average expected type of behavior among unemployed persons exists. Within this category no process of common socialization (Vergemeinschaftung) has taken place. Their individual biographical histories are far too different: Their occupational qualifications, their training prerequisites, their aspirations, and living requirements are too different.

The intersection of (vertical) stratification sociology with sociocultural issues can provide important answers to sociologically relevant patterns of lifestyles in modern societies. Joseph A. Schumpeter had already mentioned briefly in a general chapter in his book *Capitalism, Socialism and Democracy* (1942) that the development of capitalist lifestyles can easily and perhaps most impressively be described with the genesis of modern lounge suits (Schumpeter, [1942] 1947, p. 126). This example indicates that studying social change can include the process by which social and economic structures are differentiated as well as the processes of cultural change. The sociology of the stratification of unequal material distribution situations is important. How the system of classification is determined is another question that can be dealt with separately. However, these levels of distribution cannot be directly translated into either specific value patterns within society or in cultural attitudes as an expression of social life. These issues need to be dealt with by the sociology of lifestyles.

Notes

1. However, Max Weber was not the first who paid attention to the cycle between production and demand. The same issue can be found in Adam Smith's *Wealth of Nations* ([1776] 1937, p. 625), where we read that "consumption is the sole end and purpose of all production." In respect to modes of consumption, Daniel Bell maintains that a new stage of capitalism was already observed in the 1920s: "The 'new capitalism' (the phrase was first used in the 1920s) continued to demand a Protestant ethic in the area of production (the realm of work)—but to stimulate a demand for pleasure and play in the area of consumption" (1996, p. 75).
2. For a detailed introduction to different dimensions of Max Weber's work, see Collins (1986, 1998a), Kalberg (1994), Käsler (1995), and Swedberg (1998).
3. Theodor Geiger's work does not rank as a classic in the international discussion. It is thus even more interesting that Aage Soerensen (1991) refers to parallels and divergences between Geiger and Goldthorpe (see Soerensen, 1991, p. 83 n.5). See Geißler (1985) for an in-depth discussion of Theodor Geiger's (1932, 1949) present relevance.
4. Talcott Parsons did a translation of Weber's *Protestant Ethics* (first published in America in 1930, see Max Weber, 1988) to introduce the piece to American scholars. However, Max Weber and his American contemporaries were always aware of each other's writings. For instance, Max Weber cited Veblen's English-language works and Weber used some American phrases in the German original of the *Protestant Ethics*.
5. Paul DiMaggio has put his observation in definite words: "The starting point for any discussion of life styles and consumption patterns must be the work of Thorstein Veblen and Pierre Bourdieu" (1994, p. 458). For a recent discussion of Simmel, see Poggi (1993); for up-to-date relevance of Veblen, see Tillman (1996) and Penz and Wilkop (1996).
6. As we know from the sociology of knowledge, human action is organized by systems of social relevance (Alfred Schutz, [1932] 1974). Therefore,

consumption sociology has to ask for such patterns of social sense instead of taking economic behavior for granted. Baudrillard expressed this perspective in his "consumer society":

> *Consumption is neither a material practise, nor a phenomenology of "affluence". It is not defined by the food we eat, the clothes we wear, the car we can drive, nor by the visual and oral substance of images and messages, but in the organization of all this as signifying substance. Consumption is the virtual totality of all objects and message presently constituted in a more or less coherent discourse. Consumption, in so far as it is meaningful, is a systematic art of the manipulation of signs.* (1988, pp. 21–22).

7. This has been demonstrated by Granovetter and Tilly (1988) in their historically based study on "Inequality and Labor Process".
8. Thomas Kuhn (1962) described the internal academic controlling logic and semantics of topic-conjunctures as a "paradigm". Kuhn refers in his book's foreword to the fact that he is obliged to the German works of the Polish author Ludwik Fleck ([1935] 1980) for many of his ideas. Fleck described the formation of academic contexts in the semantics of "think collectives," which are forced, by means of certain thought constraints, to definite forms of thought styles. In fact, Fleck had "pre-thought" many of Kuhn's later arguments, a fact that has never been made obvious enough, neither by Kuhn (1962) nor in the ensuing discussion (see, e,g,, Baldamus, 1977). For a recent ambiguous discussion of intellectual change through a social network perspective, see the study of Collins (1998b).
9. Emil Lederer ([1929] 1979) had already expressed this with the concept of "disposition", as he referred to the fact that, only seen from the outside, the proletariat is a "massive grey layer": "A miner's disposition is continually different to that of a cobbler or a watch-maker" (1979, p. 175).
10. This seems most obvious for economists and not worth an explanation. Zablocki and Kanter (1976) have associated the emergence of several lifestyles with the social loss of value coherence: "In so doing we have attempted to call into sociological question what the micro-economist tends to take for granted—the differentiation of tastes and preferences. To the extent that a person's position in the markets for wealth and prestige still leave some degree of freedom of choice, differentiation of life styles results" (1976, p. 293). Michael E. Sobel concluded in his empirical pioneer work on lifestyles and social stratification: "While financial position is an initial condition for a lifestyle, lifestyle should not be treated as a mirror image of wealth and income" (1981, p. 170).

References

Anheimer, H. K., Gerhards, J., & Romo, F. (1995). Forms of Capital and Social Structure in Cultural Fields: Examining Bourdieu's Social Topography. *American Journal of Sociology, 100*, 859–903.

Baldamus, W. (1977). Ludwig Fleck and the Development of the Sociology of Science. In P. R. Gleichmann et al. (Eds.), *Human Figurations: Essays for Norbert Elias* (pp. 135–156). Tijdschrift.

Baudrillard, J. (1988). *The System of Objects.* Polity Press.

Becher, U. A. J. (1980). *Geschichte des modernen Lebensstils: Essen, Wohnen, Freizeit, Reisen.* C. H. Beck.

Beck, U. (1992). *Risk Society: Towards a New Modernity.* Sage.

Bell, D. (1974). *The Coming of Post-Industrial Society.* Heinemann.

Bell, D. (1996). *The Cultural Contradictions of Capitalism.* Basic Books.

Blossfeld, H.-P., & Shavit, Y. (1993). Persisting Barriers: Changes in Educational Opportunities in Thirteen Countries. In Y. Shavit & H.-P. Blossfeld (Eds.), *Persistent Inequality. Changing Educational Attainment in Thirteen Countries.* Westview Press.

Bögenhold, D. (1995). Continuities and Discontinuities in the Division of Labour Debate. Emerging Forms of Work Organization in International Perspetive. In W. Littek & T. Charles (Eds.), *The New Division of Labour.* Walter de Gruyter.

Bögenhold, D. (1996). *Das Dienstleistungsjahrhundert. Kontinuitäten und Diskontinuitäten in Wirtschaft und Gesellschaft.* Enke.

Bourdieu, P. (1979). *La distinction. Critique social du judgement.* Les éditions de minuit.

Briefs, G. (1931). Proletariat. In A. Vierkandt (Ed.), *Handwörterbuch der Soziologie* (Vol. Vol. 2). Enke.

Bryson, B. (1996). Anything but Heavy Metal: Symbolic Exclusion and Musical Dislikes. *American Sociological Review, 61*, 884–899.

Burt, R. (1992). *The Structural Hole.* Harvard University Press.

Camphell, C. (1987). *The Romantic Ethic and the Spirit of Modern Consumerism.* Basil Blackwell.

Clark, T. N., & Lipset, S. M. (1991). Are social classes dying?. *International sociology*, 6(4), 397–410.

Collins, R. (1986). *Max Weber: A Skeleton Key.* Sage.

Collins, R. (1998a). Introduction. In R. Collins (Ed.), *Max Weber. The Protestant Ethic and the Spirit of Capitalism* [orig. translated by T. Parsons]. Roxbury.

Collins, R. (1998b). *The Sociology of Philosophies: A Global Theory of Intellectual Change.* Harvard University Press.

Dahrendorf, R. (1959). *Class and Class Conflict in Industrial Society.* Stanford University Press.

DiMaggio, P. (1994). Social Stratification, Life Style, and Social Cognition. In D. B. Grusky (Ed.), *Social Stratification in Sociological Perspective: Class, Race, and Gender*. Westview Press.

Erickson, B. H. (1996). Culture, Class, and Connections. *American Journal of Sociology, 102*, 217–251.

Erikson, R., & Goldthorpe, J. H. (1992). *The Constant Flux. A Study of Class Mobilityin Industrial Societies*. Oxford University Press.

Fleck, L. ([1935]1980). *Die Entstehung einer wissenschaftlichen Tatsache*. Suhrkamp.

Geiger, T. (1932). *Die soziale Schichtung des Deutschen Volkes*. Enke.

Geiger, T. (1949). *Die Klassengesellschaft im Schmelztiegel*. Kiepenheuer.

Geißler, R. (1985). Die Schichtungssoziologie von Theodor Geiger. Zur Aktualität eines fast vergessenen Klassikers. *Kölner Zeitschrift für Soziologie und Sozialpsychologie, 37*, 755–770.

Giddens, A. (1973). *The Class Structure of the Advanced Societies*. Harper & Row.

Goldthorpe, J. H., Lockwood, D., Bechhofer, F., & Platt, J. (1968). *The Affluent Worker: Political Attitudes and Behaviour*. Cambridge University Press.

Goldthorpe, J. H., & Marshall, G. (1992). The Promising Future of Class Analysis. *Sociology, 26*(3), 381–400.

Granovetter, M., & Tilly, C. (1988). Inequality and Labor Processes. In N. J. Smelser (Ed.), *Handbook of Sociology*. Sage.

Gronow, J. (1997). *The Sociology of Taste*. Routledge.

Harris, D. (1996). *A Society of Signs?* Routledge.

Hout, M., Clem, B., & Manza, J. (1993). The Persistence of Classes in Post-Industrial Societies. *International Sociology, 3*(8), 259–277.

Kalberg, S. (1994). *Max Weber's Comparative-Historical Sociology*. University of Chicago Press.

Käsler, D. (1995). *Max Weber: Eine Einführung in Leben, Werk und Wirkung*. Campus.

Kuhn, T. S. (1962). *The Structure of Scientific Revolutions*. Chicago University Press.

Lederer, E. (1912). *Die Privatangestellten in der modernen Wirtschaftsentwicklung*. J.C.B. Mohr (Paul Siebeck).

Lederer, E. (1979 [1912]). Die Umschichtungen des Proletariats und die kapitalistischen Zwischenschichten vor der Krise. In E. Lederer (Ed.), *Kapitalismus, Klassenstruktur und Probleme der Demokratie in Deutschland 1910–1940*. Vandenhoeck & Ruprecht.

Luhmann, N. (1995). Zum Begriff der sozialen Klasse. In N. Luhmann (Ed.), *Soziale Differenzierung. Zur Geschichte einer Idee*. Westdeutscher Verlag.

Mason, R. (1998). *The Economics of Conspicuous Consumption. Theory and Thought Since 1700*. Edward Elgar.

Mayer, K.-U., & Blossfeld, H.-P. (1990). Die gesellschaftliche Konstruktion sozialer Ungleichheit im Lebensverlauf. In P. A. Berger & S. Hradil (Eds.), *Lebenslagen, Lebensläufe, Lebensstile, Soziale Welt, Special Issue, 7*. Otto Schwarz.

Nieuwbeerta, P. (1995). *The Democratic Class Struggle in Twenty Countries, 1945–1990*. Thesis Publishers.

Ossowski, S. (1963). *Class Structure in the Social Consciousness*. Routledge & Keegan.

Pakulski, J. (1993). The Dying Class or Marxist Class Theory? *International Sociology, 8*(3), 279–292.

Penz, R., & Wilkop, H. (Eds.). (1996). *Zeit der Institutionen—Thorstein Veblens evolutorische Ökonomik*. Metropolis.

Poggi, G. (1993). *Moneyand the Modern Mind: George Simmel's Philosophy of Money*. University of California Press.

Riesman, D., Reuel, D., & Glazer, N. (1950). *The Lonely Crowd: A Study of the Changing American Character*. Yale University Press.

Rose, D. & O'Reilly K. (Eds.). (1997). *Constructing Classes. Towards a New Social Classification for the UK*. Office for National Statistics and Economic and Social Research Council, Essex, UK.

Schumpeter, J. A. ([1942] 1947). *Capitalism, Socialism and Democracy*. Harper & Brothers.

Schutz, A. ([1932] 1974). *Der sinnhafte Aufbau der sozialen Welt. Eine Einleitung in die verstehende Soziologie*. Suhrkamp.

Scott, J. (1992). *Social Network Analysis: A Handbook*. Sage.

Shavit, Y., & Müller, W. (Eds.). (1998). *From School to Work: A Comparative Study of Educational Qualifications and Occupational Destinations*. Clarendon Press.

Simmel, G. ([1900] 1978). *The Philosophy of Money*. Routledge & Keegan Paul.

Smith, A. ([1776] 1937). *Wealth of Nations*.

Sobel, M. E. (1981). *Lifestyle and Social Structure. Conceptions, Definitions, Analyses*. Academic Press.

Soerensen, A. B. (1991). On the Usefulness of Class Analysis in Research on Social Mobility and Socioeconomic Inequality. *Acta Sociologica, 34*, 71–87.

Sombart, W. ([1927] 1987). *Der moderne Kapitalismus*, Vol. 3. DTV.

Stihler, A. (1998). *Die Entstehung des modernen Konsums. Darstellung und Erklärungsansätze*. Duncker & Humblot.

Swartz, D. (1997). *Culture and Power: The Sociology of Pierre Bourdieu*. University of Chicago Press.

Swedberg, R. (1998). *Max Weber and the Idea of Economic Sociology*. Princeton University Press.

Tillman, R. (1996). *The Intellectual Legacy of Thorstein Veblen*. Greenwood.

Veblen, T. B. (1899). *The Theory of the Leisure Class*.

Wasserman, S., & Faust, K. (1994). *Social Network Analysis: Methods and Applications*. Cambridge University Press.

Weber, M. ([1921] 1972). *Wirtschaft und Gesellschaft*. J.C.B. Mohr.

Weber, M. ([1930] 1988). Die protestantische Ethik und der Geist des Kapitalismus. In M. Weber (Ed.), *Gesammelte Aufsätze zur Religionssoziologie*. C. B. Mohr.

Wellman, B. (1988). Structural Analysis: From Method and Metaphor to Theory and Substance. In B. Wellman & S. D. Berkowitz (Eds.), *Social Structures: A Network Approach*. Cambridge University Press.

Zablocki, B., & Kanter, R. M. (1976). The Differentiation of Life styles. *Annual Review of Sociology, 2*, 269–298.

Zapf, W., et al. (1987). *Individualisierung und Sicherheit. Untersuchungen zur Lebensqualität in der Bundesrepublik Deutschland*. Beck.

Zukin, S., & DiMaggio, P. (Eds.). (1990). *Structures of Capital: The Social Construction of the Economy*. Cambridge University Press.

CHAPTER 3

Inequality Processes and Vertical Social Stratification: The Issue of the Middle Classes

Dieter Bögenhold and Yorga M. Permana

Introduction: Covid-19 and Globalization

The Covid-19 pandemic, which struck in early 2020 and had started in the city of Wuhan in the Peoples Republic of China, demonstrates very well how fragile and interdependent the global world system is. The virus spread over the whole globe, tackled all countries by ignoring national borders, and brought up a tremendous number of infected people among which ten thousand died. The virus brought the whole world society and economy to a lockdown, a standstill, which has never happened before. No single country proved to be immune against the evolution of the disease, and no country was successfully prepared and armed against the upcoming developments. People got ill and died everywhere, and the whole system of previous reasonable forecasting proved to be full of scientific flaws. The task of modeling economic, social, and environmental developments is always dependent upon the axiomatic input of model constructors. If applicants of those econometric models create their ideas in a sterile world of assumptions, it would be a clean world of certainty where all external variables are known and calculable or where those external variables are just ignored. In that case surprising effects, non-intended consequences, and interdisciplinary problems will not occur. Instead, we

D. Bögenhold, *Neglected Links in Economics and Society*,
https://doi.org/10.1007/978-3-030-79193-3_3

are living in a dynamic world which includes different dimensions of uncertainties that make up different degrees of complexity leading permanently to effects which are not forecasted (Merton, 1936). However, the real world is not (always) clean but (sometimes) dirty when further phenomena and consequences exist which are not included in the initial assumptions. Opposed to a model world, in the real-world many shades between black and white exist (Akerlof, 2020).

The same issue applies to the topic of globalization. Firstly, the sharp battle about the advantages and disadvantages of globalization processes which we have been observing for a few decades at least has seemingly become less controversial during last years because people started to think that there are no visible alternatives to an increased internationalization called globalization. Anthony Giddens has defined globalization as a social process of "intensification of worldwide social relations which link distant localities in such a way that local happenings are shaped by events occurring many miles away and vice versa" (Giddens, 1990, p. 64). Of course, taking this definition, we are living in an increasingly globalized world where forms of economic, social, cultural, and environmental exchange or interplay are more visible and influential than in earlier times. Apparently, the globe has turned to become a world society as this term was introduced, independently of each other, by Wallerstein (1983, 2011), N. Luhmann (1971), and John W. Meyer et al. (1981). The idea of world society claims that debate on social phenomena shall not only be referenced to individual nation-states and their very limited framework but a social universe of global world society.

Looking at the multiplication of entrepreneurial billionaires in the world (Bögenhold, 2019) shows that one reason for the enormous accumulation of such wealth is that globalization, understood as the increased economic, political, social, and cultural interconnectedness of the world, has produced many more opportunities in different parts of the world, which have enabled some people to increase their wealth vastly (Giddens, 2009, p. 525); while on the other hand, we find a lot of poverty all over the world, people suffering hunger, homeless people having no flat or no roof to stay at least and working migrants who are pushed around the world in order to raise income to try to feed their families (Case & Deaton, 2020). The bottom billion (Collier, 2007) often has no access to gas and electricity for cooking, drinking water and water toilets, education in schools, and sufficient medical care so that life expectancies are comparatively short (World Bank, 2002). Social stratification research deals with inequalities, this in individual countries and between countries.

Inequalities in the World Economy

There is considerable discontent among scholars about the history, meaning, outcomes, and processes of globalization. However, despite existing confusions and controversies that surround the concept, it generally refers to increasing interconnectedness among people, economies, and cultures at the global level which is facilitated through the massive reduction of costs of transportation and communication, and the breaking down of artificial barriers of cross-border flows of goods, services, capital, knowledge, and people as well. However, this assumption about the inevitability of integration as an essential component of globalization has been often challenged (Ritzer & Dean, 2015).

Existing literature (Bauman, 1998; Chirico, 2014; Stiglitz, 2002) supports the notion that globalization is not a uniform and neutral process, but rather that it is lacking in commonly assumed uniform effects and has multifaceted social causes and consequences. Due to the diversity and complexity of the phenomenon, existing debates on globalization are polarized (Ritzer & Dean, 2015). For an individual human being, it makes a crucial difference where one is born. As a member of a rich(er) country, people have a citizen premium where—vice versa—those from poor(er) countries suffer a citizen penalty. "Citizenship premium (or citizenship rent; the terms are used interchangeably) … refers to the boost in income one receives simply from being a citizen of a rich country, while citizenship penalty is the reduction in income from being a citizen of a poor country" (Milanovic, 2019, p. 129). Milanovic (2019) talks about the bright and the dark sides of capitalism which belong ultimately together so that he coins it an inevitable amorality of hypercommercialized capitalism (Milanovic, 2019, p. 176). This really opens up the principal question of what is legal and what is ethical or legitimate (Cohen, 2012).

The rhetorics of capitalism has been repeated numerous times (Stiglitz, 2002, 2012). Institutional economics, in recent times starting with D.G. North (1990) is all about the integration of institutional elements into a concept of the economy (Hodgson, 2000). Those institutions include the system of law and governmental institutions but all other regulations on how procedures in society are working as well. Especially, the organization of labour markets, the principles of industrial relations and the system of education. Also the working of the institution family and rules of trust and reciprocity, the principal codes of social norms governing a society which are almost interwoven with normative implications brought up by (different) religions, all these factors determine how societies concretely look. Economics in abstracto does not ask for those elements since it treats the analysis of capitalism independently if it is capitalism in Belgium, Bangladesh, Botswana, or Brazil, but those countries differ considerably among each other. These countries do not share the same level of productivity and wealth. They have different labour market data, ratios of mortality, and life expectancies; moreover, they don't share the same paths of historical development. One of the most critical neglects of economics in abstracto is that history as an important variable of development was increasingly ignored. In the twentieth century, economics has started to forget history (Hodgson, 2001). History of economic theory was abolished or pushed to different other disciplines, almost to philosophy or science theory and economic and social history as domains of the investigation were outsourced to faculties of history; they were of increasingly less interest to economists. The academic understanding of economic development is incomplete if we do not respect history and understand the social embeddedness of economic institutions and social behaviour.

Reasoning about globalization and the international system of economic and social relations is a very complicated academic issue in which we always must ask ourselves which are the specific elements in concreto and which are in abstracto. Recent neo-Marxist approaches, especially the international world-system view by Wallerstein (2011), try to add those global perspectives. Comparing international figurations of economic relations always includes the analysis of competitive economic advantages of nations. The understanding of prosperity and poverty always refers to a framework of historical explanations. Acemoglu and Robinson (2012) have dealt with the question of why similar-looking nations differ sometimes greatly in their economic and political development. It is historical processes that, via institutional drift, create the differences that may become consequential during critical junctures. Critical junctures themselves are historical turning points. And the vicious and virtuous circles imply that we have to study history to understand the nature of institutional differences that have been historically structured (Acemuglu & Robinson, 2012, p. 432).

The reader learns from Acemuglu and Robinson (2012) not only the need to dig deeply into historical issues to gain an adequate command of analysing to solve contemporary problems (see also Bögenhold, 2020) but also that economic and social developments are not simple highways always leading in the same direction. The global world is a complex puzzle with different subtle own logic, which is also integrated into international regulations of financial institutions. In this respect, Stiglitz used his famous formulation: "The global financial system is not working well for developing countries. Money is flowing uphill, from the poor to the rich" (Stiglitz, 2002, p. 245). The conclusion by Stiglitz is that "what is needed, if we are to make globalization work, is an international economic regime in which the well-being of the developed and developing countries are better balanced: a new global social contract between developed and less developed countries" (Stiglitz, 2002, p. 385).

Many contemporaries believe in capitalism as an autonomous machine that affects development, including progress and prosperity on its own, and they overlook the international perfect storm of rising inequalities (Milanovic, 2016).,especially the embeddedness of economies in global strategies of large international corporations and governmental policies which, both, enable partly the game of market forces. The most decisive factor (historically) accelerating, channeling and shaping the information technology paradigm was (and still is) the process of capitalist restructuring undertaken since the 1980s. This process led to a series of reforms (deregulation, privatization, and dismantling of the social contract between labour and capital). Four goals were pursued: (1) deepening the capitalist logic of profit-seeking in capital-labour relationships, (2) enhancing the productivity of labour and capital, (3) globalizing production, seizing the opportunity of the most advantageous conditions for production, and (4) marshalling the state's support for productivity gains and competitiveness of economies. Without new information technology, capitalist restructuring would have been much slower, with much less flexibility (Castells, 2010). Citizen premium and citizen penalty (Milanovic, 2019) are closely related to the orchestration of a world society since the living of members of one group is visibly related to the living (and working) of the other group.

Social Stratification within the Individual Nation States

The *United Nations* defines *Sustainable Development Goals where Goal No. 10 is Reducing inequality within and among countries* (United Nations, 2015). Inequality is closely related to the discussion about social stratification. Of course, we can always distinguish between differences of wealth and poverty among individual nations and the distribution of wealth and poverty *within one nation*. The British economist and inequality researcher have said regarding national and international degrees of inequality:

> *Inequality among all the world's citizens reflects the combined impact of the inequality within countries and the inequality between countries. Seen this way, the simple story of global inequality over the last hundred years is that there was first a period when inequality within rich countries was falling but inequality between countries was widening, now replaced by a period when inequality within rich countries is rising but inequality between countries is narrowing.* (Atkinson, 2015, p. 42)

The concept of stratification refers to the idea of vertical segmentation in the sense of having more or fewer resources. The evolution of the richest and the poorest people in contemporary societies is almost buffered by people being between those strata which are the core topic of our further discussion.

There is apparently an analogy to the field of geology, where always different forms of geo-material stratification are explored. The term social stratification is taken to describe the system of social order in a vertical perspective. Degrees of stratification are always relational and they express degrees of social inequality. Science is not interested in the fate of individual actors but in social categories of humans as statistical categories.

The classic idea in Marx's categorization was that access to means of production serves as the pivot point of all sociological and economic analysis. This view was universal and dominant for decades. The positioning of actors in the stratification system was located in relation to the system of industrial relations and ownership. Being wage or salary dependent implied belonging to the class of proletarians, whereas all others belonged to the class of the bourgeoisie, the class of capitalists. Marx never produced a systematic treatise of the class topic; at the end of the third volume of his famous Capital (Marx, 1977), the text ends abruptly and remains unfinished after the introduction. All that we have is a collection and interpretation of Marx's ideas from various other places in his many written works. The principal view in the materialist Marxist perspective is that relations to the system of production govern the system of stratification. Accordingly, all other dimensions of life are subordinate to or consequences of the principal material position in society.

This programme was relevant for many academics for a long time but has declined in its relevance and attraction during the last 40–50 years. An early programme in contrast to the dominant Marxist view was elaborated by Max Weber (1978), who stressed the fact of differentiation (Giddens, 1973). Although he shared Marx's view that issues of property or non-property are fundamental concerns in society, Weber concluded that, within those two categories, manifold further steps of separation can be found according to qualification and related labour market chances. He said that different individual market chances correspond with different life chances and consequently he talked about many further classes within the two main categories. As far as we identify specific market chances, we can talk about specific classes.

However, Weber also introduced the concept of status as the subjective feeling and orientation of people in terms of lifestyles and cultural expressions. The concept of lifestyle within the framework of his Protestant Ethics (Weber, 1988) is mostly used as a caricature of the modern and "standardized free" way of living. Research on social stratification asks for the position of groups of humans in relation to others based upon income, wealth, education, and further variables. Forms of social stratification can be described by objective measures of indicators. Being located higher up in the vertical social stratification of income has several serious implications since more available financial resources imply better food, living and housing, better education, health, and further life-chances. Human beings operate their activities in a social space within complex societies by socially constructed sense and cognitive mechanisms. In other words, social stratification implies a social logic of inclusion and exclusion, which means income, education and related scales of prestige create borders between different circles of people which integrate some and—vice versa—exclude others.

Nowadays, perspectives on social stratification have multiplied. Grusky et al. (2008) and Grusky and Szelényi (2018) give an introduction to and an overview of a variety of research questions. Social stratification and social inequality serve as reciprocal synonyms for unequal distribution and unequal availability of wealth in societies which have always been a pivot point of discussion in sociology. How (in)equal can societies be so that they can still be characterized as being just or fair? In parallel, during the last 20 years or so inequality has evolved to a hot topic in economics as well. The current enormous academic success of Piketty's book *Capital in the 21st Century* among members of the economics and sociology communities is a demonstration of the ongoing attraction of questions about (in)equality and stratification. Inequality has become a real interdisciplinary issue, at least between economics, sociology, and history, and the topic dominated several of the annual conferences in economics and sociology worldwide during the last decade. Besides Piketty's books (2020), several other writings emerged in parallel in economics (Stiglitz, 2012, 2015; Stiglitz et al., 2010; Atkinson, 2015, 2019).

Inequality and Middle Classes

Many research contributions dealing with inequality address primarily poverty in societies (Atkinson, 2019) and they try to scandalize low chances and discrimination practices of poor people who have low status and low income in society. Those people who have no or low income in society are excluded from the distribution of wealth, they suffer from low living and health conditions and are related to low life-expectancies. Social policy ambitions were almost to reduce poverty and to eliminate really poor people in contemporary societies. Latest with the work of Piketty (2014) the turn of attention in inequality research had turned towards the concentration of wealth at the top of incomes.

This chapter discusses one aspect of the topic of social stratification in a global world economy, namely the existence of middle classes and the question if it is getting smaller or even broader. In contrast to the majority of studies concentrating at the top or bottom strata, our research is focussing on the middle segments.

Figure 3.1 illustrates the vertical social stratification system of modern societies where there are bottom and top segments of poor and rich people and a broad middle segment between them. Poor people just try to survive by attempting to satisfy basic needs and rich people very often show distinct profiles of consumption behaviour. The vertical profile reminds us of a raindrop, and it is an open question whether the raindrop is slender or broader around its waistline. In the sociology of change and political conflict, the middle classes have always held a central function, serving as a kind of conflict buffer in modern societies which is between poverty and affluence.

The concept of stratification refers to the idea of vertical segmentation in the sense of having more or fewer resources. The middle classes are of

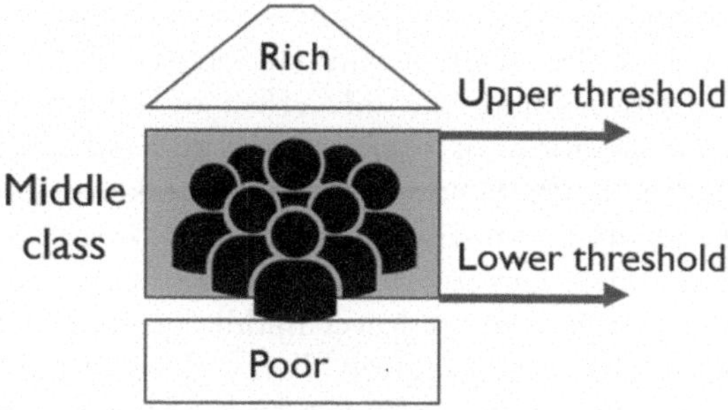

Fig. 3.1 The middle-class segment in a stratified society. (Source: Own representation)

interest for multiple reasons: (i) through the lenses of social order, integration, and political conflict, the middle classes serve as a buffer between the strata; (ii) the middle classes are defined as household groups in middle-income ranges between poverty and richness. They are open to new consumer markets, new fields to study lifestyles, and, in relation to this, new consumer behaviour; (iii) the middle classes are of interest for investigating patterns of inequality and social mobility. This last point is of particular relevance in view of the proposed decline in the middle classes in a globalized world. Is there an ongoing de-middledization as coined by Bögenhold and Permana (2018)? Since all discussion on growing (or declining) inequality refers directly to the existence of the middle classes and since the phenomenon of the middle classes is ultimately connected to consumption and consumer behaviour, the chapter explores these links in more detail, with the aim of delivering a series of strong arguments to invest further research ambitions in the topic of the middle classes, inequality, and consumer behaviour. We are convinced that poor and rich income strata have attracted a disproportionate amount of research attention, especially to scandalize different forms of having too little or too much money, whereas the middle classes have not received the research attention they deserve.

How we consume is dependent not only on the concrete society and time in which we live but also on our preferences, depending on our lifestyles and related tastes, which are almost always related to our position in the system of social classes. Therefore, the discussion in the following sections centres around the links between consumption and lifestyles in order to explain the rationality as to why people opt for this or that way of creating their own life paths and worlds of consumption. What do we want to possess, what goods are part of our dreams, for what purposes do we save money? All of these questions provide answers as to how human beings organize their lives, also in relation to material goods. Consumption practices always have the side effect of demonstrating and underlining the social position of their owner in a stratified society (Veblen, 1899; Goffman, 1979; Bourdieu, 1984). Likewise, cultural capital is related to the ability to contribute to the social processes of inclusion and exclusion (Lamont & Lareau, 1988). Another field of research is the question as to how people who are lower-middle or upper-middle classes come up with practices of consumption. Being close to poverty in particular does not allow a broad variation in strategy or issues of style beyond just managing material survival. Combining those perspectives with further variables such as gender or age opens up a variety of further research questions (Katz-Gerro, 2004).

The basic assumption behind the discussion is that the middle classes are the basic drivers of consumption. Consumption behaviour and the practices of the middle-income segments cover the vast majority of households in society. Their consumption represents what Riesman et al. (1969) once called the standard package of American consumer households, which is—again according to Riesman et al. (1969)—very much learned behaviour since late childhood. In addition, the consumption of the middle classes is widely reported by and transported through the media. In some way, consumption patterns demonstrate the social position of their users. Purchasing expensive objects can make people happy by giving them satisfaction, "joy" and "pleasure" (Veblen, 1899; see Papageorgiou et al., 2020 for similarities and dissimilarities between Veblen and Bourdieu).

The concept of stratification refers to the idea of vertical segmentation in the sense of having more or fewer resources, in analogy to the field of geology, where different forms of material stratification are investigated. Sociologists use the term social stratification to describe the system of social order from a vertical perspective. Degrees of stratification are always relational and they express degrees of social inequality. References are found to class structures, where "lifestyle" is seen as being an expressively cultural moment in consumption and the social inclusion and exclusion of groups (Bögenhold & Naz, 2018). Increasingly, problems have become clear in combining the material and cultural dimensions of investigation. What people "are" and what people "do" can no longer be conceptualized by a simple one-to-one fit (Bögenhold, 2001). In this understanding, the concept of lifestyle can provide a link between social rank and social practice. The logic of how people organize their leisure time and how they spend their income is not a simple mirror of income level but must be regarded as being embedded in social behaviour. Bourdieu (1984) sees the social world in terms of a metaphor: consider a multidimensional social sphere in which different groups of actors reflect, on the one hand, the sphere of social position and, on the other hand, the sphere of lifestyles. Material distribution in the sense of different social positions is represented in one sphere whereas, in the other sphere, the provisions of cultural resources are staked out and manifested in the form of varying lifestyles.

Other authors emphasize the growing relativity of the class concept due to increasing trends of mobility caused by education, urbanization, and changing demographic patterns, including the declining significance of the institution of the family, so that systems of stratification are becoming ever more intricate and are permanently reconfigured. Especially Beck's (2002) idea of individualization as a standardized societal principle of increased mobility has shed new light upon social stratification.

According to Collins (2013), the technological displacement of middle-class labour is not much more than 20 years old; while it took almost 200 years to destroy the working-class labour force (approximately the entire nineteenth century and three-quarters of the twentieth), the computerization of middle-class labour (since the last decade of the twentieth century) is proceeding at a much faster pace than the mechanization of the manual labour force (Collins, 2013, p. 56). Therefore, none of the previous ways to compensate for job losses will work effectively in the future. Viewing at the US, Scott and Pressman (2011) reported the double squeeze of the middle classes giving size to the top incomes and the bottom incomes as well.

Within recent discussions about the future of modern capitalist societies, many well-founded speculations rely on the interplay between continued processes of globalization, increased strength of trends in so-called digitalization, and other forms of technological progress as well as their effects on the system of social stratification and social mobility (Wallerstein et al., 2013). Pessimists argue that the twenty-first-century trajectory of technological development is likely to push the middle classes into redundancy. If this forecast comes true, it certainly has implications for the degree of societal cohesion and the mass consumer profile of consumption decisions.

What's about the Destiny of Middle Classes?

Surprisingly, there is no agreement on a definition of the middle class among scholars (Pressman, 2015). For a long period of time, distributional studies have focused on the poor and the rich while those in the middle have been forgotten (Atkinson & Brandolini, 2011). The concern to define and measure the middle class has increased in the past decade since the issue of shrinking middle classes became a major anxiety. Therefore, since there is no consensus, any attempts to define the size of the middle class are quite obviously arbitrary and open to challenge (Piketty, 2014).

In this study, we focus on the disposable household income range which is measured by the survey of European Union Statistics on Income and Living Conditions (EU-SILC) provided in the Eurostat database. We define the middle classes as those whose income lies between an absolute lower cut-off and upper cut-off near the median. The PEW Research Center (2012) defines the middle-class in the US to be between 67 percent and 200 percent of the median income.

However, we do not think that there is an exact number for either the lower or upper cut-off point because it depends on the context of the study. We follow the arguments by Ravallion (2010) and Atkinson and Brandolini (2011) which state that the lower cut-off for the middle class is equivalent to the line threshold of being at risk of poverty. In other words, those who are classified as middle class are those who are not at risk of poverty. In the EU, the at-risk-of-poverty threshold is set at 60 percent of the national median household income. Thus, we chose that number to set the lower cut-off for defining the middle class. Meanwhile, the upper cut-off differentiates between the middle class and the rich. We set 150 percent of the median as the upper cut-off for defining the middle class, as also suggested by Grabka and Frick (2008) to measure the size of the German middle class.

To sum up, this study defines the middle class as the population group with a relative income position between 60 and 150 percent of the median. As a comparison, the results are also robust when changing the lower and upper threshold into 40 percent and 130 percent of median income respectively.

Table 3.1 captures the size of the middle class in 28 EU countries (plus Norway and Switzerland) between 2005 and 2018. Nineteen out of the 30 countries are experiencing a decline in the middle classes, while the size

Table 3.1 Share of people in the bottom, middle-, and top-income groups in EU countries 2005–2018

Country	*First observation (2005)*			*Last observation (2018)*			*Point percentage change in the size of middle class*
	Poor	*Middle Class*	*Rich*	*Poor*	*Middle Class*	*Rich*	
	share of people with less than 60% of median	*share of people with 60–150% median income*	*share of people with greater than 150% of median*	*share of people with less than 60% of median*	*share of people with 60–150% median income*	*share of people with greater than 150% of median*	
European Union	16.5	63.4	20.1	17.1	62.9	20	-0.5
Luxembourg	13.7	68.6	17.7	18.3	57.4	24.3	-11.2
Sweden	9.5	76.6	13.9	16.4	67.2	16.4	-9.4
Bulgaria	18.4	60.2	21.4	22	52.2	25.8	-8
Germany	12.2	72	15.8	16	65.4	18.6	-6.6
Denmark	11.8	76.1	12.1	12.7	71.5	15.8	-4.6
Latvia	19.4	55.2	25.4	23.3	51.6	25.1	-3.6
Norway	11.4	76.8	11.8	12.9	73.5	13.6	-3.3
Netherlands	10.7	72.8	16.5	13.3	69.8	16.9	-3
Austria	12.6	70.8	16.6	14.3	68.7	17	-2.1
Estonia	18.3	55.8	25.9	21.9	54.4	23.7	-1.4
Spain	20.1	56.7	23.2	21.5	55.3	23.2	-1.4
Lithuania	20.5	53.1	26.4	22.9	51.7	25.4	-1.4
Hungary	13.5	69.6	16.9	12.8	68.7	18.5	-0.9
Italy	19.2	59.6	21.2	20.3	58.8	20.9	-0.8
Finland	11.7	72.2	16.1	12	71.5	16.5	-0.7
Romania	24.6	50.4	25	23.5	49.8	26.7	-0.6
Malta	14.3	65	20.7	16.8	64.4	18.8	-0.6
Slovenia	12.2	72.8	15	13.3	72.6	14.1	-0.2
United Kingdom	19	57.6	23.4	18.9	57.6	23.5	0
Belgium	14.8	69.3	15.9	16.4	69.6	14	0.3
Switzerland	15	65	20	14.6	65.7	19.7	0.7
France	13	68.5	18.5	13.4	69.3	17.3	0.8
Czechia	10.4	71.8	17.8	9.6	73.8	16.6	2
Cyprus	16.1	63	20.9	15.4	65.4	19.2	2.4
Croatia	20.6	56.7	22.7	19.3	59.8	20.9	3.1
Greece	19.6	56.2	24.2	18.5	60	21.5	3.8
Portugal	19.4	55.9	24.7	17.3	60.2	22.5	4.3
Slovakia	13.3	70.5	16.2	12.2	75.6	12.2	5.1
Ireland	19.7	59.6	20.7	14.9	65	20.1	5.4
Poland	20.5	55.7	23.8	14.8	66.7	18.5	11

Source: Created by Dieter Bögenhold and Yorga Permana

of the middle class across all countries has decreased by five percent, from 63.4 percent to 62.9 percent. The highest de-middledization phenomenon (Bögenhold & Permana 2018) has been experienced by Luxembourg (11.2 percent decline), Sweden (9.4 percent), Germany (6.6 percent), and Denmark (4.6 percent). Among countries in which the size of the middle class has increased, Poland (11 percent), Slovakia (5.1 percent), Ireland (5.4 percent), and Portugal (4.3 percent) are those with a significant rise while the remaining countries are more stable.

Current empirical studies on the situation of the middle classes in the US as well as in European or Asian countries (Kochhar, 2017; Pruchnik & Zowczak, 2017) show contradictory results about their survival trends, indicating different directions. The findings of the middle classes in Europe presented here indicate that some countries have suffered from a process of de-middledization. Collins' (2013) thesis of increased de-middledization seems to have some empirical evidence when confronted with selected empirical data. Our research is also rooted in recent social stratification research but the primary question is whether these observations of inequality will turn into changing patterns of consumption.

Whenever they occur, massive social, economic, and cultural changes are bound to affect the lives of children. Those changes might be direct, as in the case of war, migration, or rapid urbanization, or indirect, as their parents cope with new economic realities. In other words, contextual changes in social and economic structures already influence lifestyles, life perceptions, and consumer preferences in childhood (Kaufman et al., 2004). Their wishes and dreams become valid when they have become adults (Cross, 2010). When typical consumer households and their purchasing power are shrinking, the "average consumer", as a typical member of the middle classes, is losing their former dominance.

Among the eight countries in the EU with the highest GDP per capita, only Ireland has experienced an increase in the size of its middle class (see Figs. 3.2 and 3.3 above), while the others have experienced a declining trend. As the middle classes seem to be losing their former degree of consistency and as they are in the process of becoming fragmented, they are in danger of not representing further the "standard package" of modern consumer household profiles (Riesman et al., 1969). It may be supposed that this standard package is part of an ongoing erosion process towards the multiplication of lifestyles and consumption identities. The pluralization of society (Bögenhold, 2001; Beck, 2002) will increasingly influence a shift towards a pluralization of consumption practices as a parallel trend.

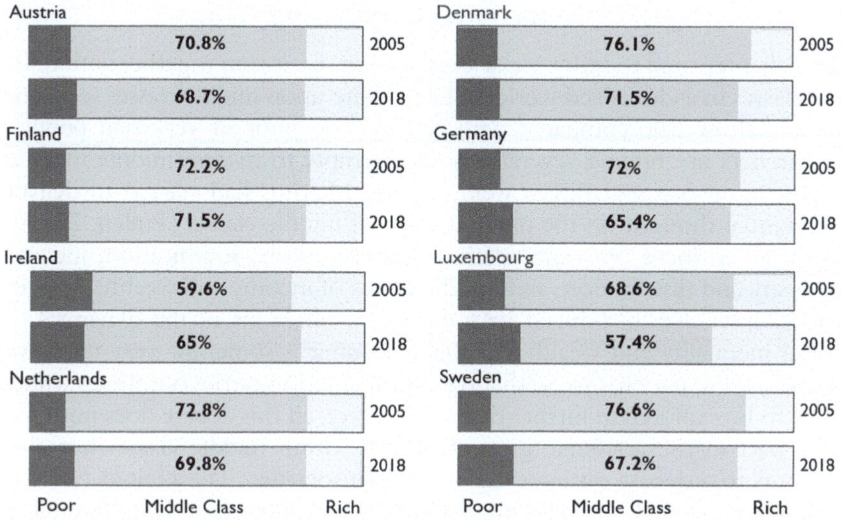

Fig. 3.2 Middle class trend in 2005 and 2018 in eight EU countries with the highest GDP per capita (Source: Own calculations based on EUROSTAT statistics)

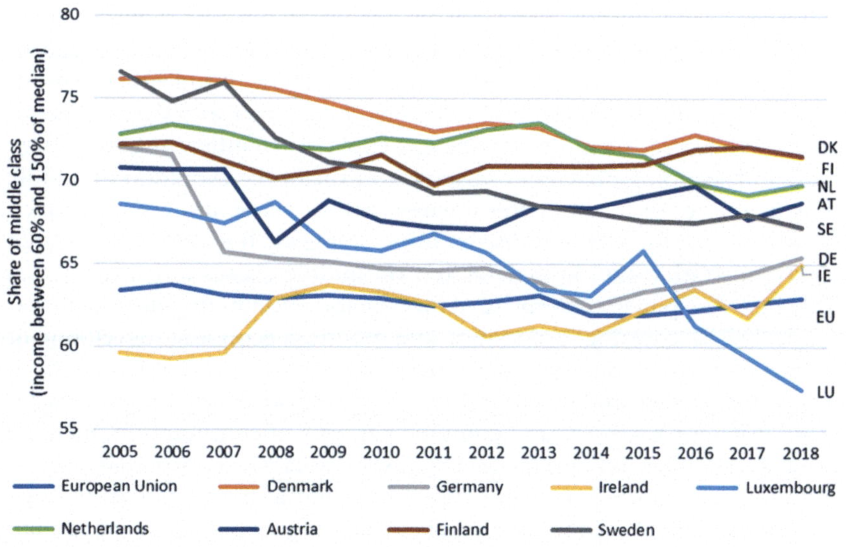

Fig. 3.3 Middle-class trends in eight countries in the EU with the highest GDP per capita (Source: Own calculations based on EUROSTAT statistics)

What's to Conclude?

This chapter tried to bring social stratification discussion together with middle classes in a globalized world. While debate upon middle classes seems to be somehow pale compared with research on poor or very rich people, researchers are finding several serious attempts to discuss middle-income segments in our societies as well. Already Malthus had started to deliver substantial thought on the phenomenon of middle classes (Pullen, 2019). We tried to focus on some relations between social stratification, income diversity and distribution, and middle zones of income and wealth. And, in this chapter, we introduced to some first evaluations of the dynamics of social inequality and wealth. All this reasoning is somehow very tentative and of preliminary nature so that the argumentation carries out theses which have to be explored in further detail. However, all this debate does not only take part in the academic ground of and within middle classes but also belongs to a debate on injustice in modern societies. The United Nations defined Sustainable Development Goals where Goal No. 10 is Reducing inequality within and among countries (United Nations, 2015). According to our empirical inspection, measures of inequality seem to point in the direction of increasing inequalities rather than reducing inequalities.

Our attempt is a synthesis of theoretical reasoning and empirical findings which shed light on a research agenda which must be explored much deeper to arrive at a broader and more adequate understanding of recent developments in a global world, in the interaction of individual nation-states and the relative success of individual states, their societies, and economies. While Pressman (2010) referred explicitly to different government taxes and spending policies in societies to explain the evolution of middle classes, a series of further determinants may be taken into account which we will try to discover and discuss more seriously. It shows that research on social stratification in general and on middle classes in particular is a truly interdisciplinary enterprise of investigation combining divergent academic lenses covering economics and political economy, development studies, industrial relations, social inequality studies, economic sociology, ethics, and gender studies altogether. The interdisciplinary nature includes many different keywords and combine patterns of consumption, income, work, and gender but also inequality, justice, social and economic change, and political economy as major topics bridging a diversity of knowledge domains and synthesizing discussions, which must be sought, found, and fitted together like puzzle pieces. All this is part of the new interdisciplinary framework of social sciences (Bögenhold, 2018).

References

Acemoglu, D., & Robinson, J. A. (2012). *Why Nations Fail: The Origins of Power, Prosperity and Poverty*. Profile.

Akerlof, G. A. (2020). Sins of Omission and the Practice of Economics. *Journal of Economic Literature, 58*(2), 405–418.

Atkinson, A. B. (2015). *Inequality: What Can Be Done?* Harvard University Press.

Atkinson, A. B. (2019). *Measuring Poverty Around the World*. Princeton University Press.

Atkinson, A. B., & Brandolini, A. (2011). *On the Identification of the 'Middle Class'*. ECINEQ Working Paper 2011–2017. Society for the Study of Economic Inequality.

Bauman, Z. (1998). *Globalization: The Human Consequences*. Columbia University Press.

Beck, U. (2002). *Risk Society: Toward a Modernity*. Sage.

Bögenhold, D. (2001). Social Inequality and the Sociology of Life Style: Material and Cultural Aspects of Social Stratification. *American Journal of Economics & Sociology, 60*, 829–848.

Bögenhold, D. (2018). Economics between Insulation and Social-Scienciation. *Journal of Economic Issues, 52*(4), 1127–1144.

Bögenhold, D. (2019). From Hybrid Entrepreneurs to Entrepreneurial Billionaires: Observations on the Socioeconomic Heterogeneity of Self-employment. *American Behavioral Scientist, 63*(2), 129–146.

Bögenhold, D. (2020). History of Economic Thought as an Analytic Tool: Why Past Intellectual Ideas Must Be Acknowledged as Lighthouses for the Future. *International Advances in Economic Research, 26*(1), 73–87.

Bögenhold, D., & Naz, F. (2018). *Consumption and Life-Styles. A Short Introduction*. Palgrave Macmillan.

Bögenhold, D., & Permana, Y. (2018). *End of Middle Classes? Social Inequalities in the Digital Age*. Discussion Paper 04-2018, Department of Sociology, University of Klagenfurt.

Bourdieu, P. (1984). *Distinction: A Social Critique of the Judgement of Taste*. Harvard University Press.

Case, A., & Deaton, A. (2020). *Deaths of Despair and the Future of Capitalism*. Princeton University Press.

Castells, M. (2010). *The Information Age. Economy, Society, and Culture*. Vol. I: The Rise of the Network Society. Oxford: Wiley-Blackwell.

Chirico, J. (2014). *Globalization: Prospects and Problems*. Sage Publications.

Cohen, J. L. (2012). *Globalization and Sovereignty. Rethinking Legality, Legitimacy, and Constitutionalism*. Cambridge University Press.

Collier, P. (2007). *The Bottom Billion: Why the Poorest Countries Are Failing and What Can Be Done About It*. Oxford University Press.

Collins, R. (2013). The End of Middle-Class Work: No More Escapes. In I. Wallerstein, R. Collins et al. (Eds.), *Does Capitalism Have a Future?* (Chapter 2). Oxford University Press.

Cross, G. (2010). Valves of Adult Desire: The Regulation and Incitement of Children's Consumption. In D. Buckingham & V. Tingstad (Eds.), *Childhood and Consumer Culture* (pp. 17–30). Palgrave Macmillan.

Giddens, A. (1973). *The Class Structures of the Advanced Societies.* Hutchinson.

Giddens, A. (1990). *The Consequences of Modernity.* Polity Press.

Giddens, S. (2009). *Sociology.* Polity Press.

Goffman, E. (1979 [1951]). *Gender Advertisements.* Macmillan.

Grabka, M. M., & Frick, J. R. (2008). The Shrinking German Middle Class–Signs of Long-Term Polarization in Disposable Income? *DIW Berlin Weekly Report, 4*(4), 21–27.

Grusky, D., Ku, C. M., & Szelényi, S. (Eds.). (2008). *Social Stratification: Class, Race, and Gender in Sociological Perspective.* Westview Press.

Grusky, D. B., & Szelényi, S. (Eds.). (2018). *The Inequality Reader.* Routledge.

Hodgson, G. M. (2000). What Is the Essence of Institutional Economics? *Journal of Economic Issues, 34*(2), 317–329.

Hodgson, G. M. (2001). *How Economics Forget History.* Routledge.

Katz-Gerro, T. (2004). Cultural Consumption Research: Review of Methodology, Theory, and Consequence. *International Review of Sociology, 14*(1), 11–29. https://doi.org/10.1080/0390670042000186743

Kaufman, N. H., Rizzini, I., Wilson, K., & Bush, M. (2004). The Impact of Global Economic, Political, and Social Transformations on the Lives of Children. In N. H. Kaufman & I. Rizzini (Eds.), *Globalization and Children. Exploring Potentials for Enhancing Opportunities in the Lives of Children and Youth Globalization and Children* (pp. 3–18). Kluwer.

Kochhar, R. (2017). *Middle Class Fortunes in Western Europe.* Luxembourg Income Study (LIS), Working Paper 702.

Lamont, M., & Lareau, A. (1988). Cultural Capital: Allusions, Gaps and Glissandos in Recent Theoretical. *Sociological Theory, 6*(2), 153–168.

Luhmann, N. (1971). Die Weltgesellschaft. *Archiv für Rechts- und Sozialphilosophie, 57*(1), 1–35.

Marx, K. (1977). *Capital: A Critique of Political Economy* (Vol. 3). Progress Publishers.

Merton, R. K. (1936). The Unanticipated Consequences of Purposive Social Action. *American Sociological Review, 1*(6), 894–904.

Meyer, J. W., Boli, J., Thomas, G. M., & Ramirez, F. O. (1981). World Society and the Nation-State. *American Journal of Sociology, 103*(1), 144–181.

Milanović, B. (2016). *Global Inequality: A New Approach for the Age of Globalization.* Harvard University Press.

Milanovic, B. (2019). *Capitalism, Alone. The Future of the System That Rules the World*. Belknap Press at Harvard University Press.
North, D. C. (1990). *Institutions, Institutional Change and Economic Performance*. Cambridge University Press.
Papageorgiou, T., Michaelides, P. G., & Bögenhold, D. (2020). Veblen and Bourdieu on Social Reality and Order: Individuals and Institutions. *Journal of Economic Issues, 54*(3), 710–773.
Pew Research Center. (2012). *The Lost Decade of the Middle Class*. https://www.pewresearch.org/social-trends/wp-content/uploads/sites/3/2012/08/pew-social-trends-lost-decade-of-the-middle-class.pdf
Piketty, T. (2014). *Capital in the 21st Century*. Harvard University Press.
Piketty, T. (2020). *Capital and Ideology*. Harvard University Press.
Pressman, S. (2010). The Middle Class Throughout the World in the Mid-2000s. *Journal of Economic Issues, 44*(1), 243–262.
Pressman, S. (2015). Defining and Measuring the Middle Class. *American Institute for Economic Research* (pp. 1–27). https://www.aier.org/wp-content/uploads/2016/10/WP007-Middle-Class.pdf
Pruchnik, K., & Zowczak, J. (2017). *Middle-Income Trap: Review of the Conceptual Framework*. Asian Development Bank Institute. https://www.adb.org/sites/default/files/publication/329201/adbi-wp760.pdf
Pullen, J. (2019). Malthus on Social Classes: Higher, Lower and Middle. *Cambridge Journal of Economics, 43*(5), 1417–1435.
Ravallion, M. (2010). The Developing World's Bulging (But Vulnerable) Middle Class. *World Development, 38*(4), 445–454.
Riesman, D., Denney, R., & Glazer, N. (1969 [1955]). *The Lonely Crowd: A Study of the Changing American Character*. Doubleday.
Ritzer, G., & Dean, P. (Eds.). (2015). *Globalization*. Blackwell Publishing Ltd..
Scott, R. H., & Pressman, S. (2011). A Double Squeeze on the Middle Class. *Journal of Economic Issues, 45*(2), 333–342.
Stiglitz, J. E. (2002). *Globalization and Its Discontents*. W.W. Norton and.
Stiglitz, J. E. (2012). *The Price of Inequality: How Today's Divided Society Endangers Our Future*. W. W. Norton.
Stiglitz, J. E. (2015). Inequality in America: A Policy Agenda for a Stronger Future. *The Annals of the American Academy of Political and Social Science, 657*(1), 8–20.
Stiglitz, J. E., Sen, A., & Fitoussi, J.-P. (2010). *Mismeasuring Our Lives: Why GDP Doesn't Add Up*. The New Press.
United Nations. (2015). *Transforming Our World: The 2030 Agenda for Sustainable Development*. https://www.un.org/ga/search/view_doc.asp?symbol=A/RES/70/1&Lang=E
Veblen, T. B. (1899). *The Theory of the Leisure Class*. Macmillan.
Wallerstein, I. (1983). *Historical Capitalism*. Verso.

Wallerstein, I. (2011). *The Modern World System*. University of California Press.
Wallerstein, I., Collins, R., Mann, M., Derluguian, G., & Calhoun, C. (2013). *Does Capitalism Have a Future?* Oxford University Press.
Weber, M. (1978). *Economy and Society: An Outline of Interpretive Sociology*. University of California Press.
Weber, M. (1988). Die protestantische Ethik und der Geist des Kapitalismus. In M. Weber (Ed.), *Gesammelte Aufsätze zur Religionssoziologie* (pp. 17–206). J. C. B. Mohr.
World Bank. (2002). *Globalization, Growth, and Poverty. Building an Inclusive World Economy*. Oxford University Press.

CHAPTER 4

Social Network Analysis and the Sociology of Economics: Filling a Blind Spot with the Idea of Social Embeddedness

Introduction

Many social sciences, but especially economics and sociology, are arranged in faculties, courses, and textbooks on the basis of macro and micro analysis. Research on the connection between micro and macro perspectives has been scarce and the subject is virtually neglected (see Hoover, 2009, 2010; Colander, 1993). In economics, no consensus exists as to whether macro follows micro or vice versa. While a macro perspective dominated for a long time since Wicksell "more or less founded macroeconomics" (Blaug, 1986, p. 274), recently Rodgers (2011, ch. 2), who puts some of the discussed theoretical trends in a wider social perspective of thought, argues that micro views have gained some advantages nowadays.

In many respects, network analysis may be a tool to bridge both perspectives. Social embeddedness seems to have become "economic sociology's most celebrated metaphor" (Guillén et al., 2002, p. 4). Social network analysis may be able to translate and exemplify those popular formulations. Different network designs provide different opportunities to communicate and receive information and, as a result, they create different structures of social contacts and an unequal distribution of

Bögenhold, Dieter: Social Network Analysis and the Sociology of Economics: Filling a Blind Spot with the Idea of Social Embeddedness, in: *The American Journal of Economics and Sociology*, Vol. 72, No. 2, 2013, pp. 293–318

D. Bögenhold, *Neglected Links in Economics and Society*,
https://doi.org/10.1007/978-3-030-79193-3_4

knowledge, which serve as a kind of social capital for individual agents. Network analysis enquires of the modes and content of exchanges between people, where symbols (concepts, values, and norms), emotions (love, respect or hostility), or goods or services (especially financial subsidies and gifts) are exchanged. Network research has become an evolving cross-disciplinary subject with applications in many diverse fields of social and economic life. Even physicists show an increasing interest in network research (Scott, 2011).

The aim of the chapter is to present a compelling argument for social network analysis as a valid way to illuminate the idea of social embeddedness, since it provides dynamic aspects that are inherent in structures often commonly treated as blueprints. Social network analysis sits comfortably alongside recent discussions within the field of philosophy of economics, examining the limitations of mainstream economics. It has been argued that economics should be open to the integration of behavioural and cognitive elements (Akerlof, 2007; Akerlof & Kranton, 2000; Akerlof & Shiller, 2009; Kahneman, 2003) in order to assist the movement of economics from the world of abstract modeling to real-world phenomena. Viewing economics as a box of tools (Schumpeter, 1954, Preface) permits one to identify social network analysis as an economic technique with the potential to map with economic behaviour, institutions, and economic and social change. That is because social network analysis will foster a shift from abstract economics towards an economics dealing with real people.

If sociology can claim that traditional network research belongs on sociological terrain, then the improving reception of the literature on social networks and the growing acceptance of interdisciplinary network research necessarily requires sociological competency in the subject. In other words, institutional academic sociology can use the subject of network sociology as a positive example to demonstrate the comparative strengths of academic sociology.

By referring to the network issue in a broader sense and at different levels, one can show that specific regions, related companies and economies differ in terms of their network structures, implying that they have specific family structures and structures of interaction, communication and exchange. Consequently, different structures reflect the issue that has been expressed by the formulation of "Culture Matters" (Harrison & Huntington, 2000). In contrast to sterile neoclassical economics, which aims at universal principles in a capitalist economy, the topic of network structures, which by definition includes corresponding variability, must be regarded as a counter-weight to abstract theorizing in economics (Jones, 2006).

The current chapter addresses the challenges brought out in two major areas of discussion. First of all, the chapter tries to provide a survey of positions in the history of intellectual debate on network research. Moreover, the composition of arguments and related references is more concerned with a sociology of science. In contrast to, and in critique of, formal and abstract attempts of theorizing in economics and in sociology, the chapter intends to show that social network research highlights what cultural sciences want to express, which is that culture matters. Networks integrate the level of action and communication with issues of structural selection and social change, which is the reason that social networks can be viewed as both a theoretical and methodological concern simultaneously. Different network structures in different cultures frame individual decision making and choice (Becker, 1974) by providing specific sets of preferences (Ellison, 1995). Cultures within related times and spaces provide a differing calculus of individual rationality.

Network Research and Academic Innovation: Against the Homo Oeconomicus

When discussing sociological network theory, we follow an innovative script that invites academic and economic and policy issues of real societies and economies (as opposed to abstract societies and economies) as subjects for research. Network research, especially when applied, is increasingly interdisciplinary and provides an adequate response to the limitations of mono-disciplinary approaches (Marcovich & Shinn, 2011), which are always in danger of being quasi-autistic. It is just the intensive study of the economic development that illustrates our genuine understanding of Schumpeter, namely, that innovation is the enforcement of "new combinations" (Schumpeter, [1911] 1963, pp. 100–102) of ways to produce.

Referring to differences in economic structures between countries and within countries, many of the differences to be found may reflect different culture-related organizational principles of economic life that are reflected by divergent social network structures, which mirror divergent training, education, and employment arrangements and, ultimately, different family structures, different systems of industrial relations, and economic mentalities. As a result, a variety of social actors can be found that cannot be reduced to the simple idealized figure of homo oeconomicus as the ideal model of a "clean" economics would have it. The idea of homo oeconomicus itself is a stereotype that does not acknowledge properly the semantic changes over time (Pearson, 2000). Nevertheless, historian David Landes (2000, p. 2) put it concisely: "Culture makes almost all the difference."

Thinking along those lines, the intersection between a perspective on social network analysis and research on institutional economics and socioeconomic systems becomes visible; both aim to understand the object of analysis in its social and historical context. Instead of referring to stereotypical classifications that emphasize generalized statements on nature, the role and function of the society or the economy, independent of specific cultural and historical contexts, economic life never takes place without an interplay with its real social and economic environment. Peter Berger put it this way: "Economic institutions do not exist in a vacuum but rather in a context of social and political structures, cultural patterns, and indeed, structures of consciousness (values, ideas, belief systems). An economic culture then contains a number of elements linked together in an empirical totality" (Berger, 1986, p. 24).

This position is constitutive for new economic sociology, which takes up a tradition going back to old institutionalism that intersected the new historical school in the German-speaking world (Schmölders, 1984) and also works simultaneously in North America (see Dorfman, 1946–1959). There is an inherent common logic between modern works in sociology and those in economics that criticize the status of mainstream economics. The term "heterodox economics" (Lee, 2009) stands for this form of critique. In the center of the related critique is the model of the homo oeconomicus as it is used in neoclassical theory. The basic assumptions are: "1. The assumption of rational, maximizing behavior by agents with given and stable preference functions, 2. A focus on attained, or movements toward, equilibrium states, 3. The absence of chronic information problems (there is, at most, a focus on probabilistic risk: excluding severe ignorance, radical uncertainty, or divergent perceptions of a given reality)" (Hodgson, 1994, p. 60).

In our discussion, it is the first and third items of Hodgson's notion that are of interest: human beings have motives, which may be viewed as rational or irrational by observers (Lauterbach, 1962; Rabin, 1998), and people have emotions by which they are governed positively or negatively (Elster, 1998; Scherer, 2011). Love, hate, or envy are expressions of human activity that are real. Human beings love human beings, yet they kill people on occasion, they take part in lotteries, or they present gifts and cheat elsewhere (see, for emotions, Turner & Stets, 2009; Stets & Turner, 2007). Human beings do not share the same network structures but have divergent communication structures and related modes of interaction. Communication processes are asynchronous—everybody cannot speak with everybody else, but only a few people in specific groups communicate regularly with selected others, and consequently information in society is not shared equally. The topic of social networks tries to highlight the blind spots of neoclassical theory (Smelser & Swedberg, 1994). Society is conceptualized as a configuration of different patterns of interactions that party overlap and partly coexist. The question of the institutional framing and the relevance of culture is not only the legitimacy of doing appropriate analysis on economies and societies (Jones, 2006), but it is a *conditio sine qua non* if one wants to avoid a sterile economic discussion that neglects diverse social networks and structures of motivations in order to arrive at generalized statements.

Society in Abstracto Versus in Concreto: An Epistemological View

Differentiation of academic subjects and disciplines, especially in the second part of the twentieth century, brought increasing autonomy to the disparate sections of social sciences, and consequently academic communication between individual branches of the subject decreased. An archipelago of new academic islands emerged, most with an intensive island life, but the communication traffic between each was scarce and almost silent. Economics suffered from a loss of access to sociological and behavioural contexts, and came to favor a priori assumptions regarding human action. The trend ran parallel with a shift in economic theorizing towards formalized modeling and theory building instead of real-world analysis (Mikl-Horke, 1999, ch. 13) but modeling itself became differentiated and contradictory (Morgan, 2011).

As scientific theorems became more formal and abstract, dimensions such as space and time lost their significance, theorizing became increasingly non-historical and non-cultural since sterility was precisely the aim. In economics, a substantial number of positions neglected culture for that very reason, and often with quite offensive arguments. In that respect, there is a parallel between the approach of Karl Marx and formulations in neoclassic theory and its related idea of homo oeconomicus. Marx thinks human actors are treated simply as agents of roles, as personifications of economic categories, which function like actors interpreting a specific script (Marx, 1977, p. 16). In terms of their methodological procedures, economists engaged in marginal utility theory proved to be quite similar. Karl Menger and associates assumed that human needs that are relevant for economic life occur at different stages, which lead—from stage to stage—to decreasing ratios of satisfaction and finally to the marginal utility of the last available unit. This idea was not based upon empirical psychological research because it was not regarded as necessary. Deductive reasoning came up with a priori statements instead.

Arguing against Menger, there was Gustav Schmoller, who opposed Menger in what came to be called the first battle of methods in social sciences. Schmoller's intention was to criticize the abstract nature of those models solely based on non-empirical assumptions. Schmoller argued institutionally in favor of the cultural and historical embeddedness of observations.[1] The twentieth century represented the triumph of Menger's thought and his marginal utility theory became a foundation of a neoclassical economics clearly distinct from sociology and historicism (Hodgson, 2001).

Today, the works of Max Weber and Werner Sombart are better known both in terms of their theoretical impact and empirical content. Religious dispositions and economic mentalities were discussed in relation to the establishment of socioeconomic systems and Weber elaborated a typology of four ideal types of social action, which are the rationality of traditional action, of affective action, of value orientation, and of purposive-rational utilitarian action (Weber, 1972, pt. 1, ch. 1) of which only the last point of classification matches with the supposed rationality of homo oeconomicus.[2] Being distant to a procedure as provided in theoretical economics, Max Weber concluded that economics "argues with a non-realist human being, analogous a mathematical ideal figure" (Weber, 1990, p. 30). The questioning of the institutional framework of economic phenomena and the relative autonomy of networks corresponds with the recognition of the impact of culture within the process of economic development. According to Sombart (1982), all economies and their inherent economic lives are related to specific times and spaces, which are always embedded in a historical flux. The perspective comes very close to that of a modern interdisciplinary program, both claiming a dialogue between economics and neighbouring academic fields.

The Idea of "Social Embeddedness"

As ideas about an economy and society in concreto are increasingly accepted, so the relative autonomy of culture and its specification in different historical variations is also increasingly accepted. A plea for the academic existence of sociology must be the ultimate consequence. In particular, historical and comparative sociology, socioeconomics and economic sociology, and, of course, social network research proves to be innovative when highlighting national and international variations and specifics. In general, one can also argue that history, economics, business administration, and sociology should try to reintegrate because their topics are among the items in a complex web of reciprocal thematic interaction. The concept of the "social embeddedness" of institutional actors and human behaviour is a common label for approaches that attempt to deal with the interplay of individual and corporate actors in a dynamic and joint process. "Social embeddedness," as a term and conceptual idea, goes back to Karl Polanyi, who became especially well-known through his book, *The Great Transformation* (2001), which elaborates on the genesis of a self-regulatory market in Europe, and particularly in England. Polanyi's concept shows clear links to Durkheimian thought (Carroll & Stanfield, 2003).

Polanyi contends that all societies are regulated and limited by economic factors. Parallel to the course of the establishment of free and self-regulatory markets, Polanyi observes a process of social differentiation. Status and community dominate where an economy is integrated in non-economic institutions, but contract and society are characteristic of a separation of economy and society.

According to Polanyi, an economy is a process embedded in economic and non-economic institutions. The integration of economic life runs in three different ways, namely, through the mode of reciprocity, which is dedicated to social networks and kinship relations, through the mode of redistribution, which depends on a central organization in society, and through processes of exchange integrating the economy into a system of market prices. The semantic use of "social embeddedness" originated from anthropology (and is still to be found in substantive anthropology) but it has now been adopted by a range of other disciplines.

The impact of such a perspective is that modern economics could be linked with a constructive view that provides a new division of work between economics and the other social sciences (Granovetter, 1993). Granovetter's formulation of a "social embeddedness of economic behavior and institutions" (Granovetter, 1985) has subsequently become widely known. Granovetter focuses explicitly on the work of Polanyi and his argumentation is based upon three premises, namely, that economic action is a special case of social action, secondly, that economic action is socially situated and embedded, and thirdly, that economic institutions are social constructions. A synthesis is sought between conceptions of over-socialized and under-socialized human beings in order to articulate a theorem that takes into account both the determination of society and the relative openness of human activities as a process (Granovetter, 1993, 2002). Granovetter argues against the concept of a homo oeconomicus as used in neoclassical thought and against a model of a homo sociologicus in which an individual agent is controlled by social norms and roles.

Social network research has, partly implicitly and partly explicitly, adopted Granovetter's preambles as a research program. Economy and society are permanently "in the making" and they are best interpreted as the socially structured and motivated interaction of actors. Social actions are constituted along existing ties of contacts, which are based upon social experiences within different social circles of communication.

The Genesis of Network Research: Geometry of Social Relations and Structures of Reciprocity

The earliest network research is attributed to Georg Simmel. Although Simmel was not strictly a network researcher, he was a researcher who thought in categories quite similar to network approaches found today. Simmel portrayed society in dualistic terms, exemplified by the word pairs of universality and particularity, continuity and change, or conformism and distinction. In addition, people are dualistic and Simmel thinks of dualism as a driving force of development, which creates change.

The earliest sociologists thought of society in terms of the geometry of social relations. In the same way that geometry deals with forms capable of becoming bodies, the analysis of abstract forms was a major task for Simmel's work. Social formations are characterized and constituted through continuous repetition. Simmel's view of the cross-pressures of social circles ("Kreuzung sozialer Kreise"; Simmel, 1908) appears very similar to the modern analysis of cliques in contemporary network analysis. The dispositions of individual actors differ according to their positions in a network, and personality, in the sense of individuality, is a result of the cross-pressures of circles. Networks function as modes of social differentiation and societal trends of standardization. Finally, social structures are conceptualized as relational—and principally changing—links between human actors and organizations.

A different origin of contemporary network discussion can be seen in anthropology, where structural attributes of societies will be discussed in the context of processes of gift giving, marriages, or authority and violence. Mauss (2002, 2006) demonstrates how the giving and exchanging of gifts is organized along social norms and processes. Often, no specific economic advantage is connected to the exchange of gifts and sometimes the same things are even exchanged between two parties, suggesting that beyond the economic rationalities a specific social logic must be working.

Individual agents, families, and tribes combine with each other through the exchanges of gifts and of "throats to be cut which are 'lent' and 'repaid' " (Collins, 1988, p. 419). As a consequence, social relations emerge and are intensified so that circles of reciprocal connections between families and tribes are constructed. Although the terminology of networks is not used, the topic is obviously close. Reciprocal ties based upon different manners of exchange between actors constitute the structure of societies.

Structure as a term also has substantial meaning in the works of Lévi-Strauss. In the societies he analysed, families form alliances through marriages of dependent family members that lead to reciprocal commitments. Such alliances provide for the distribution of goods and services. Since the patterns of kinship exchange vary between societies, Lévi-Strauss addresses the dynamics of the structures by asking for specific rules for marriage practices (Lévi-Strauss, 1987) and by distinguishing between "short cycles," which unify a small number of families and that are stable over a few generations, and "long cycles," which unify many more families indirectly and families that may also be geographically separated (Collins, 1994, p. 231). The works of Mauss and Lévi-Strauss are antecedents of modern network research but their perspective is already clear and convincing. Families establish ties and create simple and complex networks. This structural approach describes the structure of societies and related dynamics and changes to these societies. The argumentation is in no way restricted to agrarian or tribal societies, but can be applied to modern societies as well.

Later, other anthropologists produced more elaborate theoretical and empirical work on networks, trying to deal with particular units and relations. British structural functionalists like Radcliffe-Brown and the "Manchester anthropologists"—John Barnes, Clyde Mitchell, Elizabeth

Bott—focused on cultural systems of normative rights and duties, which govern behaviour within specific ensembles like tribes, villages, or working groups (Wellman, 1988, p. 21).

Radcliffe-Brown is often credited as the originator of the term social network: he wrote that "direct observation does reveal to us that these human beings are connected by a complex network of social relations. I use the term 'social structure' to denote this network of actually existing relations" (Radcliffe-Brown, 1940, p. 2). Radcliffe-Brown's terminology inspired other anthropologists to discuss contemporary metaphors such as "fabric," "web," "interweaving," and "interlocking" and to extend them to formal concepts like "density" and "texture" (Scott, 2010).

The work of anthropologists in the 1950s focused on cultural systems, which had limitations when relations occurred that were transitory to close groups or categories. "Concrete ties" and "cross-cutting ties" were discussed, and network analysis started in earnest by developing systematic network concepts. In his study of a Norwegian island on which he discovered hidden networks of friendship and kinship, which sometimes crossed the hierarchical, administrative, and industrial structures, Barnes (1954) produced pioneering work. His network of relations was built upon intentional choices made by individual actors that partially reflected the class system of the island. Barnes initiated a change from a metaphoric network to a network term corresponding to modern network analysis, which is close to graph theory (Scott, 2010, p. 27).

The research programme of these anthropologists was focused on particular social relations to determine structures with inherent patterns of action. A crucial advance was added by structuralists like Harrison White and associates (White et al., 1976), who introduced the block-model analysis, which is still on the agenda in evolved form and is used by mathematicians and physicists and members of other disciplines (see Scott, 2010, p. 33). The basic premise was to use network concepts in order to arrive at a theory of social structures:

The presently existing, largely categorical description of social structure has no solid theoretical grounding; furthermore, network concepts may provide the only way to construct a theory of social structure (White et al., 1976, p. 732). Many subsequent network-related studies and research topics tried to foster "a broadly comprehensive structural analytic approach" (Wellman, 1988, p. 29).

Social Network Research as Research of Social and Economic Dynamics

Social network analysis has become a cross-disciplinary subject with applications in many diverse fields of social and economic life, and it continues to evolve. One of the most challenging fields to investigate is market dynamics, a subject very often regarded as a black box by mainstream economists (Swedberg, 2003). Markets function upon the basis of communication and social rules, which may be addressed by social-network-oriented research perspectives. At least two of the crucial research conclusions Fligstein (2001) drew in his *Architecture of Markets* are relevant for network research; these are: "What social rules must exist for markets to function, and what types of social structures are necessary to produce stable markets?" and "What is a 'social' view of what actors seek to do in markets, as opposed to an 'economic' one?" (Fligstein, 2001, pp. 11–14). Markets are always in transition, they come up, they go down, and they change. The markets are populated by actors utilizing sets of people they know and in whom they trust, while regarding other people as potentially hostile competitors. However real markets are portrayed, they always have very social traits, and economics researchers would be neglecting their duties if they were not to ask about their effects. Competition processes must also be analysed and understood as ongoing social processes that are involved in the continual reorganization (see Shackle, 1972) of choices and decisions in relation to uncertainty.

The analysis of markets and processes of innovation has involved a variety of approaches, of which just three are mentioned here. Besides the works of White, it is worth mentioning network studies interpreting markets as networks (White, 1981, 1988; Granovetter, 1985; Baker, 1984, 1990). A specific issue of research is how structures of a network influence markets and the different chances individual actors have according to their specific position in a network (Burt, 1995). The starting point of the structural approach is the assumption that "markets may be viewed as social rather than exclusively economic structures" (Baker, 1984, p. 776).[3] Burt summarizes the research idea programmatically when talking about the "social structure of completion" (Burt, 1995, later broadly reformulated as Burt, 2007).

Granovetter (1973, 1974) started to do labour market research in the 1970s, inquiring of the social processes involved in finding new jobs. His theorem of "the strength of weak ties" has since become a classic formulation. Granovetter referred to informal channels of getting information, which were introduced through microstructural perspectives. Later, Granovetter (1985, 2002) extended his argumentation to a discussion of macro-level structures when examining the social embeddedness of institutions and behaviour and when discussing different modes of structures.

Baker (1984) performed network research on the social structure of stock markets. His study distinguishes between different markets and types of markets, which are carried out by different forms of social relations. This perspective holds that network structures serve as both cause and result of social processes. Finally, when referring to the ideas of Burt (1995), Baker (1984), or Granovetter (1974), it is important to note that they all centre on the question "Where do markets come from?" (White, 1981) and favour a type of answer with a strong link to social foundations. New information, ideas, and opportunities come up through different forms of strong or weak ties between people in different clusters (see Bögenhold & Marschall, 2008).

Social Network Analysis: Innovation, Theory, and Methods

The modern social-science-based understanding of how economy and society are linked seems to confer legitimacy upon social network research, owing to its offering a package of different perspectives and insights. The argumentation in this chapter travels a long line within the history of thought in social network analysis. The evolution of research in the field has become remarkable and a series of journals and research committees have been founded worldwide. In the meantime, the International Network for Social Network Analysis (www.insna.org) has more than 1,700 members with very diverse academic backgrounds in 78 countries. Reading contributions in the field sometimes demands very specialized expertise in specific academic areas. Over time, the complexities increase and the applications multiply (Dehmer, 2010). While network analysis started in anthropology and sociology, employing qualitative methods and local community studies, in the last few decades, quantitative methods have made strong advances in network research. In some disciplines, like physics, large-scale analysis has become the predominant method. However, even today, qualitative studies remain a useful and valuable field for social network research, ranging from anthropology to conversation and discourse analysis and other applications. In addition, historians increasingly refer to network concepts (see, for example, Rota, 2007; Laird, 2006).

Network research studies usually strengthen and highlight the inner dynamics of societies (for an overview, see Scott, 2010; Carrington et al., 2009; Wasserman & Faust, 2009; Carrington & Scott, 2010; Stegbauer, 2008; Häußling & Stegbauer, 2010; Newman, 2010; Easley & Kleinberg, 2010; Burt, 2010). Orthodox and heterodox economics could both take advantage of these conceptual ideas in order to instigate innovative research programmes; other disciplines, like sociology, already do so.

Social network analysis now makes a constructive contribution in many academic fields. To neglect network structures bears the risk that the social figuration processes of interaction and the basic principles that underpin them are ignored. If one does not know the modes of interaction and communication, one does not know the ways in which signs, symbols, and contents are transported. To be able to study processes of diffusion requires information about ties and links of exchange. All processes of innovation and the diffusion of innovation are highly dependent upon communicative acts of people belonging to different networks, sharing and providing information through different media (Rogers, 2003). Whether related to the innovation of production systems in diverse commercial fields, or to customers and their consumer behaviour and social lifestyles, all hierarchies of preferences are crystallized in and through networks and constructed by opinion leaders. Networks are always the media holding (diverse) knowledge and the media through which that knowledge is modified.

One of the most intriguing questions is whether the way in which networks function has changed over time. Due to the increased prevalence of modern electronic communication systems, we not only have electronic markets but also new forms of private exchange through the Internet or by cell phone (Wellman & Haythornthwaite, 2002). Does this development create new patterns of communication and network structures? How are network structures linked to increased social and occupational mobility? Has the relevance of family-based ties decreased in the era of individualization and globalization or is the opposite in fact evident? Do demographic changes have an impact on network structures? Will the increasing number of elderly people in society lead to changing network structures? Catalogues of questions could be formed to provide grounds for justifiable further research.

Since social network research has evolved so rapidly in recent decades, two specific questions have assumed great importance and must be answered explicitly: (i) Does network research still fit into one single academic subject? The answer must promptly follow that network research has become too diverse to be identified as part of one discipline. Network research has become a kind of cross-disciplinary way of thinking and, as such, it might become a new academic area in its own right. (ii) What is the status of social network research? Is it a theory or is it a research method?

To answer, one should first clarify what is meant by theory. Half a century ago, Schumpeter (1954) wrote that a scientific economist can be distinguished from a simple economist by a command of techniques classified in different fields, that is, economic history, statistics, economic sociology, and theory and applied fields. In this context, the word theory is always written with quotation marks—as "theory"—to underline that it is problematic to talk about theory as if a common understanding of the term existed. In fact, there is no unanimously agreed definition of theory at all; different types of theory coexist (see, for recent contributions, Bunge, 1996; Haller, 2003, ch. 1; Schülein, 2009, p. 42–65) and the question of when an academic statement acquires the status of theory remains a moot point (Turner, 1988, p. 4). Reviewing several existing pieces of literature dealing with the question of whether social network analysis is primarily theory or instead a method shows that we have not yet found any coherent answers. The basic denominator is that social network analysis seems to be something of a hybrid (Bögenhold & Marschall, 2010). Universally, network research is qualified as an important instrument, but the difficulty remains of how to describe the status of network analysis. More than 20 years ago, Wellman (1988, p. 20) said: "Some have hardened it into a method, whereas others have softened it into a metaphor" and Collins referred to network analysis as a "technique in search of a theory" (Collins, 1988, p. 412).

Turner (1988, p. 528) says that the potential for network analysis as a theoretical approach is great because it captures an important property of social structure—patterns of relations among social units, whether people, collectivities, or positions. However, Turner's judgement is that network analysis is still overly methodological in nature and that it is concerned with generating quantitative techniques for arraying data in matrices and then converting the matrices into descriptions of particular networks (whether as graphs or as equations). As long as that is the case, network sociology will remain primarily a tool for empirical description. Second, there has been little effort to develop principles of network dynamics, per se. Few seem to ask theoretical questions within the network tradition itself. For example, how does the degree of density, centrality, equivalence, bridging, and brokerage influence the nature of the network and the flow of relations among positions in the network? There are many empirical descriptions of events that touch on this question but few actual theoretical laws or principles (Turner, 1988, p. 529).

Strategically, networks provide a link between micro and macro perspectives. They integrate the level of action and communication with issues of structural selection and social change. Networks serve as "sets" of preferences and social contacts between individual agents and groups of people. The bloodstream of society runs through networks. Whereas many writers treat the functioning of markets as something close to a black box, in which offer and demand equalize somehow, network analysis sheds far more light on the processes and informs us of how economic dynamics are often based upon social dynamics in which personal experiences and trust play important roles. Markets as well as many other institutions provide resources to human actors through different levels of inclusion, which function through principles of social networks (Burt & Talmud, 1993). That the status of social network analysis remains unresolved and weak (the theory versus method debate) implies that there is room for further input here.

From Social Network Analysis to Social Capital

Discussion on social network analysis often elicits mention of the term social capital, as if both terms are interchangeable. It seems appropriate to conclude the current chapter by adding some brief reflection on the relationship between social networks and social capital. The answer is very simple, since social networks can serve as social capital for individuals or groups of people, sets of specific networks, which one actor has compared to those of another actor, may be understood and used as a kind of economic resource.

Even the debate on social capital is marked by a long history of ideas going back to early neighbourhood and community studies, starting in the middle of the twentieth century. However, the works of Bourdieu (1983) and Coleman (1988, 1990) addressed social capital more specifically and conceptually. Addressing "capital as power" (Nitzan & Bichler, 2009), Bourdieu (1983) is primarily interested in inquiring about the analytical position of social resources and strategies in the context of economy and society. How can individuals, groups, or classes enhance their life-chances, careers, and quality of life? What many previous social network researchers have thought about, but rarely articulated, is explicitly elaborated as a conceptual perspective embedded in a broader scenario. Bourdieu (1983) distinguishes between economic capital, which he interprets in a classic sense as material and financial capital and assets, cultural capital, which includes an interpretation of human capital, and can be further split into subsections, and, finally, social capital. Individuals or collectives own different amounts of capital consisting of different compositions of the three sources of capital. Finally, capital of one sort can partly be instrumentalized to realize capital profits of another sort. Bourdieu's perspective left behind a narrow social network perspective and started focusing on the more principal issues of order and restructuring of complex societies and their social inequalities. Social capital is interpreted as the volume of social resources of a person's networks.

Coleman (1990) searches for the "social foundations of social theory" and has devoted a substantial chapter (Chap. 12) of his *Foundations of Social Theory* to a discussion of social networks. He says that social capital and human capital are often complementary (Coleman, 1988).

> *Social capital, in turn, is created when the relations between people change in ways that facilitate action. Physical capital is wholly tangible, being embodied in observable material form; human capital is less tangible, being embodied in the skills and knowledge acquired by an individual; social capital is even less tangible, for it is embodied in the relations between people. Physical capital and human capital facilitate productive activity, and social capital does so as well.* (Coleman, 1990, p. 304)

Coleman (1990) does not restrict social capital to resources based upon social networks, but includes in his definition institutional interpretations as well. Those include family structures, societal forms of trustworthiness, systems of production and regulation, religion, education, and language. All these dimensions differ between and within societies and generate different levels of social capital.

The potential for further applications, and also for problems, becomes obvious as basic social network research starts to become diversified, opening itself to societal mentalities and their religions, social and psychological dispositions, and different institutions of societal order. Social capital became open to being multiplied and instrumentalized (Ostrom & Ahn, 2001; Burt, 1997). Policy studies, management and organization theory, and the practical policies of national and global policymakers started to employ social capital as a strategic concept for the use of an increasing number of associations. Putnam's (Putnam et al., 1993) networks of civic engagement, Fukujama's (1995) comparisons between different social structures in different societies as sources of different economic competitive structures of economies, and many other studies that followed analysed links between social networks, social capital, and economic development (Sabatini, 2008; Barr, 2009; Chamlee-Wright, 2008; Chalupnicek, 2010), as did monographs, handbooks, and encyclopedias (Easley & Kleinberg, 2010; Field, 2008; Svendsen & Haase Svendsen, 2009).

Debate on social capital has emerged and the term has become a policy instrument, and sometimes social capital sounds like a hackneyed phrase. It refers to political economy and some further distinct thematic areas but all of the applications are grounded on the premise that the procedures of a complex economic and social life have serious social roots that together constitute a powerful plea for an integrated socioeconomics in research and in teaching, which can only be understood as part of an institutional interpretation linking different academic areas. Recent ideas stem from their own history of ideas and economic and social thought. As always, it is fruitful to start from a broader perspective to see the conceptual lines of continuity and change. We started with the idea that cultures matter and that sterile conceptions close to central ideas of neoclassic economics fail. Accepting that premise and moving forward logically, we can see that network analysis and research on social capital provide useful arguments as to why these "social dimensions" fit with institutional thought.

Different capital structures correspond with different network designs and vice versa. Divergent network arrangements provide different opportunities to communicate, receive information, and create different structures of cultural capital. Network analysis explores modes and contents of exchanges between different agents when symbols, emotions, or goods and services get exchanged. This chapter tried to argue that social network analysis has become a cross-disciplinary subject with applications in diverse fields of social and economic life. The message of the chapter was to highlight that social network analysis provides a tool to foster the understanding of social dynamics by looking between micro and macro areas and filling the gap. Social network analysis enhances recent debate on social and economic changes and may get rid of some limitations of the cognitive and explanatory potential of economics.

Notes

1. Pearson (1999) argues that the concept of a German Historical School of Economics is itself infelicitous. For a substantial discussion of Schmoller's position, see Schumpeter (1926).
2. Weber (1988) noted the coincidence between the Protestant ethic and the rise of capitalism. It is interesting to see that Weber quoted Th. Veblen (1899) who—vice versa—already had a frequent exchange with contemporary European authors (see Loader & Rick, 1995).
3. The cultural approach employs ethnographic (Abolafia, 1998) or historical (Zelizer, 1985, 1988) methods and the political approach underlines the role of institutions and the role of governmental influences for the functioning of markets (Fligstein, 2001).

References

Abolafia, M. Y. (1998). Markets as Cultures. An Ethnografic Approach. In M. Callon (Ed.), *The Laws of the Markets* (pp. 69–85). Blackwell Publishers.

Akerlof, G. A. (2007). The Missing Motivation in Macroeconomics. *The American Economic Review, 97*(1), 5–36.

Akerlof, G. A., & Kranton, R. E. (2000). Economics and Identity. *Quarterly Journal of Economics, 115*(3), 715–753.

Akerlof, G. A., & Shiller, R. J. (2009). *Animal Spirits: How Human Psychology Drives the Economy, and Why it Matters for Global Capitalism.* Princeton University Press.

Baker, W. E. (1984). The Social Structure of a National Securities Market. *American Journal of Sociology, 89*(4), 775–811.

Baker, W. E. (1990). Market Networks and Corporate Behavior. *American Journal of Sociology, 96*(3), 589–625.

Barnes, J. A. (1954). Class and Committees in a Norwegian Island Parish. *Human Relations, 7*(1), 39–58.

Barr, T. (2009). With Friends Like These. Endogenous Labor Market Segregation with Homogenous, Nonprejudiced Agents. *American Journal of Economics and Sociology, 68*(3), 703–746.

Becker, G. S. (1974). Theory of Social Interaction. *Journal of Political Economy, 82*(6), 1063–1093.

Berger, P. L. (1986). *The Capitalist Revolution.* Basic Books.
Blaug, M. (1986). *Great Economists Before Keynes. An Introduction to the Lives and Works of One Hundred Great Economists of the Past.* Cambridge University Press.
Bögenhold, D., & Marschall, J. (2008). Metapher, Methode, Theorie. Netzwerkforschung in der Wirtschaftssoziologie. In C. Stegbauer (Ed.), *Netzwerkanalyse und Netzwerktheorie. Ein neues Paradigma in den Sozialwissenschaften* (pp. 387–400). VS-Publishers.
Bögenhold, D., & Marschall, J. (2010). Weder Methode noch Metapher. Zum Theorieanspruch der Netzwerkanalyse bis in die 1980er Jahre. In R. Häußling & C. Stegbauer (Eds.), *Handbuch Netzwerkforschung* (pp. 283–291). VS-Publishers.
Bourdieu, P. (1983). Forms of Capital. In J. G. Richardson (Ed.), *Handbook of Theory and Research for the Sociology of Education* (pp. 214–258). Greenwood Press.
Bunge, M. (1996). *Finding Philosophy in Social Science.* Yale University Press.
Burt, R. S. (1995). *Structural Holes: The Social Structure of Competition.* Harvard University Press.
Burt, R. S. (1997). The Contingent Value of Social Capital. *Administrative Science Quarterly, 42*(2), 339–365.
Burt, R. S. (2007). *Brokerage and Closure: An Introduction to Social Capital.* Oxford University Press.
Burt, R. S. (2010). *Neighbor Networks. Competitive Advantage Local and Personal.* Oxford University Press.
Burt, R. S., & Talmud, I. (1993). Market Niche. *Social Networks, 15*(2), 133–149.
Carrington, P., & Scott, J. (Eds.). (2010). *Handbook of Social Network Analysis.* Sage.
Carrington, P. J., Scott, J., & Wasserman, S. (2009). *Models and Methods in Social Network Analysis.* Cambridge University Press.
Carroll, M. C., & Stanfield, J. R. (2003). Social Capital, Karl Polanyi, and American Social and Institutional Economics. *Journal of Economic Issues, 37*(2), 397–404.
Chalupnicek, P. (2010). The Capital in Social Capital: An Austrian Perspective. *American Journal of Economics and Sociology, 69*(4), 1230–1250.
Chamlee-Wright, E. (2008). The Structure of Social Capital: An Austrian Perspective on its Nature and Development. *Review of Political Economy, 20*(1), 41–58.
Colander, D. C. (1993). The Macrofoundations of Micro. *Eastern Economic Journal, 19*(4), 447–457.
Coleman, J. S. (1988). Social Capital in the Creation of Human Capital. *American Journal of Sociology, 94*, 95–120.
Coleman, J. S. (1990). *Foundations of Social Theory.* Harvard University Press.
Collins, R. (1988). *Theoretical Sociology.* Hartcourt Brace Jovanovich.
Collins, R. (1994). *Four Sociological Traditions.* Oxford University Press.

Dehmer, M. (Ed.). (2010). *Structural Analysis of Complex Networks*. Birkhäuser.
Dorfman, J. (1946–1959). *The Economic Mind in American Civilization* (Vol. 5). Viking Press.
Easley, D., & Kleinberg, J. (2010). *Networks, Crowds, and Markets: Reasoning About a Highly Connected World*. Cambridge University Press.
Ellison, C. G. (1995). Rational Choice Explanations of Individual Religious Behavior: Notes on the Problem of Social Embeddedness. *Journal for the Scientific Study of Religion, 34*(1), 89–97.
Elster, J. (1998). Emotions and Economic Theory. *Journal of Economic Literature, 36*(1), 47–74.
Field, J. (2008). *Social Capital*. Routledge.
Fligstein, N. (2001). *The Architecture of Markets*. Princeton University Press.
Fukuyama, F. (1995). *Trust: The Social Virtues and the Creation of Prosperity*. Free Press.
Granovetter, M. S. (1973). The Strength of Weak Ties. *American Journal of Sociology, 78*(6), 1360–1380.
Granovetter, M. S. (1974). *Getting a Job: A Study of Contact and Careers*. Harvard University Press.
Granovetter, M. S. (1985). Economic Action and Social Structure: The Problem of Embeddedness. *American Journal of Sociology, 91*(3), 481–510.
Granovetter, M. S. (1993). The Nature of Economic Relationships. In R. Swedberg (Ed.), *Explorations in Economic Sociology* (pp. 3–41). Russell Sage Foundation.
Granovetter, M. S. (2002). A Theoretical Agenda for Economic Sociology. In M. F. Guillén, R. Collins, P. England, et al. (Eds.), *The New Economic Sociology. Developments in an Emerging Field* (pp. 35–60). Russell Sage Foundation.
Guillén, M. F., Collins, R., England, P., & Meyer, M. (2002). The Revival of Economic Sociology. In M. F. Guillén, R. Collins, P. England, et al. (Eds.), *The New Economic Sociology: Developments in an Emerging Field* (pp. 1–32). Russell Sage Foundation.
Haller, M. (2003). *Soziologische Theorie im systematisch-kritischen Vergleich*. UTB.
Harrison, L. E., & Huntington, S. P. (Eds.). (2000). *Culture Matters. How Values Shape Human Progress*. Basic Books.
Häußling, R., & Stegbauer, C. (Eds.). (2010). *Handbuch Netzwerkforschung*. VS-Publishers.
Hodgson, G. M. (1994). The Return of Institutional Economics. In N. J. Smelser & R. Swedberg (Eds.), *The Handbook of Economic Sociology* (pp. 58–75). Princeton University Press and Russell Sage.
Hodgson, G. M. (2001). *How Economics Forgot History*. Routledge.
Hoover, K. D. (2009). *Microfoundational Programs*. Paper Prepared for the First International Symposium on the History of Economic Thought: The Integration of Micro and Macroeconomics from a Historical Perspective, University of São Paulo.

Hoover, K. D. (2010). Idealizing Reduction: The Microfoundations of Macroeconomics. *Erkenntnis, 73*, 329–347.

Jones, E. L. (2006). *Cultures Merging. A Historical and Economic Critique of Culture*. Princeton University Press.

Kahneman, D. (2003). A Perspective on Judgment and Choice: Mapping Bounded Rationality. *American Psychologist, 58*(9), 697–720.

Laird, P. W. (2006). *Pull: Networking and Success Since Benjamin Franklin*. Harvard University Press.

Landes, D. (2000). Culture Makes Almost All the Difference. In L. E. Harrison & S. P. Huntington (Eds.), *Culture Matters. How Values Shape Human Progress* (pp. 2–13). Basic Books.

Lauterbach, A. (1962). *Psychologie des Wirtschaftslebens*. Rororo.

Lee, F. S. (2009). *A History of Heterodox Economics. Challenging the Mainstream in the Twentieth Century*. Routledge.

Lévi-Strauss, C. (1987). *Anthropology and Myth*. Blackwell.

Loader, C., & Rick, T. (1995). Thorstein Veblen's Analysis of German Intellectualism: Institutionalism as a Forecasting Method. *American Journal of Economics and Sociology, 54*(3), 339–355.

Marcovich, A., & Shinn, T. (2011). Where is Disciplinarity Going? Meeting on the Borderland. *Social Science Information, 50*(3–4), 582–606.

Marx, K. (1977). *Das Kapital. Kritik der politischen Ökonomie* [1864] (MEW Vol. 23.) Dietz Publishers.

Mauss, M. (2002). *The Gift: The Form and Reason for Exchange in Archaic Societies*. Routledge.

Mauss, M. (2006). *A General Theory of Magic*. Routledge.

Mikl-Horke, G. (1999). *Historische Soziologie der Wirtschaft*. Oldenbourg.

Morgan, M. (2011). *The World in the Model*. Cambridge University Press.

Newman, M. (2010). *Networks: An Introduction*. Oxford University Press.

Nitzan, J., & Bichler, S. (2009). *Capital as Power. A Study of Order and Reorder*. Routledge.

Ostrom, E. & Ahn, T. K. (2001). *A Social Science Perspective on Social Capital: Social Capital and Collective Action*. Research Paper: Indiana University.

Pearson, H. (1999). Was There Really a German Historical School of Economics? *History of Political Economics, 31*(3), 547–562.

Pearson, H. (2000). Homo Economicus Goes Native, 1859–1945: The Rise and Fall of Primitive Economics. *History of Political Economy, 32*, 933–998.

Polanyi, K. (2001). *The Great Transformation: The Political and Economic Origins of Our Time*. Beacon Press.

Putnam, R. D., Leonardi, R., & Nanetti, R. Y. (1993). *Making Democracy Work: Civic Traditions in Modern Italy*. Princeton University Press.

Rabin, M. (1998). Psychology and Economics. *Journal of Economic Literature, 36*(1), 11–46.

Radcliffe-Brown, A. R. (1940). On Social Structure. *Journal of the Royal Anthropological Institute of Great Britain and Ireland, 70*(1), 1–12.
Rodgers, D. T. (2011). *Age of Fracture.* Harvard University Press.
Rogers, E. M. (2003). *Diffusion of Innovations.* Basic Books.
Rota, M. F. (2007). *Is Social Capital Persistent?: Comparative Measurement in the Nineteenth and Twentieth Centuries.* Economic History Working Papers (103/07). Department of Economic History. London: London School of Economics and Political Science.
Sabatini, F. (2008). Social Capital and the Quality of Economic Development. *Kyklos, 61*(3), 466–499.
Scherer, K. R. (2011). On the Rationality of Emotions: or, When are Emotions Rational? *Social Science Information, 50*(3–4), 330–350.
Schmölders, G. (1984). Historische Schule. In O. Issing (Ed.), *Geschichte der Nationalökonomie* (pp. 107–120). Franz Vahlen.
Schülein, J. A. (2009). Soziologische Theorie und ihr Gegenstand. In J. A. Schülein, G. Mikl-Horke, & R. Simsa (Eds.), *Soziologie für das Wirtschaftsstudium* (pp. 14–115). UTB.
Schumpeter, J. A. (1926). Gustav von Schmoller und die Probleme von heute. In *Jahrbuch für Gesetzgebung, Verwaltung und Volkswirtschaft im deutschen Reich* (pp. 337–388). Duncker & Humblot.
Schumpeter, J. A. (1954). *History of Economic Analysis.* Oxford University Press.
Schumpeter, J. A. (1963). *The Theory of Economic Development.* Oxford University Press.
Scott, J. (2010). *Social Network Analysis.* Sage.
Scott, J. (2011). Social Network Analysis: Developments, Advances, and Prospects. *Social Network Analysis and Mining, 1*(1), 21–26.
Shackle, G. L. S. (1972). *Epistemics and Economics.* Cambridge University Press.
Simmel, G. (1908). Die Kreuzung sozialer Kreise. In G. Simmel (Ed.), *Soziologie. Untersuchungen über die Formen der Vergesellschaftung* (pp. 305–344). Duncker & Humblot.
Smelser, N. J., & Swedberg, R. (1994). The Sociological Perspective on the Economy. In N. J. Smelser & R. Swedberg (Eds.), *Handbook of Economic Sociology* (pp. 3–26). Russel Sage Foundation and Princeton University Press.
Sombart, W. (1982). Wirtschaft. In A. Vierkandt (Ed.), *Handwörterbuch der Soziologie* [1931]. (pp. 209–216). Enke.
Stegbauer, C. (Ed.). (2008). *Netzwerkanalyse und Netzwerktheorie. Ein neues Paradigma in den Sozialwissenschaften.* VS-Publishers.
Stets, J. E., & Turner, J. (Eds.). (2007). *Handbook of the Sociology of Emotions.* Springer.
Svendsen, G. T., & Haase Svendsen, G. L. (Eds.). (2009). *Handbook of Social Capital.* Edward Elgar.

Swedberg, R. (2003). Economic and Sociological Approaches to Markets. In R. Swedberg (Ed.), *Principles of Economic Sociology* (pp. 104–131). Princeton University Press.

Turner, J. H. (1988). *The structure of sociological theory.* Homewood, IL: Dorsey Press.

Turner, J., & Stets, J. E. (Eds.). (2009). *The Sociology of Emotions.* Cambridge University Press.

Veblen, T. B. (1899). *The Theory of the Leisure Class. An Economic Study in the Evolution of Institutions.* Macmillan.

Wasserman, S., & Faust, K. (2009). *Social Network Analysis.* Cambridge University Press.

Weber, M. (1972). *Wirtschaft und Gesellschaft.* Mohr.

Weber, M. (1988). Die protestantische Ethik und der Geist des Kapitalismus [1904]. In M. Weber (Ed.), *Gesammelte Aufsätze zur Religionssoziologie* (pp. 17–206). Mohr.

Weber, M. (1990). *Grundriß zu den Vorlesungen über Allgemeine (theoretische) Nationalökonomie.* Mohr.

Wellman, B. (1988). Structural Analysis: From Method and Metaphor to Theory and Substance. In B. Wellman & S. D. Berkowitz (Eds.), *Social Structures. A Network Approach* (pp. 19–61). Cambridge University Press.

Wellman, B., & Haythornthwaite, C. (Eds.). (2002). *The Internet in Everyday Life.* Blackwell.

White, H. C. (1981). Where Do Markets Come From? *American Journal of Sociology, 87*, 517–547.

White, H. C. (1988). Varieties of Markets. In B. Wellman & S. D. Berkowitz (Eds.), *Social Structures: A Network Approach* (pp. 226–260). Cambridge University Press.

White, H. C., Boorman, S. A., & Breiger, R. L. (1976). Social Structures from Multiple Networks. I. Blockmodels of Roles and Positions. *American Journal of Sociology, 81*(4), 730–780.

Wiseman, B. (Ed.). (2009). *The Cambridge Companion to Lévi-Strauss.* Cambridge University Press.

Zelizer, V. A. (1985). *Pricing the Priceless Child. The Changing Social Value of Children.* Basic Books.

Zelizer, V. A. (1988). The Proliferation of Social Currencies. In M. Callon (Ed.), *The Laws of the Markets* (pp. 58–68). Blackwell Publishers.

PART II

Orthodoxy, Heterodoxy, and Limits of Rationality

CHAPTER 5

From Heterodoxy to Orthodoxy and Vice Versa: Economics and Social Sciences in the Division of Academic Work

The Rise of Economics and Orthodoxy and Heterodoxy

This chapter addresses some questions about the development of economics. Where is economics coming from and where is it going to, what is the domain of economics and how far coexist different approaches in economics? We observe dichotomic labelling in economics that distinguishes between mainstream and heterodox economics but these opposed monoliths are both diverse themselves. The attempt to define both camps clearly is especially difficult since both concepts have vague borders and both are embedded in overall changing contexts of scientific changes for decades. The basis of this chapter is that mainstream economics does not remain the same when acknowledging historical changes and the same is valid for heterodox economics. Changes occur permanently that modify boundaries of the two camps and that also affect potential convergencies. Orthodox economics is a synonym for mainstream economics. Heterodox economics seems to be a counter project to orthodox economics and seems to be in itself a loose coupling of different approaches with the common denominator of being non-mainstream (Lee, 2009). In a situation that orthodox

Bögenhold, Dieter: From Heterodoxy to Orthodoxy and Vice Versa: Economics and Social Sciences in the Division of Academic Work, in: *The American Journal of Economics and Sociology*, Vol. 69, 2010, No. 5, pp. 1566–1590.

D. Bögenhold, *Neglected Links in Economics and Society*,
https://doi.org/10.1007/978-3-030-79193-3_5

and heterodox economics are moving forward and claiming new areas of positions, orthodox positions can partially converge with those being formerly heterodox. The argumentation is concerned with the organization and development of modern economics. The evolution of tendencies may bring up new fields of research and may also foster some new bridges between orthodoxy, heterodoxy, and further fields of social sciences. The discussion takes two examples (out of possibly many more) to highlight interdisciplinary links for the benefit of a holistic integration. It will be shown that an increasing integration of the history of economic thought will provide methodological tools that must serve as necessary background for recent activity in economics. Finally, the chapter argues in favour of an integration of network analysis, which may be a reasonable strategy to fill the micro–macro gap.

The question of what is the matter of economics has a long tradition. The often-quoted statement by Jacob Viner, "economics is what economists do" (quoted in Barber, 1997, p. 87), was completed already by Frank Knight when he added "and economists are those who do economics" (quoted in Buchanan, 1964, p. 213). Looking at activities of economists shows that the domain of economics is always in transition. Since no clear borders exist that provide rational marks for the area of economics, even such current understanding is not much further than it was at times of Viner or Knight.

The divisional order of economics is characterized by practice that mirrors the multiplicity of academic production and a somehow occidental development rather than a systematic reasoning on how to design an academic subject. With respect to the definition of what economics is and how it is organized into different subfolders, two trends overlap each other. (i) We have a long-term trend of the development of economics in which the discipline increasingly gained firm ground and recognition and in which a process of differentiation started to evolve. This trend took part within the last one and a half centuries. The field of economics also started to become a professional system with clear curricula, degrees, academic societies, and university departments with an increasing number of publications and related journals. (ii) Parallel to the consolidation process of economics, the subject formed borderlines with neighbouring fields that were formerly an ultimate part of economics. Looking over the course of the last hundred years, topics of economics have modified and multiplied.

One of Max Weber's book titles was *Wirtschaft und Gesellschaft* ([1921] 1972), which was later repeated by Parsons and Smelser in their study

"Economy and Society" (1956), indicating the ultimate link between both items. However, since the middle of the twentieth century a point of development was reached when the broad scenario, including different academic domains of social sciences, especially those of economics, history, and sociology, was not practiced and studied anymore. Specialization has occurred by which specific aspects of economy or society became subject of further investigation. "Few persons competent in sociological theory," Parsons and Smelser explained, "have any working knowledge of economics, and conversely few economists have much knowledge of sociology" (Parsons & Smelser, 1956, p. xviii). Earlier, classic authors had practiced interdisciplinary investigation working as a matter of course, without specific methodological explanation and without knowing that they did interdisciplinary work by a view of later times.

Historically, the rise of modern economics was closely connected to the rise of neoclassical theory, which had its foundations in the marginal utility theory. Related economists tried to establish a kind of economics that was defined as being theoretical and—in this sense—universal and general. "Pure" economics (Walras, [1874] 1954) was a credo trying to do economics in a way like other natural sciences were practicing too, having clear procedures and the aim to arrive at laws.

In order to apply economic discussion to modern capitalism in general statements, formulated relationships had to be abstract in an understanding that they could be used for all modern capitalist economies independently of concrete time and space. Getting a level of abstraction was seen as closely connected to the utilization of mathematics. Due to this understanding, the rise of neoclassical economics was very much a rising import of mathematics as a tool to formalize statements. This mathematization of economics was clearly expressed by, for example, looking at Jevons, who wrote in his introduction: "It is clear that Economics, if it is to be a science at all, must be a mathematical science" (Jevons, 1871, introduction).

Bringing a complex development to a very brief denominator, much of twentieth-century development in economics is the establishment of neoclassic thought, which is taught as textbook knowledge to undergraduate students and that dominates wide parts of the non-university public and public policy (Freeman, 2009). Clear relationships concerning many items like growth, prices, trade, or employment are done at very general levels as if economies exist in a vacuum having no institutions and no contextual framing of time and space. "Pure economics" served to be a program of abstractness that had problems when confronted with competing empirical material since pure economics was related to an economy in a vacuum. This type of thought emerged and became a predominant paradigm of thought during the twentieth century, which in its nucleus served to be a kind of academic religion (Nelson, 2001).

Simultaneously, a variety of new special fields of economics were founded that did not exist decades before; among them were, for example, industrial economics, labour economics, small business economics, household economics, and economics of aging. Many further new areas evolved and served as impressive examples of the general trend of academic specialization and differentiation. The more complex economics became, the smaller the real terrain of neoclassical theory remained, although the general image of economics, especially when looking from the outside at the field, is still neoclassical orthodoxy. Talking about the mainstream economics overlaps somewhat with general ideas of neoclassical thought that we find even today in textbooks for undergraduate courses.

From Abstract to Concrete Economies: Revival of Institutionalist Thought and Heterodox Economics

Multiplying economics in a sense of widening the horizon and of pluralization of perspectives is devoted to a small share of pioneers whereas the majority is working steadily with conventional issues in traditional ways, doing research and teaching as they always did. Doing academic routines in "convoy" (Bögenhold, 1995) is a topic that we find carefully described in philosophy of science as a systematic organizing principle where competing styles of thought are formed into camps of thought (Fleck, 1980; Kuhn, 1962; Collins, 2002). For economics, Lee and Harley (1998) and Lee (2010) showed that these camps survive through diverse subtle methods of reciprocal reverence systems.

Principally speaking, theoretical economics became increasingly an abstract science during the twentieth century, trying to bring the complexity of economic life into formulas. Abstractness is combined with sterility in order to arrive at universal statements (or laws) that apply universally. The German Historical School and the Institutional School, especially in North America, went down in the course of the twentieth century (Dorfman, 1955), but seemingly major ideas are going to be recovered in recent times since many ideas of those schools converge with ideas of heterodox economics and arguments for economic institutionalism (Lee, 2009). Although institutionalism was practiced by well-known names during the first half of the twentieth century (Dorfman, 1946–1959), mainstream economics was closely related to neoclassical thought and its variations.

Especially in the last 10 or 20 years, an increasing number of voices started to criticize the assumptions of the type of thought connected to the abstract modelling (Lee, 2004). Among these assumptions, the concept of the human actor seemed to be the most problematic one since the homo oeconomicus serves to be a function rather than a living human body. Also ideas of symmetric information and of economic equilibrium were not taken for granted by a growing number of economists. Hodgson (1994) summarizes the basic premises that proved to become more and more problematic: "(1). The assumption of rational, maximizing behavior by agents with given and stable preference function; (2). a focus on attained, or movements toward, equilibrium states; and (3). the absence of chronic information problems (there is, at most, a focus on probabilistic risk: excluding severe ignorance, radical uncertainty, or divergent perceptions of a given reality" (Hodgson, 1994, p. 60).

What many mainstream economists took for granted for a long time started now to be questioned at an increasing scale: Who is the actor, does the actor have gender, biography, emotions, religion, location, and preferences and why does the actor do what he or she does? Hodgson (1994) lists eight different items of critique that formed different zones of critique: (1) Institutionalism eschews atomism and reductionism in economic analysis, typically positing holistic or organistic alternatives. (2) Instead of the rational, calculating agent of neoclassical theory, institutionalism sees human behaviour as normally driven by habit and routine, but occasionally punctuated by acts of creativity and novelty. (3) Instead of an exclusive focus on individuals as units of analysis, institutionalism regards self-reinforcing institutions as additional or even alternative analytical units. (4) The conception of the economy is of an evolving, open system in historical time, subject to processes of cumulative causation—instead of approaches to theorizing that focus exclusively on mechanical equilibria. (5) Institutionalism sees individuals as situated in and moulded by an evolving social culture, so that their preference functions are not given and fixed but are in a process of continuous adaptation and change. (6) Likewise, technology is regarded evolving, and as a primary motivating force in socioeconomic development—in contrast to a theoretical framework that takes technology as fixed and exogenous. (7) There is a pervasive concern with the role and significance of power and of the conflict between both individuals and institutions in socioeconomic life. (8) Instead of an utilitarian framework that evaluates human and welfare in terms of individual utility or pleasure and separates considerations of means from those of ends, there is a focus on the identification of real human needs and on the design of institutions that can further assist their identification and clarification (Hodgson, 1994, p. 69).

Taking these points together, one can conclude that modern economies are contexted by societies in which they are embedded. Practically, economies are never abstract but always concrete. The concern of time and its academic equivalent, which is history, and the concern for spatial dimensions and its variations match with the slogan that culture matters (Harrison & Huntington, 2000). In general, institutionalist approaches have no other aim than highlighting that different social organizations and institutions (including religion, language, law, family structures and networks, systems of education, and industrial relations) make differences when trying to come up with statements regarding general principles of capitalist societies and economies. If culture makes differences (Jones, 2006), capitalism does not exist in a vacuum but in a context with specific social regimes of living and producing. Trying to understand varieties of capitalism (Elsner & Hanappi, 2008) is the ultimate acknowledgement that culture and institutional specifications matter, which finally means that academic domains of sociology matter.

Early institutionalist authors did historical studies highlighting religious systems as a crucial factor for the development of capitalism (among those Weber, 1988). Recent business historians come back to the fact to acknowledge "cultural factors in economic growth" (Cochran, 1960) and they postulate that the really fundamental problems of economic growth are non-economic" (Buchanan & Ellis, 1955, p. 405). If "culture makes almost all the difference" (Landes, 2000) the further conclusion must be that not only sociology but also history matters. The concrete historical changes provide the different colors of different variants of capitalism. As we know, capitalism in Singapore differs from capitalism in Zimbabwe, which differs from capitalism in Switzerland.

Accepting the idea that economies and societies are not filled by abstract but by real entities, one has to refer to concrete coordinates of time and space (Ostrom, 2005). If economics rediscovers history, the recent history of economic thought does a break with recent mainstream and goes beyond abstractivism. Increasing (new) discussion about path-dependency (David, 2007) wants to rediscover history. North is right when he says that the only empirical laboratory for social and economic change available for economists is the past (North, 1997, p. 1). All these considerations meet fully with a program of evolutionary (nonequilibrium) economics, which goes back to Joseph A. Schumpeter (1942, 1963).

It would require much more than a footnote to discuss what is new in recent developments, also what is new in new institutional economics (NIE) compared to an old one (OIE). A major conclusion is that we find a turn in economics that newly takes up elements of thought that belonged to nonmainstream or to heterodox economics. The question how the academic paths fit together is getting increasingly difficult. Where are borderlines and overlappings between heterodox and orthodox economics (Davis, 2007)? The observation is that these camps are diffusing slightly. Heterodox economics will certainly not convert into neoclassical thought but established economists who are conventionally regarded as representatives of mainstream economics are partially crossing borders and take the liberty of doing interdisciplinary profits and advantages. This way, so-called orthodoxy seems to become more fragmented and splits up between a small share of innovative pioneers and traditionalists being still close to hard-core neoclassical thought.

Why Do Actors Do What They Do?

Among the many critiques of abstract and sterile economics one critique seems to be the loudest, the type of the human agent and his/her motivation. While homo oeconomicus is a figure that fits into all times and societies, having no sex, age, family, and no biographical history, real-world parameters show that there are differences. So, already Max Weber concluded that economics "argues with a non-realist human being, analogous a mathematical ideal figure" (Weber, 1990, p. 30, transl. D.B.). Being distant to such a procedure as provided in theoretical economics, Weber distinguished between four ideal types of social action, which are the rationality of traditional action, of affective action, of value-orientation, and of purposive-rational utilitarian action (Weber, 1972, part 1, ch. 1) of which only the last point of classification matches with the supposed rationality of homo oeconomicus.

Classical economics started with the conception of "self-interest" for reasons that can be reconstructed logically. Parsons did a sociology of economic thought and concluded that the abstraction was due to the "fact of finding a plausible formula for filling a logical gap in the closure of a system" (Parsons, 1940, p. 188), which is characterized by Parsons as a doctrine. Thinking in terms that culture matters implies that people are guided by, at least, a set of goals that are implicit or explicit, conflicting or overlapping. Social psychology and phenomenology contributed much information about these spheres and a sociology of emotions is based upon the premise that people are not fully rationally controlled (Stets & Turner, 2007). Although already famous economists like J. M. Keynes or J. A. Schumpeter referred to nonrational and psychological categories to integrate into their framework of thought (Bögenhold, 2009), economic orthodoxy ignored those voices for a long time since an acknowledgment would imply that a clean model would get dirty.

In the last few decades, an increasingly large number of Nobel laureates were awarded for behavioural works or they referred to more differentiated explanations as orthodoxy did (for a history of Nobel laureates and their programs, see Vane & Mulhearn, 2005). Herbert Simon (1955, 1962) coined the (famous) term of a bounded rationality. Later D. G. North added that economics treats the issue of motivation of human being like a black box: "Although I know of very few economists who really believe that the behavioral assumptions of economics accurately reflect human behavior, they do (mostly) believe that such assumptions are useful for building models of market behavior in economics and, though less useful, are still the best game in town for studying politics and the other social sciences. I believe that these traditional behavioral assumptions have prevented economists from coming to the grips with some very fundamental issues and that a modification of these assumptions is essential to further progress in the social sciences. The motivation of these actors is more complicated (and their preferences less stable) than assumed in received theory. More controversial (and less understood) among the behavioral assumptions, usually, is the implicit one that the actors possess cognitive systems that provide true models of the worlds about which they make choices." (North, 1990, p. 17). Reading North is like reading ultimate voices by heterodox economists. It has become difficult to discover the concrete rifts between heterodox economics and some sort of innovative economics when looking closer at the nature of contents rather than at the flags of camps and their associations.

In the meantime, reverences to psychology have been practiced increasingly. Kahneman (2003) got highly recognized for his pioneering work in economic psychology. He received the Sveriges Riksbank Prize in Economic Science in memory of Alfred Nobel, also awarded to Akerlof. Akerlof (2007) in his function of an outgoing president of the American Economic Association recently did a plea to turn academic concentration towards issues of motivation and cognitive structures. Elsewhere, Akerlof and Kranton (2000) referred to dimensions like identity and social norms, which belong much more to sociological or psychological ground than an economic one. Akerlof and Shiller worked out in their study *Animal Spirits* (2009) that a functioning of the whole capitalist system is heavily based upon sociopsychological foundations. They (2009) take up several questions that were taken up by J. M. Keynes earlier. What sounds very convincing and very evident with everyday life observations must sound revolutionary by those who practiced orthodox (neoclassical) economics during most of the twentieth century. Here, innovative (mainstream) economics partially meets with heterodox economics. It is very important to acknowledge that nothing remains as it always has been, not even economics. The dichotomy of heterodoxy versus orthodoxy seems to have got new puzzles, which have to be taken into account.

Observing recent trends correctly indicates that daily life of text book teaching may remain what it has been for a long time but other fractions tend to converge due to the fact that new times produce new questions and provoke new combinations. Nearly 20 years ago, Frey ([1992] 1999) realized: "In sociology and many parts of political science, but implicitly also in law, a model of human behaviour is generally assumed which differs strongly from the economic concept. People's actions are taken to be influenced by moral and social factors. These social determinants of human behaviour are acquired by socialization and internationalisation processes" (Frey, [1992] 1999, p. 9). Seemingly, the message has gained further recipients. In this respect, a lot of recent offensives towards heterodox economics seem to have forgotten their own academic history. A sociology of the academic division and the related changes through the twentieth century shall argue in favour of the increased necessity to reintegrate the social sciences (Mikl-Horke, 1999). A broader history of economic and sociological thought may demonstrate that recent discussion has origins that go back for more than a century in the history of economic thought. Although sketchy and perhaps sometimes only between the lines, this chapter tries to highlight some continuities in discontinuities and vice versa: economics tends to have not completely lost the link to society but it is obviously in a position now to enter again the classic unit of economy and society and economics and sociology.

Where to Go and Where to Meet? Research Ground for Future Interdisciplinary Economics

Even the future of academic development is rather difficult to forecast, too complex is the interplay of different factors and of individual contributions by authors within quasi "open" developments. Scientific progress is often contingent and never rational in a sense that it follows arithmetic rules of combinations. The "market" for ideas is not perfectly an efficient or perfect market. Academic progress is also related to a series of mistakes by which intellectual resources are wasted, and as a consequence there are indeed intellectual gems laying unexploited, waiting for someone to grasp (Boettke, 2000).

What we have discussed so far is that the frontier of orthodox economics goes seemingly into a direction that tends to converge partially with some ideas of earlier heterodox critique. Newest economics takes up again academic perspectives that were provided by old institutional thought asking for concrete economies in concrete societies. Of course, many new thematic arenas have opened up during the last hundred years (among them game theory, transaction cost theory, principial agent theory, public choice theory, welfare economics, and many others) so that comparisons between up-to-date economics and earlier forms suffer seriously in many respects. However, reading the signs of current days correctly, tendencies towards an increasing level of abstractness and sterility seem to find an increasing number of opponents rather than supporters. Heterodox economics as a denominator serves to be almost defined negatively as being not mainstream economics. A narrower look shows that the term is a rather wide umbrella hiding specific camps of discussion that are sometimes contradictory and opponents among each other, for example, from Marxian economics to Austrian economics, or that are restricted just to individual authors and related discussion as, for example, on Veblen or Keynes.

The chapter will conclude by dropping two thematic fields that may provide reasonable ground where orthodox and heterodox economics should engage in order to draw chances to get established as common research fields that bridge the somehow sterile confrontation between orthodoxy. The areas to be mentioned are (1) to invest increasingly into history of economic thought, and (2) to import network research in order to bridge the micro–macro gap and to arrive at a more adequate understanding of market processes.

History of Economic Thought: Looking Back to Gain Orientation for the Future

If students start to get into a new academic discipline as, for example, medicine, biology, or economics, they usually want to learn what is the current state of thought. A majority of people do not want to learn which discussion was on the agenda 50 or 100 years ago but what are predominant portraits of recent debate. What is uncontested terrain, which are competing theories, and where could be academic profit of future engagement? The difficult matter is that academic progress and its change must be conceptualized as a series of processes of shortcomings, which appear backwards as a never-ending story of failures or mistakes to express it starkly. Evolutionary economists take as their credo to look at the inner dynamics of change to arrive at an understanding of principles; theoretical economists should treat their subject similarly. One has to gain a careful understanding of the history of the own discipline to see the bigger and the smaller lines that have led to recent discussion and the current state of the art. In such light, recent discussion gets much more colours and our current knowledge comes up in a historically transcendent way as a snapshot in a series of academic overcomes, being failures or innovations.

Economic theory evolves in specific contexts of social life and societal organization. In some way, they mirror the times of their origins and serve as a diagnosis of related systems of thought. As Boettke (2000) puts it:

> *The use of intellectual history instrumentally follows both from the idea that all that is important in the past is not necessarily contained in the present, and the idea that mining the past might offer concepts which point the way to more productive theory construction today. Following this path, we may find dead-ends in current trends of thought which force us to reconsider the earlier moment of choice and then imagine the path that could have been followed instead .... But reading an old work in eco- nomics is not unlike watching a silent film or news clips of an old baseball game .... There are works in the past from which we can still learn important ideas which are useful for addressing the problems we find pressing today. Intellectual errors are made all the time, knowledge gained*

> *in one period can be lost due to the fads and fashion which govern the world of ideas There are works in the past from which we can still learn important ideas which are useful for addressing the problems we find pressing today. Intellectual errors are made all the time, knowledge gained in one period can be lost due to the fads and fashion which govern the world of ideas.* (Boettke, 2000)

These intellectual entrepreneurial profit opportunities have their sources in the awareness of a flux of different positions and paradigms, authors, and interests (Boulding, 1971).

History of economic thought (HET) is often counted as being part of the plurality of heterodox economy (Lee, 2010), but it is also taught in very classic mainstream departments although being currently in strong defence to keep positions. Heterodox economics is not only a part of the pluralism in economics but it is also very pluralist in itself. Sometimes we find cumulative histories of academic processes describing how knowledge in economics changed and accumulated, in other cases history of economics is mostly concerned with specific camps of thought (for example, OIE or Marxism) or with individual authors and their influence (Becker et al., 2009). Since it should be an integral part of the identity of a profession (and a profession member) to be familiar with the tradition of the own discipline, further investment in the history of economic thought should be a unifying issue for future orthodox and heterodox thought in economics. Since we need to know the own intellectual history in order to find innovative academic concepts for the future, dealing with the history of economic thought is also a tool to undertake economics of the future.

Although plenty of excellent books in the area of history of economics are available (Backhouse, 2002; Blaug, 2006; Canterbery, 2005; Heilbroner, 2000), one of the major and basic books in this area is still J. A. Schumpeter's *History of Economic Analysis* (Schumpeter, 1954). The preface of the book gives a thorough discussion why histories of science are necessary for systematic reasons, and this not only in economics but also in other academic fields. In his (substantial) introduction to his study, Schumpeter raises explicitly the question "why do we study the history of economics?" and he continues to add his own answer, which is concerned with the issue why we study the history of any science in general and with economics specifically.

According to Schumpeter, there are four main reasons to study history. First of all, it would have pedagogical advantages. He argues that for the students it is very difficult to approach a field without knowing how it is related to the specific historical time. For a thorough understanding an historical background is required. One could affirm that the methods that are presently in use already embody what has been done in the past, and what is not part of it is not important anymore and is not worth taking into consideration. However, actually our present methods and their results are meaningful only with reference to the historical background. "Scientific analysis is not simply a logically consistent process that starts with some primitive notions and then adds to the stock in a straight-line fashion. It is not simply progressive discovery of an objective reality" (Schumpeter, 1954, p. 4).

The second reason is that when reading "old" theories, one could find other interpretations of them or new ideas; Schumpeter writes "our minds are apt to derive new inspirations from the study of the history of science" (Schumpeter, 1954, pp. 4–5). In his discussion, Schumpeter adds an example: "The productivity of this experience may be illustrated by the fact that the fundamental ideas that eventually developed in the theory of (special) relativity occurred first in a book on the history of mechanics" (Schumpeter, 1954, p. 5).

The third cause is that history can give us insights into the ways of the human mind. Particularly in the history of science, various types of logic are used and scientific performances are self-revelatory by nature, that is, they reveal the mental processes that have been made in order to achieve a certain law or theory. "Scientific habits or rules of procedure are not merely to be judged by logical standards that exist independently of them; they contribute something to, and react back upon, the logical standards themselves" (Schumpeter, 1954, p. 5). Finally, the fourth point deals especially with economics, which is described as a unique historical process. For Schumpeter, all his points noted before apply also for economics directly: Fundamentally this process does not differ from the analogous processes in other fields of knowledge but "much more than in, say, physics is it true in eco- nomics that modern problems, methods, and results cannot be fully understood without some knowledge of how economists have come to reason as they do. In addition, much more than in physics have been lost on the way or remained in abeyance for centuries" (Schumpeter, 1954, p. 6).

Given these insightful instructions by Schumpeter as a plea for increased or, at least, continuous attempts to invest in a history of economics, one has to consider Schumpeter's writing also as a good exemplification of what a history of economic writings can highlight, which is that brilliant ideas are often hidden and neglected for (too) long a time. If one wants to analyse a painting hanging on a wall, one must try to go a few steps backwards to see the painting as a whole in order to get a sense of the full composition. The same applies for dealing with science and economics specifically. History of economic thought is a neglected academic area of necessary contextualizing of knowledge in order to provide a more sufficient working compass.

Bridging Micro and Macro: Networks as Social Embeddedness

In the second chapter of the same introduction, Schumpeter (1954) continued to discuss the division of academic areas in economics, which he coins "techniques of economic analysis." He writes that what distinguishes a scientific economist from a simple economist is a command of techniques that we classify in different fields, that is, economic history, statistics, economic sociology and theory, and applied fields. In this context, the wording of theory is always written with quotation marks to underline that it is problematic to talk about theory so as if a commonly used understanding exists. In fact, there is no ultimately defined understanding of theory at all; different types of theory coexist (see, for recent contributions, Bunge, 1996; Haller, 2003, Ch. 1; Schülein, 2009, pp. 42–65) and the question when an academic statement receives the status of being theory remains still on the agenda. The simple missing of empirical data is not an ultimate indication that such a piece must be automatically qualified for being theoretical. For our discussion on convergencies, divergencies, and challenges of orthodox, heterodox, and future economics the suggestion is still very important to open up a perspective that economic history, economic sociology, and further applied sciences belong to the techniques of economic analysis. From today's point of observation, we find a proposal for—interdisciplinary—working to find appropriate academic answers when dealing with economic issues.

Economics is seen as a box of tools. The suggestion to acknowledge economic history is already treated earlier in our discussion. To address economics with the slogan "history matters" stands for the need to acknowledge concrete economies. Nobody will hope to understand the economic phenomena of any, including the present, epoch who has not an adequate command of historical facts and an adequate amount of historical sense or of what may be described as historical experience. The historical report cannot be purely economic, but must try to evaluate how economic and noneconomic facts are related to one another. Schumpeter talks about institutional facts that are not purely economic ones (Schumpeter, 1954, pp. 12–13).

Finally, a further fundamental field of economic techniques is regarded within economic sociology, which shall be, among other topics, responsible for behavioural and institutional contributions. "Economic analysis deals with the questions how people behave at any time and what the economic effects are they produce by so behaving; economic sociology deals with the question how they came to behave as they do. If we define economic behavior widely enough so that it includes not only actions and motives and propensities but also the social institutions that are relevant to economic behavior such as government, property inheritance, contract, and so on, that phrase really tells us all we need" (Schumpeter, 1954, p. 21).

Having economic sociology and economic history conceptualized as techniques of economic analysis, we are very close to a (newly) modern understanding of a wide social science based on understanding how economy and society are linked together. Since they ultimately belong together by nature, it is increasingly necessary to take attention of these facts by doing a science of economic life. Ideas by Schumpeter provide a manual on how a reasonable division of academic works may look like. Being on that ground, one of the tools that has evolved during the last decades is social network analysis. Social network analysis goes back to Georg Simmel, who started reflecting on different social circles people have. This type of thought differs considerably from a view in economics at that time that conceptualized a type of man where information is shared equally. In a real world, people have asymmetric information, which is, among other things, based upon different sets of resources about who to know and with whom to talk. Social network analysis interprets these circumstances as different individual webs of group affiliations. In his "Die Kreuzung sozialer Kreise", Simmel (1908) investigated the intersection of social circles, which were concentric in premodern societies and that are partially overlapping in modern ones. Later, anthropologists like Mauss or Levy Strauss treated these exchange networks in their own studies (Collins, 1988). Different network designs provide different opportunities to communicate, to receive information and so they create different structures of cultural capital. In the meantime, one has to distinguish between ego-centred network analysis and organizational network analysis, which host different discussion camps. Network analysis asks for modes and contents of exchanges between people or organizations where symbols (concepts, values, norms), emotions (love, respect or hostility), or goods or services (especially financial subsidiaries and gifts) get transported (Turner, 1998, Ch. 38). Network research studies usually strengthen and highlight the inner dynamics of societies (for an overview, see Scott, 2009; Carrington et al., 2009; Wasserman & Faust, 2009; Barr, 2009; Marin & Wellman, 2010) and the principal premise is that the presently existing, largely categorical description of social structure has no solid theoretical grounding; furthermore, network concepts may provide the only way to construct a theory of social structure (White et al., 1976, p. 732). Network study research has become a cross-disciplinary evolving subject with applications in many diverse fields of social and economic life. Among them, research on market dynamics is one of the most challenging ones to shed light on a subject that is very often left as a black box by mainstream economists (Swedberg, 2003). Markets function upon a basis of communication and social rules, which may be addressed by social network-oriented research perspectives. At least two of the crucial research conclusions Fligstein (2001) drew in his *Architecture of Markets* are relevant for network research, which are: "What social rules must exist for markets to function, and what types of social structures are necessary to produce stable markets?" and "What is a 'social' view of what actors seek to do in markets, as opposed to an economic one?" (Fligstein, 2001, p. 11, 14). Markets are always in transition, they come up, they go down, they change. These markets are carried out by actors having sets of people they know and whom they trust while other people may be regarded as hostile competitors. However concrete markets may look, they always have very social traits, and economics would fall short of not asking for those issues. Competition processes must also be analysed and understood as ongoing social processes that are involved in social structures and that are permanently in processes of reorganization (White, 1981, 1988; Burt, 1995).

Orthodox and heterodox economics could both take advantage of these conceptual ideas in order to innovate their research program. Although only very sketchily discussed here, an idea of the strategic potential of social network analysis might have become transparent. In many respects, network analysis is an excellent exemplification of what the term of social embeddedness can deliver. Network analysis furnishes those popular formulations that have become "economic sociology's most celebrated metaphor" (Guillén et al., 2002, p. 4). Social embeddedness was introduced by Granovetter's (1985) article in which he discussed "social embeddedness of economic behaviour and institutions" (Granovetter, 1985) without forgetting to hint at the fact that Karl Polanyi in his study *The Great Transformation* (Polanyi, 1944) used the term much earlier by showing competing modes through which people are integrated into societies, market exchange, reciprocity, and mechanisms of redistribution. All these systems that provide resources to human actors through different levels of inclusion function through principles of social networks. An economist that wants to arrive at an appropriate understanding of the dynamics of economic affairs in societies and at a global level cannot afford to neglect those social dimensions (Bögenhold & Marschall, 2008).

Conclusions

Orthodox economics and heterodox economics are abstractions. Orthodox economics is always in progress and gets permanent new colours losing old ones. Orthodox economics is best characterized as such economics that are on the agenda and that receive public legitimation. Heterodox economics wants to oppose mainstream economics by dealing with a series of forgotten or neglected matters that are also in defence since these topics often do not fall into the catalogue of defined topics valuable for public funding. In some way, one may portray this frontal system as two opposed camps that have better or worse financial funding because of being legitimate or illegitimate sciences. However, this portrait is a bit crude since orthodox economics is pluralist in some respects and heterodox economics as well (Colander, 2010; Fine & Milonakis, 2009). Heterodox economics can be defined best as being not mainstream, but behind the denominator one finds a variety of different topics around quite divergent pieces of thought that may be completely exclusive of each other. Therefore heterodox economics, which started a hundred years ago, was identified with some very well-known "heterodox" economists but heterodox economics has evolved by multiplying and getting pluralistic in the meantime.

The same may be stated for orthodox economics, which splits up into a few innovators and a majority of people working in routines doing a type of economics that has always been done before. But orthodox economics has also broadened the range of topics, specializations, and applications so that even here tendencies of fragmentation and heterogeneity are visible. A careful analysis must ask if there is common ground between heterodoxy and orthodoxy or if common ways to future terrains exist that may be interesting for the creative elites of both camps to arrive at a state of future economics that is unified by thoroughly discussed serious research questions that try to go down to the ground of common subjects instead of just sharing around own flags of camps.

The argumentation in this chapter tried to discuss tendencies within mainstream economics that lead to the fact that some—by Sveriges Riks bank prizes publicly honoured—economists tend to leave traditional ground by opening up for fields that belong to heterodox economics, history, psychology, and sociology. Noneconomic social sciences should observe and analyse these trends very carefully in order to react with strategies for this increased social-scienciation of economics. It may also be that orthodox economics breaks apart into further pieces of affiliation and schools of thought. In case the discussed tendencies have a piece of evidence, heterodox economics, history, psychology, and sociology can come up with a charming offence of "welcome back," unifying at their terrain. Despite all logic of academic strategies, a few (of some) topics were discussed that provide a need for further investment such as into history of economic thought, which is almost in defence. Looking around at recently established departments of economics, we find a trend that an increasing number of professors have never spent substantial time in reading about heroes of the own discipline but running computer programs in which models are calculated based on a few abstract axiomatic premises. However, modern times need people who sensitively raise questions concerning the tools of analysis and the final rationale of knowledge to acquire. Serious scientists must be like captains at sea, always looking at the horizon and observing how weather and winds are changing instead of looking too narrowly at the waves around.

A point of further discussion was that up-to-date economics is increasingly willing to open up for topics of cognitive structures and motivation. Even raising these items explicitly is a revolt against ideas of the abstraction of homo oeconomicus. Economic sociology and economic psychology share many of these insights since they belong commonly to their academic identity but they should be curious as well as careful when meeting with those new wielders of economics. Cooperation is explicitly the philosophy of a programme of interdisciplinarity, which was not only claimed by Schumpeter in his *History of Economic Analysis* but for which he also argued for and reflected on. Many recent interesting pieces of discussion may be synthesized, one of them seems to be a tremendously evolving discussion in the area of network analysis, which promises to bridge the micro–macro gap and that potentially helps to make an appropriate understanding of economic and social structures more dynamic, especially research on markets or organizations may find challenges here.

References

Akerlof, G. A. (2007). The Missing Motivation in Macroeconomics. *American Economic Review, 97*(1), 5–36.

Akerlof, G. A., & Kranton, R. E. (2000). Economics and Identity. *Quarterly Journal of Economics, 115*(3), 715–753.

Akerlof, G. A., & Shiller, R. J. (2009). *Animal Spirits: How Human Psychology Drives the Economy, and Why it Matters for Global Capitalism*. Princeton University Press.

Backhouse, R. (2002). *The Ordinary Business of Life. A History of Economics from the Ancient World to the Twenty-First Century*. Princeton University Press.

Barber, W. J. (1997). Reconfigurations in American Academic Economics. A General Practitioner's Perspective. *Daedalus, 126*(1), 87–103.

Barr, T. (2009). With Friends Like These. Endogenous Labor Market Segregation with Homogenous, Nonprejudiced Agents. *American Journal of Economics and Sociology, 68*(3), 703–746.

Becker, J., Grisold, A., Mikl-Horke, G., Pirker, R., & Rauchenschwandtner, H. (2009). *Heterodoxe Ökonomie*. Metropolis.

Blaug, M. (2006). *Economic Theory in Retrospect*. Cambridge University Press.

Boettke, P. J. (2000). *Why Read the Classics in Economics?* Unpublished Paper, George Mason University.

Bögenhold, D. (1995). Mythenjäger im Konvoi. In D. Bögenhold et al. (Eds.), *Soziale Welt und soziologische Praxis. Festschrift zum 65. Geburtstag von Heinz Hartmann*. Vandenhoek & Ruprecht.

Bögenhold, D. (2009). Die Psychologie im Wirtschaftsleben. Keynes und Schumpeter als Pioniere. In G. Raab & A. Unger (Eds.), *Der Mensch im Mittepunkt wirtschaftlichen Handelns*. Pabst Science Publishers.

Bögenhold, D., & Marschall, J. (2008). Metapher, Methode, Theorie. Netzwerkforschung in der Wirtschaftssoziologie. In C. Stegbauer (Ed.), *Netzwerkanalyse und Netzwerktheorie. Ein neues Paradigma in den Sozialwissenschaften*. VS-Publishers.

Boulding, K. (1971). After Samuelson, Who Needs Adam Smith? *History of Political Economy, 3*(2), 225–237.

Buchanan, J. M. (1964). What Should Economists Do? *Southern Economic Journal, 30*(3), 213–228.

Buchanan, N. S., & Ellis, H. S. (1955). *Approaches to Economic Development*. Twentieth Century Fund.

Bunge, M. (1996). *Finding Philosophy in Social Science*. Yale University Press.
Burt, R. S. (1995). *Structural Holes: The Social Structure of Competition*. Harvard University Press.
Canterbery, R. (2005). *A Brief History of Economics. Artful Approaches to the Dismal Science*. World Scientific Publishing.
Carrington, P. J., Scott, J., & Wasserman, S. (2009). *Models and Methods in Social Network Analysis*. Cambridge University Press.
Cochran, T. C. (1960). Cultural Factors in Economic Growth. *The Journal of Economic History, 20*(4), 515–530.
Colander, D. (2010). Moving Beyond the Rhetoric of Pluralism: Suggestions for an Inside-the-Mainstream Heterodoxy. In R. Garner, E. K. Olsen, & M. Starr (Eds.), *Economic Pluralism*. Routledge.
Collins, R. (1988). *Theoretical Sociology*. Hartcourt Brace Jovanovich.
Collins, R. (2002). *The Sociology of Philosophers*. Harvard University Press.
David, P. A. (2007). Path Dependence: A Foundational Concept for Historical Social Science. *Cliometrica, 1*, 91–114.
Davis, J. B. (2007). *The Turn in Recent Economics and Return of Orthodoxy*. Research Paper, University of Amsterdam.
Dorfman, J. (1946–1959). *The Economic Mind in American Civilization* (Vol. 5). Viking Press.
Dorfman, J. (1955). The Role of the German Historical School in American Thought. *American Economic Review, 45*(2), 17–28.
Elsner, W., & Hanappi, H. (Eds.). (2008). *Varieties of Capitalism and New Institutional Deals*. Edward Elgar.
Fine, B., & Milonakis, D. (2009). *From Economics Imperialism to Freakonomics*. Routledge.
Fleck, L. (1980). *Entstehung einer wissenschaftlichen Tatsache*. Suhrkamp.
Fligstein, N. (2001). *The Architecture of Markets*. Princeton University Press.
Freeman, A. (2009). *The Economists of Tomorrow*. No. 15691.MPRA Paper.
Frey, B. ([1992] 1999). *Economics as a Science of Human Behaviour. Towards a New Social Science Paradigm*. Kluwer.
Granovetter, M. S. (1985). Economic Action and Social Structure: The Problem of Embeddedness. *The American Journal of Sociology, 91*(3), 481–510.
Guillén, M. F., Collins, R., England, P., & Meyer, M. (2002). The Revival of Economic Sociology. In M. F. Guillén, R. Collins, P. England, & M. Meyer (Eds.), *The New Economic Sociology: Developments in an Emerging Field*. Russell Sage.
Haller, M. (2003). *Soziologische Theorie im Systematisch-Kritischen Vergleich*. UTB.
Harrison, L. E., & Huntington, S. P. (Eds.). (2000). *Culture Matters. How Values Shape Human Progress*. Basic Books.
Heilbroner, R. L. (2000). *The Wordly Philosophers*. Penguin Books.

Hodgson, G. M. (1994). The Return of Institutional Economics. In N. J. Smelser & R. Swedberg (Eds.), *The Handbook of Economic Sociology*. Princeton University Press and Russell Sage.

Jevons, W. S. (1871). *Theory of Political Economy*. McMillan.

Jones, E. L. (2006). *Cultures Merging. A Historical and Economic Critique of Culture*. Princeton University Press.

Kahneman, D. (2003). A Perspective on Judgment and Choice: Mapping Bounded Rationality. *American Psychologist, 58*(9), 697–720.

Kuhn, T. S. (1962). *The Structure of Scientific Revolutions*. University of Chicago Press.

Landes, D. (2000). Culture Makes Almost All the Difference. In L. E. Harrison & S. P. Huntington (Eds.), *Culture Matters. How Values Shape Human Progress*. Basic Books.

Lee, F. S. (2004). To be a Heterodox Economist: The Contested Landscape of American Economics, 1960s and 1970s. *Journal of Economic Issues, 38*(3), 747–763.

Lee, F. S. (2009). *A History of Heterodox Economics. Challenging the Mainstream in the Twentieth Century*. Routledge.

Lee, F. S. (2010). Pluralism in Heterodox Economics. In R. Garner, E. K. Olsen, & M. Starr (Eds.), *Economic Pluralism*. Routledge.

Lee, F. S., & Harley, S. (1998). Peer Review, the Research Assessment Exercise and the Demise of Non-Mainstream Economics. *Capital and Class, 22*(3), 23–53.

Marin, A., & Wellman, B. (2010). Social Network Analysis: An Introduction. In P. Carrington & J. Scott (Eds.), *Handbook of Social Network Analysis*. Sage.

Mikl-Horke, G. (1999). *Historische Soziologie der Wirtschaft*. Oldenbourg.

Nelson, R. H. (2001). *Economics as Religion: from Samuelson to Chicago and Beyond*. Pennsylvania State University Press.

North, D. C. (1990). *Institutions, Institutional Change and Economic Performance*. Cambridge University Press.

North, D. C. (1997). *Where Have We Been and Where Are We Going?* Manuscript.

Ostrom, E. (2005). *Understanding Institutional Diversity*. Princeton University Press.

Parsons, T. (1940). The Motivation of Economic Activities. *Canadian Journal of Economics and Political Sciences, 6*(2), 187–203.

Parsons, T., & Smelser, N. (1956). *Economy and Society: A Study in the Integration of Economic and Social Theory*. Free Press.

Polanyi, C. (1944). *The Great Transformation: The Political and Economic Origins of our Time*. Rinehart.

Schülein, J. A. (2009). Soziologische Theorie und ihr Gegenstand. In J. A. Schülein, G. Mikl-Horke, & R. Simsa (Eds.), *Soziologie für das Wirtschaftsstudium*. UTB.

Schumpeter, J. A. (1942). *Capitalism, Socialism and Democracy*. Allen & Unwin.

Schumpeter, J. A. (1954). *History of Economic Analysis*. Oxford University Press.
Schumpeter, J. A. (1963). *The Theory of Economic Development*. Oxford University Press.
Scott, J. (2009). *Social Network Analysis*. Sage.
Simmel, G. (1908). Die Kreuzung sozialer Kreise. In G. Simmel (Ed.), *Soziologie. Untersuchungen über die Formen der Vergesellschaftung*. Duncker & Humblot.
Simon, H. A. (1955). A Behavioral Model of Rational Choice. *Quartely Journal of Economics, 69*(1), 99–118.
Simon, H. A. (1962). The Architecture of Complexity. *Proceedings of the American Philosophical Society, 106*(6), 467–482.
Stets, J. E., & Turner, J. (Eds.). (2007). *Handbook of the Sociology of Emotions*. Springer.
Swedberg, R. (2003). Economic and Sociological Approaches to Markets. In R. Swedberg (Ed.), *Richard: Principles of Economic Sociology*. Princeton University Press.
Turner, J. H. (1998). *The Structure of Sociological Theory*. Wadsworth Publishing.
Vane, H. R., & Mulhearn, C. (2005). *The Nobel Memorial Laureates in Economics. An Introduction to Their Careers and Main Published Works*. Edward Elgar.
Walras, L. ([1874] 1954). Elements of Pure Economics. Richard D. Irwin.
Wasserman, S., & Faust, K. (2009). *Social Network Analysis*. Cambridge University Press.
Weber, M. ([1921] 1972). *Wirtschaft und Gesellschaft*. J. C. B. Mohr.
Weber, M. ([1904] 1988). *Die protestantische Ethik und der Geist des Kapitalismus*. In Max Weber (Ed.), *Gesammelte Aufsätze zur Religionssoziologie*. Vol. 1. Mohr.
Weber, M. ([1898] 1990). *Grundriß zu den Vorlesungen über Allgemeine (theoretische) Nationalökonomie*. J. C. B. Mohr.
White, H. C. (1981). Where do Markets Come From? *American Journal of Sociology, 87*, 517–547.
White, H. C. (1988). Varieties of Markets. In B. Wellman & S. D. Berkowitz (Eds.), *Social Structures: A Network Approach*. Cambridge University Press.
White, H. C., Boorman, S. A., & Breiger, R. L. (1976). Social Structures from Multiple Networks. I: Blockmodells of Roles and Positions. *American Journal of Sociology, 81*(4), 730–780.

CHAPTER 6

The Order of Social Sciences: Sociology in Dialogue with Neighbouring Disciplines

The Order of Social Sciences: Introductory Remarks

The development of academic thought during the twentieth century is marked by a rapid and continual process of accumulation of a vast quantity of scientific material. If the field is narrowed down and the social sciences are considered merely, a considerable accumulation of academic output is evident during the course of the twentieth century. The result is that the social sciences find themselves in an entirely different position at the beginning of the twenty-first century than the one they occupied at the end of the nineteenth or beginning of the twentieth century (Wallerstein, 1991). What is the background to this change? The increasing consolidation and delimitation of economics and the social sciences is of prime importance. Social sciences for their part have separated into autonomous subjects: history, sociology, political science, pedagogy, media studies, geography and, of course, economics, as well as a few others. Taking Michel Foucault's view as he delivered it in his famous *The Order of Things: An Archaeology of the Human Sciences* (1970), one can discover permanently new landscapes of scientific arrangements.

This chapter was initially conceived as a plenary address at the 3rd Forum of Sociology of the International Sociological Association held in Vienna in July 2016. Therefore, the audience was a sociological one, and the message was by a sociologist to sociologists, arguing that the academic subject should be framed by an acknowledgement and reflection of global

D. Bögenhold, *Neglected Links in Economics and Society*, https://doi.org/10.1007/978-3-030-79193-3_6

contours of scientific change. Permanently new topics arise in economy and society and provoke and modify the division of sciences. When discussing the up-to-date status of our academic domains it is essential to take into account that our current body of knowledge is itself part of a permanent storm of renewal. What the Greek philosopher Heraclitus said once, namely that "everything flows," must be valid for our own domains too: we have to employ historicizing reflections as a tool in order to find the current location and related opportunities and challenges.

Taking a less narrow perspective, which goes beyond sociology and takes the sociological reflections just as an example for different other disciplines and their positive or even negative destinies, the discussion provides some ideas about the academic interplay of different subjects. The whole system of social sciences can be treated as an involuntary concert, which, analogous to the Italian "concertare" or "concerto," means both, fighting, competing, struggling on the one and bringing together, harmonizing, and unifying on the other hand. The division of labour between economics, sociology, anthropology, history, psychology, and regional and urban sciences has and has always had fragile balances. It seems that economics as the only academic field in which Nobel prizes are awarded has become a rather dominant actor in the concerto, but even this view may be deceiving. One of the main messages of the chapter is that, most recently, many substantial concepts, from psychology, history, and sociology have been taken up by economists and incorporated into their body of knowledge without really or fully being informed by their early originators. This relative idea theft could be seen negatively or, indeed, positively as the emergence of new interdisciplinary domains and synergies. In fact, from a perspective of philosophical economics, one can speak about an ongoing social-scientification of economics (Bögenhold, 2010), which is increasingly incorporating ideas brought forth by neighbouring social science disciplines.

Looking Back over the Last 120 Years

Even at the beginning of the twentieth century, prominent academics in social sciences held professorships and chairs in the fields of economics. Economics existed without competition as a subject, since professorships for the newer subjects, such as sociology, that have now become standard, did not exist yet. These academics concerned themselves with themes, which, from the modern standpoint, were the property of history, sociology, business studies, economics, legal, or administrative sciences. The development of scientific disciplines goes hand in hand with other changes. The structure of professions has changed and social and economic structures have developed many new traits (Rosenberg, 2012). Furthermore, new times bring with them new questions and new discussions. To a great extent, the new contours of intellectual debate reflect the process of historical change (Gordon, 1993).

The essentially positive process by which subjects have gained recognition also has a downside. The price was an increasingly specialized knowledge, which, for systematic reasons, lost sight of respective neighbouring disciplines. Bridges between the islands of knowledge were even more rarely sought or found. This meant that forms of scientific knowledge disciplines and intra- and inter-disciplinarity faded even more into the background. The paradoxical effect is that the apparently relentless growth of both economics and sociology, which continues to the present day, is by no means combined with a process of academic consolidation. On the contrary, subjects lose out in numerous aspects, since they are scarcely able to communicate with one another any longer. The subjects appear to have become fragmented theoretically, methodically, and practically (Hollis, 2002).

The principal developments in the rise of sociology and the demarcation of different branches of economics have mainly taken place since the Second World War. Today the subjects are characterized by their impressive plurality in terms of the diversity of topics and methods. As a result, these subjects themselves have become differentiated further, to the extent that it is even more difficult to conceptualize them as closed, single-type disciplines (Rosenberg, 2012; Cedrini & Fontana, 2017; Bögenhold, 2018).

There was clearly no real correlation between the delineation of the system of disciplines and the corresponding increase in their recognition. Auguste Comte was probably the primary influence on the conception of sociology. In his Cours de Philosophie Positive (1830–1842, 1907) Comte formulated the necessity and unavoidability of academic specialization and differentiation. At the same time, he recognized the danger of isolation and insularity of knowledge.

Thus, he wrote, "It is evidently this division of various types of research amongst various groups of scholars that we have to thank for the level of development that knowledge has reached in our time. However, this division means that it is no longer possible for a modern scholar to engage himself with all disciplines at once—a kind of engagement that was easy and quite normal in the past" (Comte, 1907, p. 33). Comte argued that the expansion of the knowledge base goes hand in hand with the increasing differentiation and division of labour. The onset of this process, so the argument continued, also had a converse effect. "Even recognising the great results that have been achieved because of this division of labour, and accepting that this is now the true foundation of the general organisation of the academic world, it is still impossible, on the other hand, not to be adversely affected by this current division of labour for the reason of over-specialisation of ideas, which each person pursues with great exclusivity. … We must take care that human intellect does not finally lose its way in a host of details" (Comte, 1907, p. 33).

Comte's analysis, formulated in the 1830s, has proved to be extremely accurate. In particular, since the beginning of the new millennium, the process of increasing specialization within disciplines has reached a new level. Also, a separation of literature and science had started at that time (see Snow, 2012). Social sciences have evolved, but have disintegrated into various small and ever new academic territories, which themselves have divided further. In addition, literature and science have increasingly become separated from one another. Boundaries began to develop between them during the process of self-definition. This development led Max Weber, who, like most of the classic scholars known today, was an interdisciplinary generalist, to conclude in his famous article "Science as Vocation" that a high academic reputation can best be achieved by withdrawing to extremely specialized subject matter. "In our time, the internal situation, in contrast to the organisation of science as a vocation, is first of all conditioned by the fact that science has entered a phase of specialisation previously unknown and that this will forever remain the case. Not only externally, but inwardly, matters stand at a point where the individual can acquire the sure consciousness of achieving something truly perfect in the field of science only in case he is a strict specialist" (Max Weber, 1988, p. 134).

Through the explosion of new academic publications in sociology and in the different branches of the economic sciences, internal lines of differentiation and segmentation emerged. The subjects multiplied in a vertical and a horizontal direction, and within the course of constantly new subjects, new separate universes of discourse emerged, each with separate research organizations, global conferences, journals, curricula, academic career opportunities, as well as patterns and publication routines. Finally, a vulcanization of the research landscape in the social sciences was revealed, indicating a variety of new islands of knowledge, which increasingly shared fewer reciprocal ties and active links of information and communication (Wallerstein et al., 1996).

Compared to the situation in sociology, the situation in other academic fields, economics, history, psychology and others, was more or less the same, although slightly different between North America and Europe. While Émile Durkheim wrote in the introduction to the first issue of the journal *Année Sociologique* under his editorship that it is the destiny of sociology and economics that they will merge in the long run (quoted in Swedberg, 1991), the opposite was true. The subjects separated, although a few major authors in historical sociology like Wallerstein, Bendix, Elias, and Mann continued to work in both fields. For the most part, long-term processes were forgotten, and scientific analysis was based on short-term observations. Much later and initially in the US academic context, positions came up arguing that observations over longer time periods are a necessity for methodological reasons: "First, those shifts formed the context in which our current standard ideas for the analysis of big social structures, large social processes, and huge comparisons among social experiences crystallized. Second, they marked critical moments in changes that are continuing on a world scale today. Understanding those changes and their consequences is our most pressing reason for undertaking the systematic study of big structures and large processes. It is important to look at them comparatively over substantial blocks of space and time, in order to see whence we have come, where we are going, and what real alternatives to our present condition exist. Systematic comparisons of structures and processes will not only place our own situation in perspective, but also help in the identification of causes and effects" (Tilly, 1984, pp. 10–11).

Today, it is even difficult to speak about sociology in terms of a general understanding, since the coexistence of many sociologies can be observed. Sociology has proven to become a field, which reminds us of a patchwork rug with diverse individual "universes of discourse." Now, the International Sociological Association (ISA) has nearly 60 independent Research Committees, 3 Working Groups and 5 Thematic Groups, which have their own organizational life under the roof of sociology without feeling the need to contribute to a common project of grand theory. Taken together, the academic field looks like a diffuse bazaar of ideas, projects, and related people. Instead of coherence, sociology presents itself as a patchwork of fragmented interests, topics, and approaches. However, sociology has also evolved into some other different directions. There is not only the professional sociology, but the spheres of policy advice and critical sociology also exist and, last but not least, public sociology as introduced by Burawoy (2005). Public sociology, in particular, is an area of knowledge, which exists outside of universities and penetrates to us through schoolteachers and mass media so that everybody has some kind of command of sociological expressions as if they are part of the everyday language, for example, we talk about lifestyles, classes, family structure, or social opportunities as if we were trained sociologists (without being so). Public sociology has become manifest in the increased use of sociological terms in public communication. According to Burawoy (2005), one has to raise the questions of knowledge for whom and for what in order to define the fundamental character of sociology as an academic discipline (critically see Calhoun, 2005).

The divisional order of sociology is characterized by a practice, which mirrors the multiplicity of academic production and a rather accidental development rather than a systematic reasoning about how to design an academic subject (Backhouse & Fontaine, 2014). With respect to the definition of what sociology is and how it is organized into different subfolders, two trends overlap each other. (I) There is a long-term trend of the development of sociology in which the discipline increasingly gained firm ground and recognition and in which a process of differentiation started to evolve. This trend took place within the last century. The field of sociology also started to become a professional system with clear curricula, degrees, academic societies, and university departments, with an increasing number of publications and related journals. (II) Parallel to the consolidation process of sociology, the subject formed borderlines to neighbouring fields. Looking over the course of the last hundred years, topics of sociology have modified and multiplied.

Even today, no clear definition exists of what sociology is. Of course, sociology has to do with the study of societies. Already Norbert Elias in his attempt to contribute to the question: "What is Sociology?" (Elias, 1978) had to keep it very general: "It is customary to say that society is the 'thing' which sociologists investigate. But this reification mode of expression greatly hampers and may even prevent one from understanding the nature of sociological problems" (Elias, 1978, p. 14). The same descriptive definition can be found in the work by Giddens (2006): "Sociology is the scientific study of human life, groups, and societies. It is a dazzling and compelling enterprise, as its subject matter is our own behaviour as social beings. The scope of the sociological study is extremely wide, ranging from the analysis of passing encounters between individuals on the street to the investigation of global social processes such as the rise of Islamic fundamentalism" (Giddens, 2006, 4).

Looking at sociology from the outside, sociology is effectively identified as sociological theory, which is just one research committee within the ISA. Even the sociological theory is not a unique and common field, but is segmented into many competing approaches in which stakeholders follow their own practices and routines. For example, the fact that Jonathan Turner's *The Structure of Sociological Theory* (2004) has 36 chapters, each one portraying a separate theoretical approach, shows the heterogeneity of sociological theory. There is no stratified unique sociological theory, but diverse camps coexist. Today, sociology is a wide cosmos of knowledge and working islands regarding quality, quantity, and address labels. There is not necessarily any communication between them.

From Invitation to Sociology to Disinvitation

It was the famous book by Peter L. Berger (1963), which served as a plea for the academic subject of sociology. The book claimed a sociological perspective to investigate social phenomena: "Sociology is not a practise, but an attempt to understand" (Berger, 1963, p. 4), because "statistical data by themselves do not make sociology. They become sociology only when they are sociologically interpreted, put within a theoretical frame of reference that is sociological" (Berger 1963, p. 10). About 30 years later, the same author turned his invitation into a disinvitation (Berger, 1994) and accused the sociology of his time of having four different negative symptoms, which he called parochialism, triviality, rationalism, and ideology (Berger, 1994, p. 9). "While parochialism and triviality may be taken together, also rationalism and ideology have some internal link. The impeachment of parochialism means that sociology is too often centered with just one case or social experience or practice: Sociology, the discipline par excellence to understand modernity, must of necessity be comparative. …. It is the source of crippling failures of perception. It should be part and parcel of the training of every sociologist to gain detailed knowledge of at least one society that differs greatly from his own" (Berger, 1994, p. 9). Therefore, "triviality too is a fruit of parochialism, but in the case of sociology the more important root is methodological. … Identification of scientific rigor with quantification has greatly limited the scope of sociology" (Berger, 1994, pp. 9–10). Finally, Berger criticized sociology for being too often normative in a sense of stating how societies or social relations should be. Instead, sociology should remember the claim for an absence of value judgements: "Sociology is a rational discipline; every empirical science is. But it must not fall into the fatal error of confusing its own rationality with the rationality of the world" (Berger 1994, p. 10).

These modern forms of critique received several updates. Alexander (1995) and Münch (1991, 1995) debated about the so-called McDonaldization of sociology, asking if sociology has national specifics and identities or if the US-American standards of writing and quoting would increasingly direct and dominate the rest of world sociology. It was a time when, at different locations and in different organizations, the future of sociology in the wider context of social sciences was being questioned. And, Ulrich Beck (2005)—ten years later—said in discussing Burawoy (2005) that "all forms of … sociology are in danger of becoming museum pieces. … sociology needs to be reinvented" (Beck, 2005, p. 335).

Analogous to Berger's critique that sociology may have lost some degree of attractivity, is the relative loss of theory. Not only does sociological theory mark just one research committee among nearly 60 others, but, in general, the "current imbalance between methods and theory" (Swedberg, 2016, p. 5) has been criticized. It is said that methods "dominate modern social science" (ibid.). Although the rise of sociology after the Second World War was centred around methods, and mainly had to do with the introduction of quantification into the sociological analysis, in the future, sociological theory and also the process of theorizing should be upgraded and more strongly acknowledged in the organization of academic sociology (Swedberg, 2016, p. 20). The problem with Swedberg's claim is—despite the strong advantages the discussion delivers—that ultimately, the terms theory as well as theorizing, remain a bit empty (Bertilsson, 2016; Krause, 2016), not defining clearly where theory starts to be theory (and ends up as well) (for further perspectives see Swedberg, 2014, Zima, 2004). The plea for theory fits with Adorno's enlightenment, where he criticized the transformation of sociology into statistics and administrative science as the emergence of the known form of "administered society" (Adorno & Horkheimer, 1997, p. 264). The "imbalance" between theory and empirics is easy to state if no one has a firm idea of the ideal point of balance. Adorno, Horkheimer (1997) as well as Swedberg

(2016), each with very different ambitions, are correct in claiming that the process of gaining data cannot be regarded as an end in itself.

The Credo of the Reinvention of Sociology

What might a reinvention of sociology look like? That was already the topic in the 1990s in the study carried out by the *Gulbenkian Commission for the Restructuring of Social Sciences* (Wallerstein et al., 1996). The premise of discussion of the Gulbenkian Commission was that, in an increasingly globalized and digitalized world, the landscape of the social sciences (including the location of sociology) must be affected by those changes. Adaptation and reinventions are a consequence and the sterile division of order cannot be adequate for the future anymore. Instead, practical interdisciplinarity and reciprocal synergies will be the claim of the twenty-first century. "The degree of internal cohesiveness and flexibility of the disciplines varies today, both between disciplines and among the forms a discipline assumes around the world" (Wallerstein et al., 1996, p. 97).

As a consequence of those processes of the simultaneous multiplication and fragmentation of academic knowledge, new frontiers of academic organization (must) evolve: "What seems to be called for is less an attempt to transform organizational frontiers than to amplify the organization of intellectual activity without attention to current disciplinary boundaries. To be historical is after all not the exclusive purview of persons called historians. It is an obligation of all social scientists. To be sociological is not the exclusive purview of persons called sociologists. It is an obligation of all social scientists. Economic issues are not the exclusive purview of economists. Economic questions are central to any and all social scientific analysis. Nor is it absolutely sure that professional historians necessarily know more about historical explanations, sociologists more about social issues, economists more about economic fluctuations than other working social scientists. In short, we do not believe that there are monopolies of wisdom, nor zones of knowledge reserved for persons with particular university degrees" (Wallerstein et al., 1996, p. 98).

The division of academic branches today is a bit reminiscent of the peaceful oligopoly behaviour of firms, where terrains of competencies and power are claimed by definition and reciprocal acknowledgement instead of reasoning. Our brief points mentioned before indicate that sociology is always incorporated in a flux of societal and scientific change and many shifts have taken place within sociology, and a lot of critiques have emerged.

However, much of this discussion is centred around the topic of how sociology as an academic field could be modernized or optimized. Less discussion has been carried out on the issue of the expansion of the domain of sociology, interdisciplinary exchange, and going to new frontiers. Reinvention may also imply claiming more competences in the wider field of human sciences or in a broader modern concept of a universal social science. The integration and conversion of sociology may signify some losses of denominations and some gains of authority simultaneously.

Not only the *Gulbenkian Commission on the Restructuring of Social Sciences* (Wallerstein, 1999), but also the first *Social Science Report* by UNESCO (1999) pointed to the problem that academic competencies are often handled in an exclusive terminology. "Disciplines are classified under either the one (for example, economics, sociology, political science, as social sciences) or the other (for example, psychology, anthropology and linguistics, as human sciences)" (UNESCO, 1999, p. 12). Despite the need for specialization in academic training, transdisciplinary attempts are also necessary in order to increase the potential of insights: "There is no doubt that disciplinary separations are part of the scientific endeavour and have a clear heuristic and educational value. It is also obvious that a competent social scientist is a person with a high level of training and expertise in one of the core disciplines, without which he/she cannot cross, with relevance and usefulness, disciplinary frontiers, to cooperate with other specialists. However, at the cutting edge of science, in advanced research, interdisciplinarity or transdisciplinarity is required, combining theories and methods from different disciplines according to the nature of the research" (UNESCO, 1999, p. 12). The conclusion, which has been reported so far across different platforms of science management is that the "future is cross disciplinary" and "social science is central to science" overall (Campaign for Social Science, 2015).

Separation of Sociology from Economics, Psychology and History, and Re-integration

The division of work between sociology, economics, history, and psychology has so many fluid borders and areas of overlap that it is not only a difficult task to draw clear and sterile lines between these, but it would also not contribute to an appropriate understanding of knowledge domains (Fourcade et al., 2015). The academic silos of knowledge are overfilled; an exchange in a sense of reciprocal decomposing has become increasingly necessary. The recent question about the relationship between sociology and neighbouring disciplines such as economics, psychology, or history has not been discussed often. While Max Weber published his *Economy and Society* (1978 [1921]), with which he addressed both items equally, suggesting a coexistence between economy and society, the process of scientific differentiation over the following decades changed academic practice, its division, and related questions. In the 1950s, Parsons and Smelser wrote in their book *Economy and Society* (1956) that only a few authors competent in sociological theory have "any working knowledge of economics, and conversely ... few economists have much knowledge of sociology" (Parsons & Smelser, 1956).

It is my firm understanding that the trend described by Parsons and Smelser (1956) can also be confirmed for the relationship of sociology and psychology, and sociology and history. However, recent developments point to circumstances indicating completely new directions, which should be acknowledged. In particular, economics has started to re-open in the direction of psychology, history, and sociology. We observe an increased social-scientification of economics (Bögenhold, 2010), in which more and more contents of one or the other neighbouring disciplines are increasingly incorporated into economics. What was a process of de-coupling for most of the twentieth century has started to move in the opposite direction; this is an ongoing re-integration. When reasoning about sociology and its problems, challenges and destiny, one may be well advised to compare the scientific potentials of different academic work settings and their topical and methodological overlaps and divergences. Established subjects of sociological experiences and competencies are increasingly seen as being of interest for other academic disciplines and sociology should be aware of these—let's say—"imperialistic" advances (Granovetter, 1992, 2017; Davis, 2016; Chafim, 2016; Marchionatti & Cedrini, 2017), especially from the directions of economics and management studies. At least, sociology should be aware that there are many subjects, which are seen positively from neighbouring fields without receiving any attention here.

Looking at current international trends and topics show considerable thematic analogies in neighbouring disciplines, which should be analysed and explored in order to see how the contours of the academic landscape and division change and in which directions the development is evolving (Rosenberg, 2012). Ultimately, sociology is concerned with the question about what people do and why they do it in the way they do. Swedberg compared sociology with the cognitive sciences: "Sociologists have failed to address a number of topics that are important to theorizing, and that cognitive scientists have already been working on for several decades. … Cognitive scientists have also developed some important insights in other areas where sociologists are active but have not been particularly innovative. Studies of meaning, memory and emotions are some examples of this" (Swedberg, 2016, pp. 18–19).

Scientific progress is often contingent and never rational in a sense that it follows arithmetic rules of combinations. The "market" for ideas is not precisely an efficient or perfect market. Academic progress is also related to a series of mistakes by which intellectual resources are wasted, and, as a consequence, there are indeed intellectual gems lying unexploited and waiting for someone to grasp (Collins, 2002). However, actual textbook knowledge in economics often remained the same over decades (Granovetter, 2017).

Classic economics started with the conception of "self-interest" for reasons which can be reconstructed logically. Parsons engaged in a sociology of economic thought and concluded that the abstraction was due to the "fact of finding a plausible formula for filling a logical gap in the closure of a system" (Parsons, 1940, p. 188), which is characterized by Parsons as a doctrine. Thinking in terms that culture matters implies that people are guided by, at least, a set of goals, which are implicit or explicit, conflicting or overlapping. Social psychology and phenomenology contributed much information about these spheres and a sociology of emotions is based on the premise that people are not fully rationally controlled (Stets & Turner, 2007, Turner & Stets, 2009; Elster, 1998, 1999). Although famous economists like J. M. Keynes or J. A. Schumpeter already referred to non-rational and psychological categories to integrate into their framework of thought, economic orthodoxy ignored those voices for a long time. Over the past few decades, scientists from outside of core economics have increasingly been awarded Nobel prizes for behavioural works, for example, psychologist Herbert Simon for his theorem of "bounded rationality" (Simon, 1982) or Daniel Kahneman (2012) for his distinction between experience and memory, or the most recent Nobel laureate Richard Thaler (1994, 2016). Later, we come across Nobel laureates quoting extensively from sociological literature like Polanyi (1957) or Berger and Luckmann

(1966) for their work on institutions. D. G. North said that economics treats the issue of motivation of human beings like a black box. Another Nobel laureate in economics explicitly claims sociology as the science that is responsible for social norms and constraints. Akerlof (2007), in his function as outgoing president of the American Economic Association, recently voiced a plea to turn the academic focus towards issues of motivation and cognitive structures. Elsewhere, Akerlof and Kranton (2000) referred to dimensions like identity and social norms, which belong much more on the sociological or psychological ground than on economic terrain. Akerlof and Shiller worked out in their study "Animal Spirits" (2009) that the functioning of the whole capitalist system is heavily based on sociopsychological foundations. "Animal Spirits" (2009) takes up several questions, which were already raised by J. M. Keynes many years earlier.

Performing this turn, economics has demonstrated flexibility and moving away from conventional practice and its own textbook knowledge. The widely used concept of homo oeconomicus has started to erode in economics since Herbert Simon's "bounded rationality" (Simon, 1982). However, it was already Max Weber who had concluded that economics "argues with a non-realist human being, analogous to a mathematical ideal figure" (Weber, 1990, p. 30, transl. D.B., orig. 1898). Being distant to such a procedure as provided in "standard economics," Weber distinguished between four ideal types of social action, which are the rationality of (1) traditional action, of (2) affective action, of (3) value-orientation and of (4) purposive–rational utilitarian action (Weber, 1978, part 1, ch. 1), of which only the last point of classification matches with the supposed rationality of homo oeconomicus. Wallerstein (1999) discusses very thoroughly exactly this rationality conception in Max Weber's work; for a more general discussion of Weber see Lachmann (1979), Collins (1986), Swedberg (2003).

Further academic applications in economics may be shown where economists have crossed borders. A. Sen (1999) was recognized with a Nobel Prize for his seminal works on choice and his capability approach, which contributed to a better understanding of happiness and well-being by adding a relative perspective of interpretation. Another thematic field in which sociology makes waves is social network research as a mapping of patterns of communication and support. Even here, it is an interesting convergence between developments in economics as well as in management studies. Sociologists should know about this to claim intellectual property rights where necessary and to defend their own profession. Hodgson

(2012, p. 46) verified six Nobel laureates in economics since the 1970s who were recognized, among different topics, also for their concept of being very critical of the concept of the rational egoistic man.

The seemingly paradoxical situation is that, on the one hand, textbook knowledge is taught in economics, which is very much concerned with neoclassic economics, and on the other hand, economists are awarded the prestigious Nobel prizes, for criticizing principles of neoclassic thought. Robert M. Solow (Nobel Laureate in 1987) belonged to this last category: "All narrowly economic activity is embedded in a web of social institutions, customs, beliefs, and attitudes .... Few things should be more interesting to a civilized economic theorist than the opportunity to observe the interplay between social institutions and economic behavior over time and place" (Solow, 1985, pp. 328–329). A few years later, Douglas G. North (Nobel Laureate in 1993) argued in the same direction by sharpening the awareness for historical research: "Improving our understanding of the nature of economic change entails that we draw on the only laboratory that we have—the past. But 'understanding' the past entails imposing order on the myriad facts that have survived to explain what has happened—that is the theory. The theories we develop to understand where we have come from the social sciences. Therefore, there is a constant give and take between the theories we develop, and their application to explain the past. Do they improve our understanding—is the resultant explanation broadly consistent with the surviving historical evidence?" (North, 1977, p. 1).

What, among many other authors, Solow or North explain is the trivial fact that each economy is integrated into a permanent flux of changes. They both confirm what Schumpeter had expressed much earlier: "The essential point to grasp is that in dealing with capitalism we are dealing with an evolutionary process. ... Capitalism, then, is by nature a form or method of economic change and not only never is but never can be stationary" (Schumpeter, 1942, p. 82). When history was forgotten by wide parts of economics, works by Solow or North clearly rediscovered history for specific reasons. There is nothing else that provides empirical facts on capitalism other than the history of capitalism. Even to undertake future forecasts, one has to refer backwards. Those economic activities are embedded in social institutions, customs, beliefs, and attitudes that reflect the simple credo that culture matters, which implies that sociology matters.

If culture makes a difference, capitalism does not exist in a vacuum, but in a context with specific social regimes of living, producing, and exchange.

Institutionalist approaches have no other aim than to highlight that different social organizations and institutions (including religion, language, law, family structures and networks, systems of education and industrial relations) make differences when trying to come up with statements regarding general principles of capitalist societies and economies. As known, capitalism in Singapore differs from capitalism in Zimbabwe, which differs from capitalism in Switzerland. Accepting the idea that economies and societies are not filled by abstract but by real entities, one has to refer to concrete coordinates of time and space. If economics rediscovers history, the economic theory goes far beyond abstractivism (Hodgson, 2001). Taking culture as an analytic variable indicates different settings of norms and related behaviour (North, 1990; Jones, 2006). Culture serves as a framework of rational behaviour and is the factor, which indicates real societies as opposed to abstract ones. Historian David Landes put it concisely when he said: "Culture makes almost all the difference" (Landes, 2000, p. 2).

The concept of the "social embeddedness" (Granovetter, 1985, 2017) of institutional actors and human behaviour is a common label for approaches that attempt to deal with the interplay of individual and corporate actors in a dynamic and joint process. The impact of such a perspective is that modern economics could be linked with a constructive view that provides a new division of work between economics and the other social sciences (Granovetter, 1992). Granovetter's formulation of a "social embeddedness of economic behaviour and institutions" (Granovetter, 1985, 2017) has subsequently become widely known. It was in the same year in which Solow (1985) used the term of embeddedness. Granovetter's argumentation is based upon three premises: firstly, that economic action is a special case of social action; secondly, that economic action is socially situated and embedded; and thirdly, that economic institutions are social constructions. A synthesis is sought between conceptions of over-socialized and under-socialized human beings in order to articulate a theorem, which takes into account both the determination of society and the relative openness of human activities as a process (Granovetter, 1992, 2002).

Bounded rationality is very much to be understood in relation to asymmetric information and complexity. Bounded rationality mirrors the fact that societies, organizations, and economies are fragmented, they are organized along different lines and zones of contact, familiarity, and information exchange. In our view, modern economics could benefit significantly by integrating recent network concepts, which are a fantastic tool to bridge micro and macro perspectives (Bögenhold, 2013). Social network analysis continues to develop many themes enunciated by pioneering social psychologists. "At its best, social network analysis draws from traditions of research and theory in psychology, sociology, and other areas to describe how patterns of interpersonal relations are associated with diverse behavioral, cognitive, and emotional outcomes. Looking for the future, we are deepening interest in the psychological underpinnings of why some people more than others engage and benefit from the networks of contacts within which they are embedded" (Burt et al., 2013, p. 543).

Markets are always in transition, they come up, they go down, and they change. These markets are carried out by actors having sets of people they know and whom they trust, while other people may be regarded as hostile competitors. However concrete markets may look, they always have very social traits, and economics would fall short if it did not ask about those issues. Competition processes must also be analysed and understood as ongoing social processes, which are involved in social structures and which are permanently in processes of reorganization (Burt, 1995). The presently existing, largely categorical description of social structure has no solid theoretical grounding; furthermore, network concepts may provide the only way to construct a theory of social structure (White et al., 1976, p. 732). In many respects, network analysis is an excellent exemplification of what the term of social embeddedness can deliver. Network analysis furnishes those popular formulations, which have become "economic sociology's most celebrated metaphor" (Guillén et al., 2002, p. 4).

A point of initial discussion was that up-to-date economics is increasingly in a process of social-scientification as Bögenhold (2010) has coined it. Among the implications are an obvious willingness to open up for topics of cognitive structures and motivation. Economic sociology and economic psychology share many of the motives behind those trends, since the arguments in favour of these trends form the foundations of their own academic identity, but one should be curious as well as careful when meeting those new tendencies. Nothing should be taken for granted, but one should always try to see if pieces of the puzzle fit. As ideas about an economy and society in concreto are increasingly accepted again, so the relative autonomy of culture and its specification in different historical variations is also increasingly accepted. In case that one agrees on the formulation that culture matters, one has to agree on the formulation that sociology as the academic domain widely dealing with culture also matters. A plea for the academic existence of sociology must be the ultimate consequence. In particular, historical and comparative sociology, socioeconomics and economic sociology and, of course, social network research, prove to be innovative, when highlighting national and international variations and specifics.

The so-called "imperialism of economics," which is criticized by Granovetter (1992, 2017), increasingly looks towards traditional academic fields of history, psychology, and sociology. The public image of sociology may have declined during recent decades, but the strategic use and importance of (economic) sociology has never been greater, even if many stakeholders in sociology are not aware of this. Sociology seems to have become an upgraded discipline since social networks, communication processes, institutions, and culture are increasingly considered as core dimensions. The reciprocal integration of economy, society, and culture must be better acknowledged in academic reflections as a science of science so that disciplinary authorities will be defined accordingly.

Fig. 6.1 above gives an idea of the interplay of different academic disciplines. In order to arrive at a more modern and pluralistic attempt to overcome monodisciplinary studies, one may look at sociology and the institutional interaction with diverse blurred boundaries. Sociology covering society as well as culture is by nature a key player to understand or at least to contribute to an appropriate understanding of many recent phenomena in a globalized world. Sociology has a use in analysing and

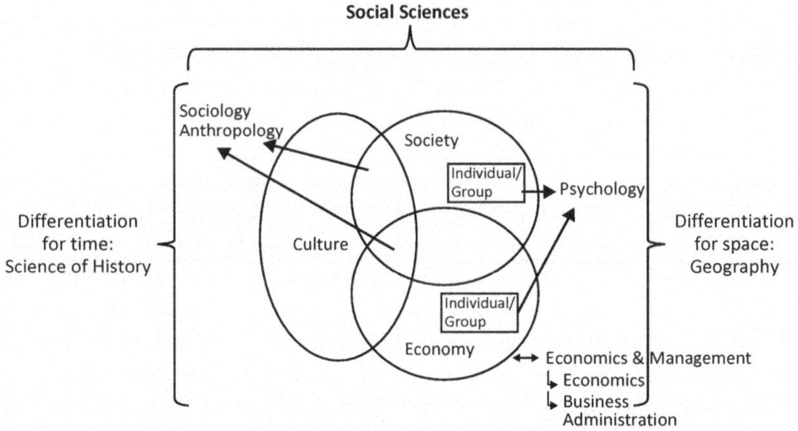

Fig. 6.1 Interplay of different academic disciplines Source: Own illustration, modification of Bögenhold (2015)

explaining phenomena of social life, firstly, and, secondly, to reason about the interplay of different academic branches in the form of the sociology of science. Wallerstein et al.'s (1996) claim to "open the social sciences" should be taken seriously. Sociology can play a crucial part in that orchestra.

Orchestrating the Social Sciences

Following the ideas of opening the social sciences, the final section will give a brief summary and outlook. In general, one can also argue that sociology, psychology, history, economics, and perhaps partly business administration should increasingly try to reintegrate, because their topics are among the items in a complex web of reciprocal thematic interaction. The concept of the "social embeddedness" of institutional actors and human behaviour is a common label for approaches that attempt to deal with the interplay of individual and corporate actors in a dynamic and joint process. Social networks, communication patterns, family structures, trust and fairness, but also distrust and crime, are all dimensions that matter when trying to analyse economies appropriately. Observing a trend of social-scientification of economics raises chances for all other social sciences to arrive at a more cooperative division of academic cooperation. Of course, talk about inter- and trans-disciplinarity is often more easily spelled out than practically achieved in a controlled manner. However, the reciprocal integration of economy, society, and culture (Granovetter, 2017) must be better acknowledged in academic reflections of a science of science so that disciplinary authorities will be defined accordingly.

Sometimes it also helps to go back in the history of intellectual thought in order to avoid the danger of reinventing the wheel. Sociology offers a rich tradition of different classics, who used a practice in which economy and society were not treated as disparate spheres, but as one and the same unit of analysis. Therefore, Max Weber's book title "Economy and Society" (Weber, 1978, in translation "economy and society") were already a manifesto. Another example is Joseph A. Schumpeter, who also worked as a scientist of sciences and who developed some ideas on the landscape of academic cooperation. Of course, he considered especially economics and surrounding sciences, but sociologists will gain profit from his explanations as well, since Schumpeter makes clear that academic sciences are not a means in itself. They have to be regarded as tools and they must be checked for the capacity to contribute to a reciprocal enhancement of a better understanding of phenomena. A universal social science is certainly more of a programme than a status, but some of Schumpeter's ideas (Bögenhold, 2013) may come quite close to that. The substantial preface to *History of Economic Analysis* (Schumpeter, 1954) can be regarded as a manual on how to refer to different academic branches and integrate them into a coherent universal social science, which is far removed from being an autistic, narrow economic science of some modern representation.

First of all, in Schumpeter's discussion theory is always written in quotation marks ("theory"), which links to the discussion initiated by Swedberg (2016): when can we speak about theory, when does a statement deserve the distinction of being a theory? Although it is not the core discussion pursued by Schumpeter, he uses the term theory as if he wants to say "so-called theory," but he explains at least three different meanings of "theory." Then, Schumpeter argues not only in favour of history as rendering a service to theory, but also in favour of "a sort of generalized or typified or stylized economic history" (Schumpeter, 1954, p. 20), which includes institutions like private property, free contracting, or government regulation. Schumpeter offers a long discussion of how much profound knowledge of history is a pre-condition for working as a modern scientist, and he is convinced that his argumentation is true for all scientific disciplines. Everybody needs to have a good command of historical facts but also of the evolution of the own academic subject in terms of the history of intellectual thought and change. Schumpeter explicitly included findings by anthropology and ethnology: "History must, of course, be understood to include fields that have acquired different names as a consequence of specialization, such as pre-historic reports and ethnology (anthropology)" (Schumpeter, 1954, p. 13).

Schumpeter was also concerned with logic, philosophy, and psychology, which are not summarized under techniques of economic analysis, but which are discussed as a basic methodological understanding of his conceptual framework. The most significant statement about economic psychology is contained in the following words: "Economics like other social sciences deals with human behaviour. Psychology is really the basis from which any social science must start and in terms of which all fundamental explanation must run" (Schumpeter, 1954, p. 27).

However, as a further important domain of knowledge Schumpeter (1954) addresses sociology, but also economic sociology: "Economic analysis deals with the questions of how people behave at any time and what economic effects do they produce by so behaving; economic sociology deals with the question how they came to behave as they do. If we define economic behaviour widely enough so that it includes not only actions and motives and propensities but also the social institutions that are relevant to economic behaviour such as government, property inheritance, contract, and so on, that phrase really tells us all we need" (Schumpeter, 1954, p. 21). There are several statements where Schumpeter speaks with great appreciation about sociology and claims that economics has to seek or to keep closer contact with sociology, because "we cannot afford [...] to neglect the developments of sociology" and especially not the "fundamental field of economic sociology in which neither economists nor sociologists can get very far without treading on one another's toes" (Schumpeter, 1954, pp. 25–26). There are also further reflections on the use of mathematics and statistics, which shall not be discussed in further detail here.

Our major point is that reading Schumpeter and other classics is an appropriate tool for finding a way back and for shedding light on contemporary questions. Weber or Schumpeter put together a series of different academic domains as if they are a bouquet of flowers and tried to select useful aspects and knowledge islands to bring them together. "Opening the social sciences" is just a catchword. At least a good manual is needed to decide how we may make use of which islands of knowledge in combination with which others. Social sciences are always confronted with the question of which knowledge is produced for whom and combined with which knowledge domains. Sociology has a very important place in the orchestra to generate knowledge, but sociology should be aware of its own positioning in the whole setting in order to know its own address and the neighbours it is surrounded by.

References

Adorno, T. W., & Horkheimer, M. (1997). *Dialectic of Enlightenment*. Verso.

Akerlof, G. A. (2007). The Missing Motivation in Macroeconomics. *The American Economic Review, 97*(1), 5–36.

Akerlof, G. A., & Kranton, R. E. (2000). Economics and Identity. *The Quarterly Journal of Economics, 115*(3), 715–753.

Akerlof, G. A., & Shiller, R. J. (2009). *Animal Spirits: How Human Psychology Drives the Economy, and Why It Matters for Global Capitalism*. Princeton University Press.

Alexander, J. (1995). How 'National' Is Social Theorizing? A Note on Some Worrying Trends in the Recent Theorizing of Richard Münch. *Revue Suisse de Sociologie, 21*(3), 541–546.

Backhouse, R. E., & Fontaine, P. (2014). Introduction. In R. E. Backhouse & P. Fontaine (Eds.), *A Historiography of the Modern Social Sciences* (pp. 1–28). Cambridge University Press.

Beck, U. (2005). How Not to Become a Museum Piece? *The British Journal of Sociology, 56*(3), 335–343.

Berger, P. L. (1963). *Invitation to Sociology. A Humanistic Perspective.* Anchor Books.

Berger, P. L. (1994). Does Sociology Still Make Sense? *Revue Suisse de Sociologie, 20*(1), 3–12.

Berger, P. L., & Luckmann, T. (1966). *The Social Construction of Reality.* Anchor Books and Doubleday.

Bertilsson, M. (2016). Theorizing—For What? *The British Journal of Sociology, 67*(1), 30–35.

Bögenhold, D. (2010). From Heterodoxy to Orthodoxy and Vice Versa: Economics and Social Sciences in the Division of Academic Work. *The American Journal of Economics and Sociology, 69*(5), 1566–1590.

Bögenhold, D. (2013). Social Network Analysis and the Sociology of Economics: Filling a Blind Spot with the Idea of Social Embeddedness. *The American Journal of Economics and Sociology, 72*(2), 293–318.

Bögenhold, D. (2015). *Gesellschaft studieren, um Wirtschaft zu verstehen.* VS Publishers.

Bögenhold, D. (2018). Economics between Insulation and Social-Scienciation: Observations by a Sociology of Economics. *Journal of Economic Issues, 52*(4), 1125–1142.

Burawoy, M. (2005). For Public Sociology. *American Sociological Review, 70*(1), 4–28.

Burt, R. S. (1995). *Structural Holes: The Social Structure of Competition.* Harvard University Press.

Burt, R. S., Kilduff, M., & Tasselli, S. (2013). Social Network Analysis: Foundations and Frontiers on Advantage. *Annual Review of Psychology, 64*(1), 527–547.

Calhoun, C. (2005). The Promise of Public Sociology. *The British Journal of Sociology, 56*(3), 355–363.

Cedrini, M., & Fontana, M. (2017). Just Another Niche in the Wall? How Specialization Is Changing the Face of Economics. *Cambridge Journal of Economics, 42*(2), 1–25.

Chafim, F. (2016). Disciplinary Division Within Social Sciences. Methodological Issues in Economic Imperialism and Economic Pluralism. *History of Economic Ideas, 24*(3), 144–164.

Collins, R. (1986). *Weberian Sociological Theory.* Cambridge University Press.

Collins, R. (2002). *The Sociology of Philosophies: A Global Theory of Intellectual Change*. Harvard University Press.
Comte, A. (1907). *Course de Philosophie Positive* (orig. 1830), Vol. 1, Paris.
Davis, J. B. (2016). Economics Imperialism Versus Multidisciplinarity. *History of Economic Ideas, 24*(3), 77–94.
Elias, N. (1978). *What Is Sociology?* Columbia University Press.
Elster, J. (1998). Emotions and Economic Theory. *Journal of Economic Literature, 36*(1), 47–74.
Elster, J. (1999). *Alchemies of the Human Mind: Rationality and the Emotions*. Cambridge University Press.
Foucault, M. (1970). *The Order of Things. An Archaeology of the Human Sciences*. Pantheon.
Fourcade, M., Ollion, E., & Algan, Y. (2015). The Superiority of Economists. *Journal of Economic Perspectives, 29*(1), 89–114.
Giddens, A. (2006). *Sociology* (5th ed.). Polity Press.
Gintis, H. (2007). A Framework for the Unification of the Behavioural Sciences. *Behavioural and Brain Sciences, 30*, 1–61.
Gordon, S. (1993). *The History and Philosophy of Social Science*. Routledge.
Granovetter, M. S. (1985). Economic Action and Social Structure: The Problem of Embeddedness. *The American Journal of Sociology, 91*(3), 481–510.
Granovetter, M. S. (1992). The Nature of Economic Relationships. In R. Swedberg (Ed.), *Explorations in Economic Sociology* (pp. 3–41). Russell Sage Foundation.
Granovetter, M. S. (2002). A Theoretical Agenda for Economic Sociology. In M. F. Guillén, R. Collins, P. England, et al. (Eds.), *The New Economic Sociology. Developments in an Emerging Field* (pp. 35–60). Russell Sage Foundation.
Granovetter, M. S. (2017). *Society and Economy: Framework and Principles*. The Beknap Press of Harvard University Press.
Guillén, M. F., Randall, C., England, P., & Meyer, M. (2002). The Revival of Economic Sociology. In M. F. Guillén, R. Collins, P. England, & M. Meyer (Eds.), *The New Economic Sociology: Developments in an Emerging Field* (pp. 1–32). Russell Sage.
Hodgson, G. M. (2001). *How Economics Forgot History: The Problem of Historical Specificity in Social Science*. Routledge.
Hodgson, G. M. (2012). *From Pleasure Machines to Moral Communities. An Evolutionary Economics Without Homo Oeconomicus*. Chicago University Press.
Hollis, M. (2002). *The Philosophy of Social Science: An Introduction*. Cambridge University Press.
Jones, E. L. (2006). *Cultures Merging: A Historical and Economic Critique of Culture*. Princeton University Press.
Kahneman, D. (2012). *Thinking, Fast and Slow*. Penguin.
Krause, M. (2016). The Meanings of Theorizing. *The British Journal of Sociology, 67*(1), 23–29.

Lachmann, L. M. (1979). *The Legacy of Max Weber.* The Glendessary Press.

Landes, D. (2000). Culture Makes Almost All the Difference. In H. Lawrence, E. Huntington, & P. Samuel (Eds.), *Culture Matters. How Values Shape Human Progress* (pp. 2–13). Basic Books.

Marchionatti, R., & Cedrini, M. (2017). *Economics as Social Science. Economics Imperialism and the Challenge of Interdisciplinary.* Routledge.

Münch, R. (1991). American and European Social Theory: Cultural Identities and Social Forms of Theory Production. *Sociological Perspectives, 34*(3), 313–335.

Münch, R. (1995). A Response to Jeffrey C. Alexander. *Revue Suisse de Sociologie, 21*(3), 547–555.

North, D. C. (1977). *Where Have We Been, and Where Are We Going?.* St. Louis, unpublished manuscript.

North, D. C. (1990). *Institutions, Institutional Change and Economic Performance.* Cambridge University Press.

Parsons, T. (1940). The Motivation of Economic Activities. *Canadian Journal of Economics and Political Science, 6*(2), 187–202.

Parsons, T., & Smelser, N. (1956). *Economy and Society: A Study in the Integration of Economic and Social Theory.* The Free Press.

Polanyi, K. (1957). *The Great Transformation: The Political and Economic Origins of Our Time.* Beacon Press.

Rosenberg, A. (2012). *Philosophy of Social Science.* Westview Press.

Schumpeter, J. A. (1942). *Capitalism, Socialism, and Democracy.* Routledge.

Schumpeter, J. A. (1954). *History of Economic Analysis.* Oxford University Press.

Sen, A. (1999). The Possibility of Social Choice. *The American Economic Review, 89*(3), 349–378.

Simon, H. A. (1982). *Models of Bounded Rationality.* MIT Press.

Snow, C. P. (2012). *The Two Cultures.* Cambridge University Press.

Solow, R. M. (1985). Economic History and Economics. *American Economic Review, 75*(2), 328–331.

Stets, J. E., & Turner, J. H. (Eds.). (2007). *Handbook of the Sociology of Emotions.* Springer.

Swedberg, R. (1991). Major Traditions of Economic Sociology. *Annual Review of Sociology, 17*, 251–276.

Swedberg, R. (2003). The Changing Picture of Max Weber's Sociology. *Annual Review of Sociology, 29*, 283–306.

Swedberg, R. (2014). *The Art of Social Theory.* Princeton University Press.

Swedberg, R. (2016). Before Theory Comes Theorizing Or How to Make Social Science More Interesting. *The British Journal of Sociology, 67*(1), 5–22.

Thaler, R. H. (1994). *Quasi Rational Economics.* Russel Sage Foundation.

Thaler, R. H. (2016). *Misbehaving. The Making of Behavioral Economics.* W.W. Norton.

Tilly, C. (1984). *Big Structures, Large Processes, Huge Comparisons*. Russel Sage Foundation.
Turner, J. H. (2004). *The Structure of Sociological Theory*. Wadsworth Publishing.
Turner, J. H., & Stets, J. E. (Eds.). (2009). *The Sociology of Emotions*. Cambridge University Press.
UNESCO. (1999). *World Social Science Report*. UNESCO.
Wallerstein, I. (1991). *Unthinking Social Science: The Limits of Nineteenth-Century Paradigms* (2nd ed.). Temple University Press.
Wallerstein, I. (1999). Social Science and Contemporary Society: The Vanishing Guarantees of Rationality. In I. Wallerstein (Ed.), *The End of the World as We Know It. Social Science for the Twenty-First Century* (pp. 137–156). University of Minnesota Press.
Wallerstein, I., et al. (1996). *Open the Social Sciences. Report of the Gulbenkian Commission on the Restructuring of the Social Sciences*. Stanford University Press.
Weber, M. (1978). *Economy and Society. An Overview of Interpretative Sociology* [German orig. 1921], 2. Vols., University of California Press.
Weber, M. ([1918–1919] 1988). Wissenschaft als Beruf. In M. Weber (Ed.), Gesammlte Aufsaetze zur Wissenschaftslehre (pp. 524–555). J.C.B. Mohr.
Weber, M. ([1898] 1990). Grundriß zu den Vorlesungen über Allgemeine (theoretische) Nationalökonomie. J.C.B. Mohr.
White, H. C., Boorman, S. A., & Breiger, R. L. (1976). Social Structures from Multiple Networks I: Blockmodells of Roles and Positions. *The American Journal of Sociology, 81*(4), 730–780.
Zima, P. V. (2004). *Was ist Theorie?* UTB.

CHAPTER 7

Bounded Rationality, Emotions, and How Sociology May Take Profit: Towards an Interdisciplinary Opening

Rationality and Max Weber and Joseph Schumpeter

Human action differs from processes in the physical world insofar as action in the social world is driven by motivation. Motivation is embedded in a framework of social goals and related preferences. Phenomenology describes very clearly that social action is led by a cognitive structure of sense and relevance, which guides people through their biographies. Such cognitive structures of sense and relevance serve as a kind of normative compass, indicating which aims are positive, neutral, or negative and how specific courses of social actions are related to those aims. Rationality has its origin in the Latin ratio, which is considered as another term for pure reason. Statements of reason can differ according to different social logics within a single society and across societies, in recent as well as in historical times (Gordon, 1993; Hollis, 2002; Swedberg, 2014).

Trying to understand the meaning of social action is one of the central fields of academic activity in social sciences (for a broader discussion see Gordon, Hollis). However, this enterprise is also the starting point of

Bögenhold, Dieter. Bounded Rationality, Emotions and How Sociology May Take Profit: Towards an Interdisciplinary Opening, in: Helmut Staubmann & Victor M. Lidz (Eds.). *Rationality in the Social Sciences. The Schumpeter/Parsons Seminar 1939/40 and Current Perspectives* (pp. 105–120). Heidelberg; New York et al.: Springer.

D. Bögenhold, *Neglected Links in Economics and Society*,
https://doi.org/10.1007/978-3-030-79193-3_7

many debates on so-called objectivity of interpretation. How can intersubjectively controlled hermeneutics be realized? Which are the parameters to measure human action? Which are, in short, the key questions asking why people do what they do and how social scientists can answer that question? Asking about rationality is closely interrelated to the question about appropriate structures of relevance, which is the domain highlighted by phenomenology. "Relevance is not inherent in nature as such, it is the result of the selective and interpretative activity of man within nature or observing nature. The facts, data, and events with which the natural scientist has to deal are just facts, data, and events within his observational field but this field does not 'mean' anything to the molecules, atoms, and electrons therein. But the facts, events, and data before the social scientist are of an entirely different structure. His observational field, the social world, is not essentially structureless. It has a particular meaning and relevance structure for the human beings living, thinking, and acting therein. They have preselected and preinterpreted this world by a series of commonsense constructs of the reality of daily life, and it is these thought objects which determine their behavior, define the goal of their action, the means available for attaining them" (Schutz, 1982, pp. 5–6).

Dealing with these sorts of questions is the domain of sociology, since sociology is by definition the science that—as Max Weber (1972) explained in his sociological categories—seeks to understand social action by interpretation in order to find explanations for the procedures and results (Lachmann, 1979). Max Weber said that it is not necessary to be Caesar in order to understand the doings of Caesar (Weber, 1972). Weber was one of the first authors who conceptualized different sources providing sense to social action. While Karl Marx, and especially Marxist thinking, idealized thought and consciousness as a kind of reflex of material conditions in society determined in one-to-one fit with the relations of production, Max Weber (1972) was led by the idea that consciousness is never right or wrong, but it always has a (relative) autonomy from the status signaled by the regime of the material world. Cultural factors, including religion and related dispositions, are factors influencing the rationality of social behaviour according to Max Weber (see Collins, 1985; Swedberg, 1998). He came up with a typology of social action based upon different sources of legitimation, which are traditional social action (actions carried out on the basis of tradition and cultural norms), affective social action (actions ultimately based upon emotions), instrumental and purposeful social action ("Zweckrationalita¨t"), and value-rational action ("Wertrationalita¨t"), where the end justifies the means. According to that typology, there is no single type of rationality, but four different types can each be separated as an ideal types; practically they overlap each other, and behaviour has different compositions of elements of rationality. Weber pointed out that broad parts of economics used a nonrealistic view of human nature that reduced people by analogy to a "mathematical ideal figure" (Weber, 1990, p. 30).

Joseph A. Schumpeter (1908) explicitly took these questions up again when he discussed assumptions and consequences of methodological individualism.[1] It was in his first book (Schumpeter, 1908) that he orchestrated a broad discussion on the need to argue atomistically or think in terms of social determinism. Especially one chapter, entitled "The Methodological Individualism" (Schumpeter 1908, Part I, Chap. 6), explained different concepts of human action and motivation. Here, Schumpeter already explicitly the term homo oeconomicus (Schumpeter, 1908, p. 85), which he used as a tool for working in the domain of "pure economics" (Schumpeter, 1954). Hodgson (2012, Chap. 2) describes different meanings of methodological individualism in contrast to "sociological individualism." Economics primarily used a narrow interpretation of the human agent in the concept of utility maximizer. Schumpeter's later paper on the use of rationality in social sciences (Schumpeter, 1991) dealt with the question of the rationality of people and the problem of interpreting this rationality (see Bögenhold, 2014 for a discussion of the interdisciplinarity of Schumpeter), which had already been raised by Max Weber. Schumpeter explicitly discussed the split between rationality as a question of the internal coherence and structure of social action and the so-called observer's rationality, the sphere of interpretation and hermeneutics on the part of academicians as "third parties.".

Despite debates about methodological premises of rationality, economics had started to choose a way of operating that mostly adopted a concept of human behaviour as egoistic utility maximizing, which corresponded exactly to the type of mathematical ideal figure already criticized by Max Weber. This type of human action was based on the idea of a homo oeconomicus as a rational agent motivated purely by economic rewards; being totally egoistic; having no biography, gender, or specific education; or other cultural attributes. Homo oeconomicus became textbook knowledge for decades until doubts about it were expressed increasingly, especially in the field of economics.

Bounded Rationality and Social Scientification of Economics

The concept of homo oeconomicus became so firmly integrated into education in economics and public reasoning on economic affairs that early discussions of its methodological underpinnings, such as those by Max Weber or Joseph A. Schumpeter, were forgotten. The rational agent served as the conception of social agents in economics. However, slowly but constantly, pioneering positions in economics started to change. Hodgson (2012, p. 46) has verified that six Nobel laureates in economics have been recognized since the 1970s for being very critical of the concept of the rational egoistic man, among other topics. The present chapter refers just to five of these figures, namely, Herbert Simon, Douglass North, Amartya Sen, Daniel Kahneman, and George Akerlof, each of whom clearly rejected the idea of rational behaviour as followed for decades before. The very interesting point here is that these names stand for a new trend in economics, which can be described as a greater turn toward a social scientification of economics (Bögenhold, 2010). Herbert Simon coined the famous formulation, bounded rationality. The term has evolved to become a kind of programme for diverse arguments against the neoclassical conception of homo oeconomicus (Larkey, 2002; Sent, 2005). Simon conducted theoretical studies as well as produced empirical works, and he was one of the firsts to use large data sets with the aid of computer simulations. Simon gained the distinction of Nobel laureate in economics in 1978 for his work, which has contributed widely to decision theory. He is regarded as an important author from the academic purviews of philosophy, psychology, organization theory, and economics. His principle matter of investigation may be described by the following question: "How do human beings reason when the conditions for rationality postulated by neoclassical economics are not met?" (Simon, 1989, p. 377). Simon criticized the neoclassic model of decision processes based upon the assumption of homooeconomicus. By contrast, the term, bounded rationality, takes into account that (I) agents often act in ways which could be characterized as nonrational behaviour driven by emotions; (II) the use of bounded rationality emphasizes that access to information is limited, since people do not share the same bits of information necessary for deciding among the alternatives in order to achieve the optimal result; (III) even in a situation of equally shared information, human beings are characterized by cognitive diversity and limited skills in evaluating the single best solution in any given situation with the information provided. According to that scenario, optimal solutions are vague and not easy to calculate. Thus, Simon talks about people trying to satisfice, a portmanteau of "satisfy" and "suffice" (Simon, 1972, p. 176), because not all aspects related to concrete decisions can be analysed adequately by human beings. Although human agents seek to come up with rational decisions, they are limited in their capabilities to find and to execute decisions, so bounded rationalities take place (Simon, 1971). The processes of decision-making are governed by psychological issues among which such factors as risk, uncertainty, and complexity play parts (Simon, 1972). Lastly, a major source of the phenomenon of bounded rationality is the limited information capacity with limited speed of information processing. The environment contains so many bits of information that people must reduce complexity and related uncertainties in order to arrive at a final decision at all, given their limited time to come up with responses (Simon, 1962). In a nutshell, Simon reflects upon traditional economic theory, which deals with conceptions of the "economic man," who was "economically engaged" and in the same sense also "rational." Simon is also guided by the idea that the same is true for the brother of the "economic man," the "administrative man," the conception of whom should also be revised and reformulated (Simon, 1955, p. 99). The evolution of organizations is a necessary effect of complex environments, which present individuals with overloading quantities of information. Within organizational settings, issues such as specialization, standardization, authority, identification, and communication are among the factors that limit the "administrative man" (Simon, 1971, pp. 102–103) and also affect the ways he is portrayed. Simon argues in favour of a more appropriate understanding of learning processes but also of the evolution of processes of behaviour. Simon has become so popular as an author, because, very often, the implications of his writings are treated as their core messages: economics is too often based on ideas of rational behaviour, which is an oversimplification. Instead, the restrictions of simple "clean" economic models should be examined in contexts of complexity. According to Simon, "the task is to replace the global rationality of economic man with a kind of rational behavior that is compatible with the access to information and the computational capacities that are actually processed by organisms, including man, in the kinds of environments in which such organisms exist" (Simon, 1955, p. 99).

Discussing Simon and his famous formulation of a bounded rationality establishes him as a milestone in the history of economic theory. However, even the emergence of the term, bounded rationality, shows that the authenticity of terms and the evolution of concepts are separate matters, which should each be an object of scientific reflection and research. The success of new combinations of things is an innovation (in ideas) in a Schumpeterian understanding (Schumpeter, [1911] 1963, pp. 100–102). We can reconstruct the survival of Simon's ideas as due to placing a spotlight on specific academic questions within a larger landscape in which a number of key questions were on the agenda of economics. However, even before Simon entered the scene, other economists had puzzled over fragments of his understanding, without creating the recognized "brand" of so-called bounded rationality. And what is true for economics is also valid for other domains of the social sciences. Thinking about rationality and so-called bounded rationality as an essence of motivation raises a plea for more integrated research involving a number of academic fields including economics and, among others, management and organization theory, neurology, psychology, sociology, and history. Hodgson (2012) has formulated the problem in the same vein: "We need an economics that builds on scientific disciplines, including psychology, neuroscience, and anthropology. These studies have recently made huge strides by incorporating insights from evolutionary theory. In the light of these studies, the critique of economic man has become irresistible" (Hodgson, 2012, p. 23).

Although Simon was awarded a Nobel Prize in the 1970s, several years passed until some of his essential messages became a kind of common knowledge. His suggestion "to turn to the literature of psychology" (Simon, 1955, pp. 99–100) was not really taken up on a greater scale until Douglass C. North, Nobel Prize recipient in economics in 1993, came up with nearly the same pragmatic formulations:

> *Although I know of very few economists who really believe that the behavioral assumptions of economics accurately reflect human behavior, they do (mostly) believe that such assumptions are useful for building models of market behavior in economics and, though less useful, are still the best game in town for studying politics and the other social sciences. I believe that these traditional behavioral assumptions have prevented economists from coming to grips with some very*

> *fundamental issues and that a modification of these assumptions is essential to further progress in the social sciences. The motivation of these actors is more complicated (and their preferences less stable) than assumed in received theory. More controversial (and less understood) among the behavioral assumptions, usually, is the implicit one that the actors possess cognitive systems that provide true models of the worlds about which they make choices* (North, 1990, p. 17)

Although North was recognized for his works on institutional economics, one clearly sees in the above quotation how much he dissented from simple and crude models that use a very narrow concept of the human being as crude economic maximizer. The same can be said regarding Amartya Sen, who highlights crucial issues that go along with individual capabilities, agency, and choice. Sen developed a kind of social relativity theory with which he explained that happiness and well-being are highly connected to individual path dependencies, comparisons, and individual choices in given situations (Sen, 1999). "Sen's notion of capabilities and functionings provides us with a better and complete understanding of the quality of life of people. Functionings refer to the current or actual life conditions of people. The levels of health, happiness, income, and nourishment are some examples of functionings a person can achieve. However, the functionings of an individual or family are the result of choices made. The standard of living reflects the amount of choices a person can make for different life achievements" (Naz, 2016, p. 4).

Kahneman is another Nobel laureate in economics, one who also has an academic background as a psychologist. Kahneman explains that social action must be interpreted as a kind of choice between alternatives (Kahneman, 2003). The word "rational" stands for reasonable in everyday speech, but for economists and decision theorists, rational has a different meaning. "The only test of rationality is not whether a person's beliefs and preferences are reasonable, but whether they are internally consistent. A rational person can believe in ghosts so long as all her other beliefs are consistent with the existence of ghosts. A rational person can prefer being hated or being loved, so long as his preferences are consistent. Rationality is logical coherence—reasonable or not" (Kahneman, 2012, p. 411).

Human beings have motives, which may be viewed as rational or irrational by observers (Lauterbach, 1962; Rabin, 1998). And people have emotions by which they are governed positively or negatively (Elster, 1998; Scherer, 2011; for historical observations, see Plamber, 2015). Love, hate, and envy are expressions of human activity that are real.

Human beings love human beings, yet they kill people on occasion, they take part in lotteries, and they present gifts but cheat elsewhere.

Finally, we may refer to Akerlof, the 2001 Nobel laureate in economics, who took up again the notion of motivation to discuss the topic in a framework of macroeconomics. Akerlof works at the level of macroeconomics and discusses motivation in a broad framework related to Keynesian ideas. The rationality of human beings and policy stakeholders, stable systems of preferences and consumption affairs, unintended consequences of social action, and the evolution of behaviour are all topics discussed in Akerlof's works. Programmatically, Akerlof (2007) claimed that economics should provide an increased acknowledgement of motivation as a key to the question of why people do what they do. Keynes (1936) referred widely to issues of psychology and social psychology in order to explain economic life in a more sound and appropriate way and discussed expectations, uncertainties, and spirits as crucial social dimensions with impact, while Akerlof also took up questions about norm regulations and other forms of commitments. In this context, Akerlof explicitly recognized a strong impact of sociology in highlighting those thematic areas: "Sociology has a further concept that gives an easy and natural way to add those norms to the utility function. Sociologists say that people have an ideal for how they should or should not behave. Furthermore, that ideal is often conceptualized in terms of the behavior of someone they know or some exemplar who they do not know" (Akerlof, 2007, p. 9).

It has been argued that economics, as presented by top scholars in the academic community, has opened itself to integration with behavioural and cognitive elements (Akerlof, 2007; Akerlof & Kranton, 2000; Akerlof & Shiller, 2009) in order to assist the movement of economics from the world of abstract modelling to realworld phenomena. These voices have evolved into a credo for a new economics. In short, Akerlof referred to cultural contexts providing different norms. Religion and religious identity provide good examples of such norms (Akerlof, 2007, p. 10) and link the discussion to issues of culture more broadly. Cultures within related times and spaces differ in the calculus of individual rationality (Gonza´les, 2012). Including culture as an analytic variable indicates a need to examine different settings of norms and related behaviour (North, 2005; Jones, 2006). Culture serves as a framework of rational behaviour and is a factor that points to real societies as opposed to abstract models. Historian David Landes put it concisely when he said: "Culture makes almost all the difference" (Landes, 2000, p. 2).

Following that line of thought, modern economics—and especially the economics that stays in the spotlight with famous Nobel laureates as key drivers—has moved considerably. The former breakthrough of Simon and his "bounded rationality" has been pushed forward by several recent authors toward a new interpretation and application of economics. One of the crucial questions to emerge has been the question of rationality and the motivation of social agents and the steps that should be taken in the direction of psychology, sociology, and cultural studies. However, time and energy are increasingly being invested academically in the direction of neurological research as well, inquiring about the functioning of the working brain, since the inner functioning processes have for decades been treated as a black box (Gazzaniga, 2011; Gazzaniga et al., 2008). In recent times we have learned that cognitive processes very often depend on physiological foundations.

Evolution of the Division Among the Social Sciences

Philosophy has long dealt with the question of rationality. Karl Popper, in particular, discussed the relativity of rationality in great depth in his so-called critical rationalism (Popper, 1959). Insofar as philosophy can be considered a reasonable contributor to many of the substantial questions of recent economics, integrating philosophical perspectives could possibly foster an appropriate understanding of the functioning processes of norms and conventions (Letsas, 2014). Grandori (2010) discusses various competing semantic concepts with respect to their similarities and divergences. If economics changes its self-portrait so significantly, one may ask if it is still the form of economics that many people have learned through the study of textbooks.

Where is economics coming from and where is it going to? What is the domain of economics and to what extent do different approaches in economics coexist? The question of what is the matter of economics has a long tradition. The oft-quoted statement by Jacob Viner that "economics is what economists do" (quoted in Barber, 1997, p. 87) was long ago completed by Frank Knight, when he added "and economists are those who do economics" (quoted in Buchanan, 1964, p. 213). Looking at the activities of economists shows that the domain of economics is always in transition. Since no clear borders exist to provide rational boundaries to the domain of economics, even a current understanding is not much further than one was at the time of Viner or Knight.

The divisional order of economics is characterized by a practice that mirrors the multiplicity of productive processes in academia, including the somehow accidental developments, rather than systematic reasoning, about the design of an academic subject. With respect to the definition of what economics is and how it is organized into different subfolders, two trends overlap. (I) We have a long-term trend in the development of economics by which the discipline increasingly gained firm ground and recognition and by which a process of differentiation began to evolve. This trend took part within the last one and a half centuries. (II) The field of economics also started to become a professional system with clear curricula, degrees, academic societies, and university departments along with an increasing number of publications and related journals. (III) Parallel to the consolidation process of economics, the subject formed border relations with neighboring fields that were formerly extended parts of economics. Looking over the course of the last 100 years, topics in economics have both modified and multiplied.

Bringing a complex development to a very brief denominator, much of the twentieth-century development in economics involved the establishment of neoclassic thought, which has been taught as textbook knowledge to undergraduate students and which has dominated wide parts of the non-university public and public policy. "Pure economics" proved to be a program of abstractness, which had problems when confronted with competing empirical materials. Pure economics was related to the concept of an economy operating in a vacuum. This type of thought emerged and became a predominant paradigm during the twentieth century. In its nucleus, it served as a kind of academic religion (Nelson, 2001).

Simultaneously, a variety of new special fields, which had not existed in the decades before, were founded within economics. Among them were, for example, industrial economics, labour economics, small business economics, household economics, and the economics of aging. Many additional areas evolved as well and became impressive fields within the general trend of academic specialization and differentiation. The more complex economics proved to be, the smaller the real terrain of neoclassic theory remained, even though the general image of economics, especially when seen from outside the field, remains neoclassic orthodoxy. How scientific change and progress occur is a topic we find carefully described in the philosophy of science as case studies of how different principles and styles of work form into competing camps of thought (Kuhn, 1962; Collins, 2002; with special reference to economics, see Wible, 1998)

If culture makes differences, capitalism does not exist in a vacuum but in a context with specific social regimes of living, producing, and exchange. Institutionalist approaches have no other aim than to highlight the respects in which different social organizations and institutions (including religion, language, law, family structures and networks, systems of education, and industrial relations) establish differences that must be considered when trying to establish statements of general principles regarding capitalist societies and economies. As we know, capitalism in Singapore differs from capitalism in Zimbabwe, which differs from capitalism in Switzerland. Accepting the idea that economies and societies are filled not by abstract but by real entities, one has to refer to concrete coordinates of time and space (Ostrom, 2005). If economics rediscovers history, the recent history of economic thought breaks with the recent mainstream and goes beyond abstractivism.

Complexity, Bounded Rationality, and Converging Economics

As far as Simon's "bounded rationality" seems to be on the right track, progress can only be measured through comparison between old and new contributions to the discussion. Simon's notion of different types of social action and related rationality points to diverse areas of earlier careful discussion that now appear neglected. Whoever talks about bounded rationality nowadays (e.g., Lovallo & Kahneman, 2000) does so on ground prepared by classic authors. In this way, reformulations sometimes come to be celebrated as new inventions. "*Animal Spirits*" (Akerlof & Shiller, 2009) takes up several questions first raised by J. M. Keynes. Simon is one of the first authors of contemporary economics who merged economics with psychology, but discussion of the social psychological dimensions of rationality can also be traced back to earlier sources in phenomenology, which described very clearly that social action is led by a cognitive structure of sense and relevance that guides people through their biographies. Such cognitive structures of sense and relevance serve as a kind of normative compass, indicating which aims are positive, neutral, or negative and how specific social actions are related to those aims.

The growing convergence between economics and psychology should not hinder an acknowledgement of the relevance of sociology and history. In sociology, Max Weber was one of the first authors who conceptualized different sources providing sense to social action. While Karl Marx and especially Marxist thinking idealized thought and consciousness in a kind of reflex to material conditions in society that determined as a one-to-one fit with the relations of production, Max Weber (1972) was led by the idea that consciousness is never right or wrong but it always has a (relative) autonomy from the status signalled by the regime of the material world. Cultural factors, including religion and related dispositions, are factors influencing the rationality of social behaviour according to Max Weber.

Thinking of rationality as a driver of social action does not imply that people can always decipher the individual elements of the forces by which they are driven. Sociology uses the term habituation to refer to deeply internalized routines of action that help to economize everyday life by avoiding the repetitious asking for the argumentative legitimation of one's own doing. In that way, habituation acts as an economy measure, since people do not have to newly seek instructions every time in order to come up with decisions (Berger & Luckmann, 1966). In contrast to sociology, psychology refers to the subconscious as a separate sphere that influences people's behaviour without giving full control to actors' decisions, as Sigmund Freud first explained (Freud, 1995). With respect to preferences in combination with lifestyles, needs, and behaviour, Maslow (1954), as a social psychologist, developed a scheme of different steps in the setting of goals for human behaviour, which he ranked in the form of a pyramid. According to Maslow, people try to meet the satisfaction of basic needs first. One way out of the dilemma was taken by Gary Becker when he considered that "behavior is driven by a much richer set of values and preferences" (Becker, 1995, p. 385), but—according to Becker—ultimately all decisions, even seemingly nonrational ones, are based upon rational decisions of selfishness. Becker put a lot of effort into explaining his idea through many examples, including choices of marriage, sports, restaurant visits, or decisions regarding family and career. But at the end, an understanding of rationality seems to become somehow self-referential, since all actions prove to be outcomes of a rational decision. If all emotion can be seen as part of rationality, the term tends to make itself obsolete, and the traditional meaning of ratio could be replaced by behaviour (Rosenberg, 2012, pp. 89–116).

A different way to foster an understanding of rationality is through the explicit addressing of emotions as a field of research (Elster, 1999; Hochschild, 2013). This method of analysis merges different disciplines and has gained considerable attention during the past two decades

(Scherer, 2011). However, talking about rationality (or nonrationality) always implies that we practically know how people think. In that way of academic practice, the brain usually serves as a black box. Sociology, psychology, or economics is increasingly moving in new directions and also toward different integrations with neurosciences. Divergent issues, such as happiness or trust capacity, can also be analysed in relation to the workings of the brain. Cognitive neuroscience can deal with memory, speed of thinking, creativity, attention, and flexibility much more adequately than traditional thinking could, as it did not try to merge different insights. Future discussion should acknowledge further developments in these fields in order to avoid discussion on the basis of "as if" assumptions. It is also very important to arrive at a better understanding about the degree to which behaviour is socially learned and embedded in specific social contexts (Lagueux, 2010) and the degree to which it is governed by neurotransmitters and neuromodulators. Given the fact that human behaviour has proven to be more complex than what can be expressed in monocausal and linear assumptions of rational man who has no social context and who lives without being captured by institutions and related norms, constraints, and opportunities, without having social attributes such as age, biography and life history, family, gender, occupation, and education and without belonging to a specific concrete time or space, the rationality concept remains a vague and empty term.

Further Research Grounds of Universal Social Sciences

Scientific progress is often contingent and never rational in a sense that it follows arithmetic rules of combinations. The "market" for ideas is not precisely an efficient or perfect market. Academic progress is also related to a series of mistakes by which intellectual resources are wasted. As a consequence, there are, indeed, intellectual gems lying unexploited and waiting for someone to grasp (Boettke, 2000).

Newest economics once again takes up academic perspectives that were provided by (old or new) institutional thought, asking about concrete economies in concrete societies. Of course, many new thematic arenas have opened up during the last hundred years (among them game theory, transaction cost theory, principal agent theory, public choice theory, welfare economics, and many others), so that comparisons between up-to-date economics and earlier forms suffer from a lack of integrity in many respects. If students start to get into a new academic discipline, such as medicine, biology, or economics, they usually want to learn the current state of thought. A majority of people do not want to find out which discussions were on the agenda 50 or 100 years ago but are interested instead in the predominant portraits of recent debates. What is uncontested terrain, which are the competing theories, and where can there be academic profit in future engagement? The difficult matter is that academic progress and its change must be conceptualized as a series of processes of shortcomings, which retrospectively appear as a never-ending story of failures or mistakes, to express it starkly. Since it should be an integral part of the identity of a profession (and a profession's member) to be familiar with the tradition of its own discipline, further investment in the history of economic thought should be a unifying issue for the future of economics. Since we need to know the intellectual history in order to find innovative academic concepts for the future, dealing with the history of economic thought is also a tool to undertake economics of the future.

A manual on how to treat the issues academically is still provided by Joseph A. Schumpeter's *History of Economic Analysis* (Schumpeter, 1954). The preface of the book gives a thorough discussion of why histories of science are necessary for systematic reasons, not only in economics but also in other academic fields. In his substantial introduction to his study, Schumpeter explicitly raised the question, "Why do we study the history of economics?" He continued to add his own answer, which was concerned with the issue why we study the history of any science in general and of economics specifically. Just as evolutionary economists take as their credo the look at the inner dynamics of change to arrive at an understanding of principles, theoretical economists should treat their subject analogously. One has to gain a careful understanding of the history of one's own discipline to see the larger and smaller lines that have led to recent discussion and to the current state of the art. In this light, recent discussion gains much more color, and our current knowledge comes up in a historically transcendent way as a snapshot within a series of new intellectual positions, be they failures or innovations. Economic theories evolve in specific contexts of social life and societal organization. In some way, they mirror the times of their origins and serve as a diagnosis of related systems of thought.

Economics is seen as a box of tools, and it always contains "theory" (always written with quotation marks by Schumpeter 1954), economic history, sociology, political economy, statistics, and some additional fields. Finally, Schumpeter explained that "psychology is really the basis from which any social science must start and in terms of which all fundamental explanation must run" (Schumpeter, 1954, p. 27).

Bounded Rationality and Social Networks

Discussing the seminal ideas by Simon, we should acknowledge more explicitly the obvious links to social network analysis, which has a strong anchor in the field of sociology and which has diffused and evolved increasingly toward many neighboring fields. Bounded rationality is very much to be understood in relation to asymmetric information and complexity. Bounded rationality mirrors the fact that societies, organizations, and economies are fragmented; they are organized along different lines and zones of contact, familiarity, and information exchange. In our view, modern economics could benefit significantly by integrating recent network concepts, which are fantastic tools for bridging micro- and macro-perspectives. "Network models of advantage use structure as an indicator of how information is distributed in a system of people" (Burt et al., 2013, p. 529). Social network analysis also continues to develop many themes enunciated by pioneering social psychologists. "At its best, social network analysis draws from traditions of research and theory in psychology, sociology, and other areas to describe how patterns of interpersonal relations are associated with diverse behavioral, cognitive, and emotional outcomes. Looking to the future, we are deepening interest in the psychological underpinnings of why some people more than others engage and benefit from the networks of contacts within which they are embedded" (Burt et al., 2013, p. 543). On the other hand, discussion that refers to psychological differences of human natures also urgently requires an understanding of social facts and vice versa (Walker & Lynn, 2013), a point celebrated by E. Durkheim's analysis of suicide (Durkheim, 1951) long ago.

Markets are always in transition, they come up, they go down, and they change. Markets are carried out by actors who know and trust sets of people while perhaps also regarding other people as hostile competitors. However concrete markets may look, they always have social traits, and economics would fall short if it did not ask about such issues. Processes of competition must also be analysed and understood as ongoing social processes involved in social structures and permanently in processes of reorganization (Burt, 1995; Bögenhold, 2013) and closely linked to different formations of habits (Hodgson & Knudsen, 2004). The presently existing, largely categorical descriptions of social structure have no solid theoretical grounding, but network concepts may provide the only way to construct a theory of social structure (White et al., 1976, p. 732). In many respects, network analysis is an excellent exemplification of what the term of social embeddedness can deliver. Network analysis furnishes the popular formulations that have become "economic sociology's most celebrated metaphor" (Guillen et al., 2002, p. 4).

Different capital structures correspond to different network designs and vice versa. Divergent network arrangements provide different opportunities to communicate, to receive information, and to create different structures of cultural capital. Network analysis explores modes and contents of exchanges between different agents when symbols, emotions, or goods and services are exchanged. An initial point of discussion was that up-to-date economics is increasingly willing to open up to topics of cognitive structure and motivation. Economic sociology and economic psychology share many of the same motives behind these trends, since the arguments in favour of the trends form the foundations of their own academic identity.

But one should be curious as well as careful when meeting these new tendencies. Nothing should be taken for granted; one should always try to see whether pieces of the puzzle fit.

Conclusion

The title of the chapter is "Bounded Rationality, Emotions, and How Sociology May Take Profit." "Bounded rationality" stands for the work of Herbert Simon, but we have seen that Simon had several followers who have pushed the academic discussion much further forward. Of course, many questions were raised, but many definite answers have not been given. Rationality is the social grammar that provides the sense for social action. It is a driver that has sources in different domains. Social sense is learned and depends upon biographies and life courses with social embeddedness in terms of culture, space, and time. The social context of judgement and decision serves as a framework. It oscillates with modes of social action, so that beginning and end are intertwined. Even the workings of the brain, as viewed in the domain of neuroscience, must be studied with a linkage to society (Pickersgill, 2013). Asymmetric information and social capital, asymmetric social support through diverse social ties, and asymmetric distribution of aspiration are among the social premises of diverse behaviour. Taken together, all these factors contribute to an understanding stating that economics alone "can't explain the modern world" (McCloskey, 2011). These topics suggest that diverse branches of research and knowledge may benefit from further cooperation. Reasoning about rationality and her sister irrationality indicates that—besides economics and social psychology—sociology matters. The observed social scientification of economics helps to highlight several strengths that sociology commands by nature of its domain: societies in contexts.

References

Akerlof, G. A. (2007). The Missing Motivation in Macroeconomics. *The American Economic Review, 97*(1), 5–36.

Akerlof, G. A., & Kranton, R. E. (2000). Economics and Identity. *Quarterly Journal of Economics, 115*(3), 715–753.

Akerlof, G. A., & Shiller, R. J. (2009). *Animal Spirits: How Human Psychology Drives the Economy, and Why It Matters for Global Capitalism*. Princeton University Press.

Barber, W. J. (1997). Reconfigurations in American Academic Economics. A General Practitioner's Perspective. *Daedalus, 126*(1), 87–103.

Becker, G. (1995). The Economic Way of Looking at Behavior. *Journal of Political Economy, 101*(3), 385–409.

Berger, P. L., & Luckmann, T. (1966). *The Social Construction of Reality*. Anchor Books/Doubleday.

Boettke, P. J. (2000). *Why Read the Classics in Economics?* George Mason University: Unpublished Paper.

Bögenhold, D. (2010). From Heterodoxy to Orthodoxy and Vice Versa: Economics and Social Sciences in the Division of Academic Work. *The American Journal of Economics and Sociology, 69*(5), 1566–1590.

Bögenhold, D. (2013). Social Network Analysis and the Sociology of Economics: Filling a Blind Spot with the Idea of Social Embeddedness. *The American Journal of Economics and Sociology, 72*(2), 293–318.

Bögenhold, D. (2014). Schumpeter as a Universal Social Theorist. *The Atlantic Economic Journal, 42*(2), 205–215.

Buchanan, J. M. (1964). What Should Economists Do? *Southern Economic Journal, 30*(3), 213–228.

Burt, R. S. (1995). *Structural Holes: The Social Structure of Competition*. Harvard University Press.

Burt, R. S., Kilduff, M., & Tasselli, S. (2013). Social Network Analysis: Foundations and Frontiers on Advantage. *Annual Review of Psychology, 64*(1), 527–547.

Collins, R. (1985). *Max Weber: A Skeleton Key*. Sage.
Collins, R. (2002). *The Sociology of Philosophers*. Harvard University Press.
Durkheim, E. (1951). *Suicide: A Study in Sociology*. The Free Press.
Elster, J. (1998). Emotions and Economic Theory. *Journal of Economic Literature, 36*(1), 47–74.
Elster, J. (1999). *Alchemies of the Human Mind: Rationality and the Emotions*. Cambridge University Press.
Freud, S. (1995). *The Basic Writings of Sigmund Freud*. Random House.
Gazzaniga, M. S. (2011). *Who's in Charge? Free Will and the Science of the Brain*. Harper Collins.
Gazzaniga, M. S., Ivry, R. B., & Mangun, G. R. (2008). *Cognitive Neuroscience* (The Biology of the Mind). Norton.
Gonza´les, A. M. (2012). Emotional Culture and the Role of Emotions in Cultural Analysis. In A. M. Gonza´les (Ed.), *The Emotions and Cultural Analysis* (pp. 1–15). Ashgate.
Gordon, S. (1993). *The History and Philosophy of Social Science*. Routledge.
Grandori, A. (2010). A Rational Heuristic Model of Economic Decision Making. *Rationality and Society, 22*(4), 477–504.
Guillen, M. F., Randall, C., England, P., & Meyer, M. (2002). The Revival of Economic Sociology. In M. F. Guille´n, R. Collins, P. England, & M. Meyer (Eds.), *The New Economic Sociology: Developments in an Emerging Field* (pp. 1–32). Russell Sage.
Hochschild, A. (2013). *So How Is the Family?* University of California Press.
Hodgson, G. M. (2012). *From Pleasure Machines to Moral Communities. An Evolutionary Economics Without Homo Oeconomicus*. Chicago University Press.
Hodgson, G. M., & Knudsen, T. (2004). The Complex Evolution of a Simple Traffic Convention: The Functions and Implications of Habit. *Journal of Economic Behavior & Organization, 54*(1), 19–47.
Hollis, M. (2002). *The Philosophy of Social Science: An Introduction*. Cambridge University Press.
Jones, E. L. (2006). *Cultures Merging. A Historical and Economic Critique of Culture*. PUP.
Kahneman, D. (2003). A Perspective on Judgment and Choice: Mapping Bounded Rationality. *The American Psychologist, 58*(9), 697–720.
Kahneman, D. (2012). *Thinking, Fast and Slow*. Penguin.
Keynes, J. M. (1936). *The General Theory of Employment, Interest and Money*. Macmillan.
Kuhn, T. S. (1962). *The Structure of Scientific Revolutions*. University of Chicago Press.
Lachmann, L. M. (1979). The Method of Interpretation. In L. M. Lachmann (Ed.), *The Legacy of Max Weber* (pp. 17–48). The Glendessary Press.
Lagueux, M. (2010). *Rationality and Explanation in Economics*. Routledge.

Landes, D. (2000). Culture Makes Almost all the Difference. In L. E. Harrison & S. P. Huntington (Eds.), *Culture Matters. How Values Shape Human Progress* (pp. 2–13). Basic Books.

Larkey, P. D. (2002). Ask a Simple Question. A Retrospective on Herbert Alexander Simon. *Policy Science, 35*(3), 239–268.

Lauterbach, A. (1962). *Psychologie des Wirtschaftslebens.* Rowoldt.

Letsas, G. (2014). The DNA of Conventions. *Law and Philosophy, 33*(5), 535–571.

Lovallo, D., & Kahneman, D. (2000). Living with Uncertainty: Attractiveness and Resolution Timing. *Journal of Behavioral Decision Making, 13*(2), 179–190.

Maslow, A. H. (1954). *Motivation and Personality.* Harper & Row.

McCloskey, D. N. (2011). *Bourgeois Dignity: Why Economics can't Explain the Modern World.* Chicago University Press.

Naz, F. (2016). Understanding Human Well-being: How Could Sen's Capability Approach Contribute? *Forum for Social Economics., 49*(3), 316–331.

Nelson, R. H. (2001). *Economics as Religion: From Samuelson to Chicago and beyond.* Pennsylvania State University Press.

North, D. C. (1990). *Institutions, Institutional Change and Economic Performance.* Cambridge University Press.

North, D. C. (2005). *Understanding the Process of Economic Change.* Princeton University Press.

Ostrom, E. (2005). *Understanding Institutional Diversity.* Princeton University Press.

Pickersgill, M. (2013). The Social Life of the Brain: Neuroscience in Society. *Current Sociology, 61*(3), 322–340.

Plamber, J. (2015). *The History of Emotions.* Oxford University Press.

Popper, K. (1959). *The Logic of Scientific Discovery.* Routledge.

Rabin, M. (1998). Psychology and Economics. *Journal of Economic Literature, 36*(1), 11–46.

Rosenberg, A. (2012). *Philosophy of Social Science.* Westview Press.

Scherer, K. R. (2011). On the Rationality of Emotions: Or, When are Emotions Rational? *Social Science Information, 50*(3/4), 330–350.

Schumpeter, J. A. (1908). *Das Wesen und der Haptinhalt der theoretischen Nationalokonomie.* Duncker & Humblot.

Schumpeter, J. A. (1954). *History of Economic Analysis.* Oxford University Press.

Schumpeter, J. A. (1963). *The Theory of Economic Development.* Oxford University Press.

Schumpeter, J. A. (1991). The Meaning of Rationality in the Social Sciences. In R. Swedberg (Ed.), *The Economics and Sociology of Capitalism (pp. 316–318).* Princeton University Press.

Schutz, A. (1982). *Collected Papers, Vol. I, The Problem of Social Reality, (1961 firstly).* Martinus Nijhoff.

Sen, A. (1999). The Possibility of Social Choice. *American Economic Review, 89*(3), 349–378.

Sent, E.-M. (2005). Simplifying Herbert Simon. *History of Political Economy, 37*(2), 227–232.

Simon, H. A. (1955). A Behavioral Model of Rational Choice. *Quarterly Journal of Economics, 69*(1), 99–118.

Simon, H. A. (1962). The Architecture of Complexity. *Proceedings of the American Philosophical Society, 106*(6), 467–482.

Simon, H. A. (1971). *Administrative Behavior. A Study of the Decision-Making Process in Administrative Organization.* Macmillan.

Simon, H. A. (1972). Theories of Bounded Rationality. In C. B. McGuire & R. Radner (Eds.), *Decision and Organization. A Volume in Honor of Jacob Marschak* (pp. 161–176). North Holland Publishing.

Simon, H. A. (1989). The Scientist as a Problem Solver. In D. Klahr & K. Kotowsky (Eds.), *Complex Information Processing. How Do Human Beings Reason* (pp. 375–398). Erlbaum.

Swedberg, R. (1998). *Max Weber and the Idea of Social Science.* Princeton University Press.

Swedberg, R. (2014). *The Art of Social Theory.* Princeton University Press.

Walker, M. H., & Lynn, F. B. (2013). The embedded self: A social networks approach to identity theory. *Social Psychology Quarterly, 76*(2), 151–179.

Weber, M. (1972). *Wirtschaft und Gesellschaft.* J.C.B. Mohr.

Weber, M. (1990). *Grundriß zu den Vorlesungen uber Allgemeine (theoretische) National Ökonomie.* J.C.B. Mohr.

White, H. C., Boorman, S. A., & Breiger, R. L. (1976). Social Structures from Multiple Networks I: Blockmodells of Roles and Positions. *The American Journal of Sociology, 81*(4), 730–780.

Wible, J. R. (1998). *The Economics of Science. Methodology and Epistemology as If Economics Really Mattered.* Routledge.

PART III

History of Economic and Social Thought

CHAPTER 8

History of Economic Thought as an Analytic Tool: Why Past Intellectual Ideas Must Be Acknowledged as Lighthouses for the Future

Economics within Social Sciences: Specialization and Differentiation

Economic theory as a body of common knowledge is never stationary nor a stable set of monolithic systems of academic belief but it is always embedded in changes of intellectual thought and related processes of struggle. What the ancient Greek philosopher Heraklitus meant by "everything flows," is also valid for social sciences. John Maynard Keynes came up with his observation very clearly:

> *The ideas of economists and political philosophers, both when they are right and when they are wrong, are more powerful than is commonly understood. Indeed, the world is ruled by little else. Practical men, who believe themselves to be quite exempt from any intellectual influences, are usually the slaves of some defunct economist.* (Keynes, 1936, p. 383)

Bögenhold, D. (2020). History of Economic Thought as an Analytic Tool: Why Past Intellectual Ideas Must Be Acknowledged as Lighthouses for the Future, in: *International Advances in Economic Research*, 2020, 26(1), 73–87.

D. Bögenhold, *Neglected Links in Economics and Society*,
https://doi.org/10.1007/978-3-030-79193-3_8

When an economic crisis occurs, as was the case in 2008, contemporaries tend to question certainties of belief systems including academic systems of knowledge. Existing paradigms evolve to become a subject of inquiry. Among those new topics is a claim to acknowledge the history of economic thought (HET) as an important, although neglected, domain of economic inquiry. During the last decades, HET has mostly been abolished or has disappeared in many contemporary teaching curricula in economics. When the latest methods in econometrics and mathematical procedures are put into the reading schedule in university education, reading of the history of our own discipline appears to be nearly forgotten. In general, the study of the history of economic thought is held in low esteem by "mainstream economists and sometimes openly disparaged as a type of antiquarianism" (Blaug, 2001, p. 145). An unforecasted crisis, such as the economic crisis and downturn in 2008, teaches us that our academic understanding of economic processes may be incomplete, that our analysis of economic relationships must be more comprehensive, integrating further perspectives of thought, and that contemporaries cannot afford to have a good command of economics without a working knowledge of the changes in and the tradition of our own subject.

Although there exist active professional societies in many countries which try to celebrate and foster the history of economic thought, especially the US-based History of Economics Society (HES) and the European Society for the History of Economic Thought (ESHET), which each have an annual conference, maintain journals, and many further activities, it does not look as if those societies and related scholars belong to the core faculties of the subject economics. Practice tells us that courses in history of economics are taught less and less, and in many institutions, they are no longer part of the curriculum (Roncaglia, 2014). Many even raise the question of whether the history of economics should be considered a subject of history rather than of economics (Kates, 2013).

However, can we learn anything by reading the history of economic theory, and, if yes, what may it be? Peter Boettke raised the pertinent question: Why, indeed, read the classics in economics?

> *There are antiquarian reasons—reading the works of the great political economists of the past does give us a glimpse of the genius of an earlier age. But reading an old work in economics is not unlike watching a silent film or news clips of an old baseball game. It is quaint and romantic to look in on the past, but it*

> *is useful to remember that this world we sometimes worship from afar was a world without indoor plumbing, without modern transportation.* (Boettke, 2000, p. 1)

This chapter is about the question why it is not only useful but also necessary to invest into history of economic thought. It is difficult to clarify the domain of economics in clear words when teaching undergraduates. Usually we operate with simplifications, which highlight a general theory as a body of "cohesive ideas set within a structure that seems internally consistent" (Wunder, 2010, p. 23). As Viner put it in 1917: "There is a tendency among economists to fear over much for the integrity of their science and to try to maintain its borders intact by carefully avoiding encroachment on the fields of other science" (Viner, 2017, p. 236). At a first glance, such a monolithic view of theory may be convincing, since it does not acknowledge contradictions, empirical failures, a plurality of competing paradigms and, especially, ignores change.

> *Methodology used by economists today is very different from what was used 30 years ago, and what was used 30 years ago was very different from the methodology used by such great economists as Adam Smith and David Ricardo. The economic methodology that is taught in undergraduate courses today is the result of centuries of intellectual debate, and the origin of this body has been filled with differing thinkers often in violent disagreement with each other.* (Wunder, 2010, p. 23)

Many contemporary academic disciplines, not only economics, are experiencing a flood of material in terms of publications and new people (Bögenhold, 2010). The topics have multiplied in many directions and whole new areas of discourse have emerged (Chafim, 2016), each with separate research organizations, global conferences, journals, curricula, academic career opportunities, as well as patterns and publication opportunities. Parallel, shifting disciplinary boundaries have been observed inside and outside economics (Cedrini & Fiori, 2016). During the second part of the twentieth century, an organizational segmentation began, which provided proof of Max Weber's statement given in his famous article "Science as Vocation" (1988a), namely that the individual can achieve something really substantial on academic ground only in a situation of increased specialization:

> *In our time, the internal situation, in contrast to the organization of science as a vocation, is first of all conditioned by the facts that science has entered a phase of specialization previously unknown and that this will forever remain the case. Not only externally, but inwardly, matters stand at a point where the individual can acquire the sure consciousness of achieving something truly perfect in the field of science only incase he is a strict specialist.* (Weber, 1988a, p. 526)

A variety of new specialized fields of economics were founded, among them industrial economics, labour economics, small business economics, household economics, economics of aging, but most notably game theory and diverse applications in combination with econometrics. Use of advanced statistics and econometrics have expanded substantially (Weintraub, 2002; Morgan, 2012), which can be summarized broadly as diverse sorts of "mathiness" (Romer, 2015). Taken together, one may conclude that we have entered *The Age of the Applied Economist* (Backhouse & Cherrier, 2017) where elegant theoretical reasoning and historical foundation are being lost. Discussing *The Future of the History of Economics* (Davis et al., 2002) showed the need to acknowledge the history of economics and other social sciences, but also serious practical weaknesses in doing so in times when the history of economics is out of fashion. This chapter will primarily present the perspective of Joseph A. Schumpeter, who dealt in detail with the questions of how to deal with historiography as a tool for appropriate economics in his substantial introduction to the *History of Economic Analysis* (1954). While points of discussion and neglect of history occurred for many years, it is less known that Schumpeter (1954) already pointed out very clearly that history of thought must be acknowledged because it provides a manual to gain systematic knowledge in order to be better equipped for research on future developments.

Loss of History of Economic Thought

Recently there has been a tricky situation in economics. On the one hand, there is increased specialization, abstractness, and mathiness, and on the other hand, there are ongoing tendencies toward processes of an increased pluralization of economics (Hodgson et al., 1992; Schabas, 1992; Davis, 2006), but there is obviously no specialization for HET anymore. Economics was applauded for its empiricism in the direction of further social sciences (Lazear, 2000; Fourcade et al., 2015) or blamed for having forgotten its social foundations (Buckley & Casson, 1993; Granovetter, 2002; Davis, 2016; Chafim, 2016; Marchionatti & Cedrini, 2017). Many new areas have evolved and serve as impressive fields of the general trend of academic specialization and differentiation. The more complex economics has become, the smaller the real terrain of neoclassical theory remains; although the general image of economics, especially when looking from the outside, still shows a dominance of neoclassical orthodoxy. However, mainstream economics is also fragmented and always changing (Cedrini & Fontana, 2018). The twenty-first century looks back at this scientific period of development, differentiation, and consolidation as a feature of the twentieth century.

Economics has changed and the types of economists are changing. The former link, which was maintained by economics and further social science domains, especially philosophy, was exchanged for the link of econometrics and mathematics. Mainstream economics became increasingly associated with abstractness and formalism, which went along with an ongoing trend that the history of economic theory was disregarded. In other words, economics has started to forget history (Hodgson, 2001). History of economic theory was abolished or pushed to different disciplines (philosophy or science theory). Hodgson argued that:

> *prowess with formal technique has replaced the broader intuitive, methodological and historical intellectual grounding required of the great economist. Such qualities were emphasized and personified by both Alfred Marshall and John Maynard Keynes. Today, economists are no longer systematically educated in economic history, the philosophy of science or the history of their own discipline.* (2007, p. 19)

What Heilbroner wrote in 1979, namely that the history of economic thought is taught on a very small scale, has become even smaller since then.

> *The history of economic thought is not in very high esteem these days. Few universities include it as a prescribed portion of the standard training curriculum for budding economists. The history of thought is usually taught in a single semester in which the student dashes through Physiocracy to Smith and Ricardo, stops for a moment to regard from afar the mysterious figure of Karl Marx, learns about the Marginalist Revolution, and is finally delivered safely to the arms of Modern Economics when he reaches the 1930s and the General Theory is born.* (Heilbroner, 1979, p. 192)

Practically, history of economic thought is regarded as something which is disappearing (Vaughn, 1993; Backhouse, 1994; Samuels, 1997; Fogarty & Naples, 1998; Laidler, 2001), a fact which was already noted in the early 1960s (Winch, 1962), since many contemporaries did not acknowledge history of economic thought as part of the domain of economics (Blaug, 2001). What Boulding (1971) reported more than 45 years ago, namely that modern graduates have rarely read a piece which is older than 10 years, is still true (Roncaglia, 2014). The half-life knowledge of publications is getting shorter and shorter.[1] Also the number of publications in history of economics has declined compared to the total of publications in economics while a large body of those publications are concentrated in just five highly specialized journals (Marcuzzo & Zacchia, 2016, p. 36).

The trade-off is that recent graduates of economic studies are more competent in the application of mathematics and statistics and ambitious computer simulations than in having a working knowledge of the history of a specific subject. In mathematics, the small multiplication table is a precondition for the larger multiplication tables, but in modern economics, one can skip the elementary steps contained within the history of economic ideas. In other words,

> *recruitment and professional advancement are almost on the basis of technical competence, rather than on knowledge of the real economy or of the evolution of economics as a discipline. This bias towards formalism has become deeply ingrained and institutionalized in the academy. It is compounded by the fragmentation of the profession into technical specialisms, often lacking the generalist background that enables communication and synthetic advance.* (Hodgson, 2007, p. 19)

History of Economic Thought and Historiography

History of economic thought is practically historiography. Talk about historiography oscillates between the two quite different perspectives of writing history in practice as used by social and economic historians and methodological reflections on the use of history as a heuristic tool. The double-sided understanding of historiography as data collecting and synthesizing for economies and societies on the one hand and of a methodological tool to arrive at a deeper understanding of processes inherent to sciences and their change, on the other hand, is not always clearly separated in practice.

The term "historiography," literally "the writing of history," carries two distinct meanings.

> *On the one hand, it refers to historical accounts of the past, in contrast to the past itself. On the other hand, the term is used in a meta-theoretical sense as the reflection on how historians account for the past. Historiography in this second sense has two aspects. It may refer either to the particular historical methods employed by the historian, or to a broader reflection on the methodology underlying her historical research. According to the broader interpretation, historiography is to the practice of the history of economics what the methodology of economics is to the practice of economics. An additional complexity arises because both history and methodology of economics are meta-discourses ... in respect to the discipline of economics, which increasingly draw upon one another.* (Klaess, 2003, p. 491)

Just reading a contemporary piece in economics (or any other social science) does not allow one to get the full sense of that piece if one does not understand the context of creation. Ideas, it was said, have their own history; telling the story of an idea's development was "internal" or "absolutist" history (Emmet, 2003, p. 533).

> *However, there is a difference between arguing that ideas are determined by their context and interpreting the historical meaning of texts. Rather than seeking the link between ideas and historical events, historical reconstructions seek to reconstruct the sense (meaning) that someone gave a particular text at some historical point. The most obvious form of historical reconstruction is the effort to understand the original author's meaning.* (Emmet, 2003, p. 533)

However, Kurz (2016) indicated that not only is it important to remember that the huge changes in the economy over the last few centuries have also changed our view of the economy and society (Kurz, 2016, p. 3), but that the history of economic thought is also changing. Each generation writes its own history, new knowledge is always created and each generation is "keen not only on being original but on being perceived as such. But each generation also searches for meaningful progenitors so it can share in their renown and brilliance" (Kurz, 2016, p. 2).

We may distinguish between history of economic thought, which is a kind of intellectual history, while other concepts focus more on the history of economic theory. Marcuzzo and Zacchia (2016) distinguished between history of economics and history of economic thought, raising the question of whether they differ. While the first attempts to understand the ideas of past thinkers and how and why those ideas have developed and changed through time (Biddle, 2003), the second is much more concerned with very concrete authors, meaning (Faccarello & Kurz, 2016) that most research in the history of economic.

> *involved textual exegesis or interpretation; that in a sense the work of most historians of economic thought has been similar to the work of theologians seeking the true interpretations of scriptural writings, or legal scholars and judges seeking the true intent of legislators.* (Biddle, 2003, p. 2)

Both versions are at the intersection with philosophy and methodology of economics. Empirical studies on journal publications in the area of history of economic thought show clearly the trend that research on individual authors has gone down (Marcuzzo, 2008; Marcuzzo & Zacchia, 2016). A third topic is economic history. Economic history deals with different empirical facts in a series of social arrangements and physical processes by which human societies have produced the material conditions of human life since the emergence of the human species, mostly devoted to the development of modern economic growth (Headlee, 2010). Douglas V. North and R.W. Fogel, two Nobel laureates in economics during the 1990s, worked exactly on those grounds, empirically and methodologically (Greif & Mokyr, 2017; Hodgson, 2017; Diebolt & Haupert, 2018) making a plea for institutional and historical economics and for the need to collect data.

Younger and Older Historical Schools

The first "battle of methods", which is well-known under its German noun Methodenstreit, contained some very principal arguments which provide a brilliant background understanding for up-to-date debates (Richter, 2001). Although the debate between Menger and Schmoller was rather sketchy and polemical, the confrontation between inductive and deductive ways to generate scientific statements makes it a classic piece. This chapter tries to embed recent discussion on the issue of realism versus formalism in the scenario of the history of economic thought. The first battle of methods was 120 years ago. This controversy has existed since the first conflict between Gustav Schmoller and Carl Menger, which is still unresolved (Schumpeter, 1926; Swedberg, 1991). It can be reduced to the principal question of inductive versus deductive working strategies. While Menger, contemporary with Walras, designed marginal utility theory (Grenznutzentheorie) and was a supporter of abstraction and modelling (Menger, 1883), Schmoller (1883) believed that empirical research must be carried out to test the theory.

The question of the degree of abstraction (empirical closeness or distance), together with the degree of restriction of scientific theorems, will be addressed with empirical data. This circumstance can further be formulated around the question of the relationship between theory and empiricism in social studies and economics. The aim of theorizing is to explain and describe the connections between different variables representing functions in society where classification difficulties arise when the number of variables is high and their sphere of reference is complicated. The clarity of arguments has been expressed repeatedly, namely the questions of empiricism versus theory, presentation of data versus generalization, and historical reconstruction versus formal theorizing.

The younger and older historical schools in German economics were close to this version of economic history. The German Historical School represented an approach in economics, which had its zenith during the late nineteenth and the first two decades of the twentieth century in Germany. The German Historical School is an essential part of the history of economic thought and it is ultimately identified as a (German) way of old institutionalist thought (Dorfman, 1959). Behind the label are different authors and related debates covering nearly 80 years from the 1840s until the 1920s, in which academic procedures, methodological standpoints and normative orientations were perpetually changing. The German Historical School did not ultimately unify researchers through a unique view without contradictions, since remarkable conflicts occurred between authors commonly identified as members of that school. However, the common bond was that all people associated as members of the historical school were, to a certain degree, concerned with a type of research, which had a focus on historical investigation in relation to economic topics. The profile is most clear as an approach of historicism competing with attempts in economics to formalize economic observation and analysis by universalizing and neglecting the framework of time and space. The credo of the historical school was that researchers should dive into the ocean of economic history with its manifold historical details in order to gather sufficient details that may be generalized (Shionoya, 2001, 2005).

From today's point of view, the German Historical School is of interest because it represents a trend of thought which has many convergences with current ideas of new institutional economics and with economic sociology. The idea of social embeddedness of social behaviour and institutions has some intellectual closeness, provides one of the reasons that the German Historical School is perceived to be going through a revival. Another important factor for the relevance of the German Historical School lies in the methodological concerns connected to the schools and their debates. The first two (so-called) "battles of methods" in the social sciences took place on the grounds of that school and involved different proponents. Their arguments are still important pieces in the history of intellectual ideas and methodological concerns.

Literature distinguishes between an "older," "younger," and "youngest" historical school (Herbst, 1965). The "older" historical school is represented by writers such as Wilhelm Roscher (1817–1894), Bruno Hildebrand (1812–1878), or Karl G. A. Knies (1821–1898). The "younger" historical school has its most famous representative in the figure of Gustav Schmoller (1838–1917), but authors like Karl Bücher (1847–1930) and Lujo Brentano (1844–1931) are also still well known. For the "youngest" school, commonly Max Weber (1864–1920), Werner Sombart (1863–1941), and Arthur Spiethoff (1873–1957) are counted as the most prominent representatives (Shionoya, 2001).

The "older" historical school was not really a school, because the leading authors differed in what they were practicing and they were not very distant from other practices of doing economics. Roscher, Hildebrand, or Knies claimed not only the use of statistical data but also conducted methodological reflections on the use of employing statistics. Hildebrand also wrote about the evolutionary character of economic civilization where historical progress was thought of as a ladder starting from the barter economy evolving through monetary economy up to the banking industry. Roscher and Knies both conducted historically informed and inspired macroeconomics, which was also guided by ethical ideas. Wealth is not an end-in-itself of economy and society but one of the major questions closely related to issues of life-standards and their measurement. Later, Weber discussed Roscher and Knies and the logical implications of doing historical economics carefully and substantially by emphasizing that despite all forms of preliminary thought, Roscher and Knies contributed considerably to the substantial development of historical economics in the nineteenth century (Weber, 1988b).

The subsequent "younger" historical school summarized many of those ideas, which were formerly created and consolidated academics substantially. The common denominator was that profound studies in many economic sectors were undertaken and research programmes were set up that studied economic sectors, geographic regions, or individual branches or occupations in detail in a historical view in order to investigate their related dynamics. Karl Bücher and Gustav Schmoller dealt with the processes of the establishment of modern mass production with limits to growth (Bögenhold, 2000). Lujo Brentano and Gustav Schmoller were programmatically engaged in finding a politically contrasting programme for the social question of working classes, poverty, housing and living conditions in general. They endeavoured to find a political–academic perspective, which was distant to that of evolving Marxism. What the German Historical School had in mind was a kind of social-reformism within the borders of the constitutional society, which was labelled as "Katheder-Sozialismus" (socialism provided by professors), which was later regarded as a derogatory term by the left-wing workers' movement for not being radical enough.

Schmoller was the informal leader of the "younger" German Historical School, having submitted several books and further studies in which he undertook historically informed studies by using diverse sources. Being an influential professor in Berlin, Schmoller was consulted by the policy administration in Berlin and he converted his networks into power. Schmoller's position was strengthened further once he became president of the Verein für Socialpolitik [Society for Social Policy], which was founded by Schmoller and associates in 1872. The Verein für Socialpolitik was the first academic organization of mainly German speaking economists and still exists today as a major economic organization joining economists of Germany, Austria, and Switzerland. The annual conferences were often focused on academic discussion around concrete social problems connected to the rapid industrial-capitalist explosion (housing, handicraft production, working conditions, etc.).

When Schmoller was at the peak of his career, he saw himself confronted with published critiques by the Austrian economist Carl Menger who argued against Schmoller and the German Historical School in general (Backhaus & Hansen, 2000; Louzek, 2011). Menger, who originated marginal utility theory, which later served to be the consolidation of neoclassic theory in economics, argued against the methodological principles of the German Historical School. Menger's message was that the German Historical School was far from being a theoretical science (Bögenhold, 2008). The historical-analytic and in some ways reconstructive-narrative method of the historical school would not be sufficient to meet with the requirements of a theoretical science. The dispute between Menger and Schmoller serves as the first battle of methods in economics. The methodological implications of the controversy are concerned with questions about the status of theory and different methods to practice science. At the end, one can conclude that the controversy was about inductive versus deductive methods. The history of economic thought and the sociology and philosophy of science both treat this still unresolved battle as a classic piece in the history of intellectual ideas. According to the literature, a "youngest" German Historical School also existed. Max Weber, Werner Sombart, and Arthur Spiethoff are regarded as major representatives. Arthur Spiethoff is acknowledged as one of the founding fathers of conducting research on business cycles by employing historical methods. Max Weber and Werner Sombart both conducted historical research, which was connected to the rise of modern capitalism with a strong emphasis on cultural variables for its interpretation. Weber was a professor of economics, whose famous *Economy and Society* (1972) was published posthumously. His work was concerned with reflections on a sociology of science and a sociology of religion. Weber's typology of human motives and behaviour with a categorization of (ideal) types of action argues against current ideas of a simpleminded homo oeconomicus, which Weber regarded as a non-realistic figure close to a mathematical ideal case.

Weber was an initiator and major proponent of the second battle of methods in which he attacked, again, Schmoller and this research, which was typical for many members of the Verein für Socialpolitik (Swedberg, 2000). Textbooks speak about the value judgement debate where Weber said that ethical orientation might be fine but it was also a long way from being a science. He claimed the objectivity of economic statements. Discussions at the annual conferences of the Verein für Socialpolitik were very controversial, such that many members dissolved their membership.

Sombart always assisted Weber in his fights for "objectivity." He succeeded Schmoller's chair after Schmoller's retirement and was well known for his historically, culturally, and hermeneutically inspired economics. With his major work *Der moderne Kapitalismus* (Sombart, [1902/1927]

1987), attempted "an historical and systematic exposition of Europe's economic life from its beginning to the present day" (Sombart, 1982). Sombart's approach was similar to that of Max Weber but with far less emphasis on the role of religious institutions. More than any other thinker, Sombart was responsible for the general introduction and acceptance of the term "capitalism" as a description of the modern business economy.

The "youngest" German Historical School is of central concern for the current discussion on interdisciplinarity since convergences between economics, historical scholarship, religious studies, and sociology were practised at that time (1880–1930) as a matter of course. Economies were not taken in abstracto but always in concreto, which is not too far from the credo of new institutional thought. Taken as a whole, the German Historical School lost influence over the course of the twentieth century, but it seems that some major ideas are showing signs of recovery in recent times, since many ideas of that school converge with ideas of pluralist economics and arguments for economic institutionalism.

Contemporary discussion is far removed from those debates, which ran a hundred years ago under the slogan of historical schools. Recent economics has become "cleaner" and more theory-driven, but even mainstream authors now write about parallels between old and new institutional economics. Recent scholars, and especially students, should be trained to have some idea of the underlying trends and tendencies of the own academic field. History of economic thought belongs to those tools, which are important to keep the engine of changes visible and to learn to understand directions of change.

Why Study History of Economic Thought?

Ten years after the last serious economic crisis, contemporaries still criticize the obvious inability of economics to forecast those economic occurrences appropriately. "What's wrong with modern economics?" was one of the most reported questions. Of course, answers may be diverse and complex, but the fact remains that the best mathematical and econometric modelling techniques did not manage to forecast the development. If economics is a science and more than an ex-post reporting branch, one must expect that economics is better equipped and also more self-reflexive. In these times, several questions and claims were brought onto the agenda, which must serve as a table of contents for a separate discussion.

Of course, one of the comments was that the academic subject and also recent education in economics has become more invested in the history of economic thought, especially as a tool to learn the context of thought and historical knowledge, mistakes and progress. If students receive degrees in economics without having read about, for example, Smith, Keynes, Schumpeter or Hayek, economics is in danger of extinction, and losing economic and social context and the meaning of Begriffsgeschichte or Dogmengeschichte (history of economic terms). We are observing new trends in the mainstream of economics in the sense that the social-scientific nature of economics is increasing (Bögenhold, 2000, 2008). There are noticeable trend boundary shifts within and outside of economics (Cedrini & Fiori, 2016). However, economists do not systematically acknowledge the appropriate foundation of thought in the social sciences where contemporary authors should always try to draw links to such authors as Marshall, Weber, Pareto, and Keynes in order not to unknowingly reinvent ideas which existed already. Not only has the teaching of history of economic thought fallen out of fashion but, consequently, publishing in this field has as well. Marcuzzo and Zacchia (2016) showed that we are experiencing a decline of publications in the area of HET which are concentrated in a small number of journals.

It is interesting enough that Joseph A. Schumpeter in his *History of Economic Analysis* (1954) already provided the methodological advice, why history of economic theory is (always) needed and why historiography is about more than watching old movies (Bögenhold, 2014). Schumpeter argued not only in favour of economic history as rendering a service to economic theory, but also in favour of "a sort of generalized or typified or stylized economic history" (Schumpeter, 1954a, p. 20), which includes institutions like private property, free contracting, or government regulation.

According to Schumpeter, there are multiple reasons to study history, pedagogical advantages, new ideas, and new insights into the workings of the human mind. First of all, regarding the pedagogical advantages, he argued that for students it is very difficult to approach a field without knowing how it relates to the specific historical time. For a thorough understanding, a historical background is required. One could affirm that methods presently used already embody what has been done in the past, and what is not a part thereof is no longer important. However, present methods and results are meaningful only with reference to their historical background. "Scientific analysis is not simply a logically consistent process that starts with some primitive notions and then adds to the stock in a straight-line fashion. It is not simply progressive discovery of an objective reality" (Schumpeter, 1954, p. 4).

The second reason is that in reading "old" theories, one may discover other interpretations of new ideas; Schumpeter wrote that "our minds are apt to derive new inspirations from the study of the history of science" (Schumpeter, 1954, pp. 4–5). In his discussion, Schumpeter added an example. The productivity of this experience may be illustrated by the fact that the fundamental ideas that eventually developed into the theory of special relativity occurred first in a book on the history of mechanics (Schumpeter, 1954, p. 5).

The third cause is that history can give us insights into the manner in which the human mind works. Particularly in the history of science, various types of logic are used. Scientific performances are self-revelatory by nature; that is, they reveal the mental processes that have taken place in order to arrive at a certain law or theory. "Scientific habits or rules of procedure are not merely to be judged by logical standards that exist independently of them; they contribute something to, and react back upon, the logical standards themselves" (Schumpeter, 1954, p. 5).

Finally, the fourth point deals with economics in particular, which is described as a unique historical process. Fundamentally this process does not differ from analogous processes in other fields of knowledge, but,

> *much more than in, say, physics is it true in economics that modern problems, methods, and results cannot be fully understood without some knowledge of how economists have come to reason as they do. In addition, much more than in physics have results been lost on the way or remained in abeyance for centuries.* (Schumpeter, 1954, p. 6)

Given these insightful instructions by Schumpeter as a plea for increased, or at least continuous, attempts to invest in history of economics, one also has to consider Schumpeter's writings as exemplifying what the history of economic writings can highlight. Brilliant ideas are often hidden and neglected for long periods of time. If one wants to analyse a painting hanging on a wall, one must take a few steps back to see the painting as a whole in order to get a sense of the full composition. The same applies to dealing with science and economics specifically. History of economic thought is a neglected academic topic, necessary for contextualizing knowledge, which provides a more sufficient working compass for further study (Kates, 2013). If we are really serious that economics is a part of social sciences (Marchionatti & Cedrini, 2017), we have to look for links to neighbouring fields of economics in the social sciences. Anthropology, sociology, (social-)psychology and, of course, history are those neighbours (Bögenhold, 2018) which always provide fruitful ideas and links to prevent economics from becoming sterile and too insulated.

If modern crises have any benefits, one may be to trigger a careful revision of the systematics of sciences, of tools and common bodies of knowledge. A science without a necessary understanding of the roots of the subject is hard to accept. A graduate in economics who has never read a single line of one of the prominent classic authors of economics is a tragic caricature of a professional person. There are also systematic reasons. New knowledge in economics is made up of, above all, old particles of knowledge combined in new ways (Kurz, 2016, p. 4). Going back to Boulding's (1971) rhetorical question of whether Adam Smith was still needed after Samuelson was published, economics as well as other social sciences have to learn to interpret their subjects as a permanent over-writing process of academic failures by which we can learn about directions of new knowledge.

Note

1. "The antihistorical school, which is now so common in the United States, where the history of thought is regarded as slightly depraved entertainment, fit only for people who really like medieval Latin, so that one became a fully-fledged, chartered Ph.D. economist without ever reading anything that was published more than ten years ago ..." (Boulding, 1971, pp. 232–33).

References

Backhaus, J., & Hansen, R. (2000). Methodenstreit in der Nationalökonomie. *Journal for General Philosophy of Science, 31*(2), 307–336.

Backhouse, R. E. (1994). Why and How Should We Study the History of Economic Thought? *History of Economic Ideas, 2*(2), 113–123.

Backhouse, R. E., & Cherrier, B. (Eds.). (2017). The Age of the Applied Economist: The Transformation of Economics Since the 1970s. *History of Political Economy, 49*(Supplement), 1–33.

Biddle, J. E. (2003). Research Styles in the History of Economic Thought. In W. J. Samuels, J. E. Biddle, & J. B. Davis (Eds.), *A Companion to the History of Economic Thought* (pp. 1–10). Blackwell.

Blaug, M. (2001). No History of Ideas, Please, We're Economists. *The Journal of Economic Perspectives, 15*(1), 145–164.

Boettke, P. F. (2000). Why Read the Classics in Economics?. *Library of economics and liberty*. http://www.econlib.org/library/Features/feature2.html

Bögenhold, D. (2000). Limits to Mass Production: Entrepreneurship and Industrial Organization in View of the Historical School of Schmoller and Sombart. *International Review of Sociology: Revue Internationale de Sociologie, 10*(1), 57–71.

Bögenhold, D. (2008). Economics, Sociology, History: Notes on Their Loss of Unity, Their Need for Re-integration and the Current Relevance of the Controversy Between Carl Menger and Gustav Schmoller. *Forum for Social Economics, 37*(2), 85–101.

Bögenhold, D. (2010). From Heterodoxy to Orthodoxy and Vice Versa: Economics and Social Sciences in the Division of Academic Work. *The American Journal of Economics and Sociology, 69*(5), 1566–1590.

Bögenhold, D. (2014). Schumpeter as a Universal Social Theorist. *The Atlantic Economic Journal, 42*(2), 205–215.

Bögenhold, D. (2018). Economics Between Insulation and Social-Scienciation. *Journal of Economic Issues, 52*(4), 1127–1144.

Boulding, K. E. (1971). After Samuelson Who Needs Adam Smith? *History of Political Economy, 3*(2), 225–237.

Buckley, P., & Casson, M. (1993). Economics as an Imperialist Social Science. *Human Relations, 46*(9), 1035–1052.

Cedrini, M., & Fiori, S. (2016). Shifting Boundaries, Within and Outside Economics. *History of Economic Ideas, 24*(3), 11–25.

Cedrini, M., & Fontana, M. (2018). Just Another Niche in the Wall? How Specialization is Changing the Face of Economics. *Cambridge Journal of Economics, 42*(2), 427–451.

Chafim, F. (2016). Disciplinary Division Within Social Sciences. Methodological Issues in Economic Imperialism and Economic Pluralism. *History of Economic Ideas, 24*(3), 144–164.

Davis, J. B. (2006). The Turn in Economics: Neoclassical Dominance to Mainstream Pluralism? *Journal of Institutional Economics, 2*(1), 1–20.

Davis, J. B. (2016). Economics Imperialism Versus Multidisciplinarity. *History of Economic Ideas, 24*(3), 77–94.

Davis, J. B., Weintraub, E. R., Mirowski, P., Brewer, A. A., & Backhouse, R. E. (2002). *The Future of the History of Economics, HOPE Annual Supplement* (Vol. 34). Duke University Press Books.

Diebolt, C., & Haupert, M. (2018). A Cliometric Counterfactual: What If There Had Been Neither Fogel Nor North? *Cliometrica, 12*, 407–434.

Dorfman, J. (1959). *The Economic Mind in American Civilization* (Vol. 5). Viking Press.

Emmet, R. M. (2003). Exegesis, Hermeneutics, and Interpretation. In W. J. Samuels, J. E. Biddle, & J. B. Davis (Eds.), *A Companion to the History of Economic Thought* (pp. 523–537). Blackwell.

Faccarello, G., & Kurz, H. D. (Eds.). (2016). *Handbook on the History of Economic Analysis Volume III*. Edward Elgar.

Fogarty, E. A., & Naples, M. I. (1998). The Presence of History: A Survey of Articles on the History of Economic Thought and Methodology in the Economic Literature Index, 1969–1995. *Journal of Economic Issues, 32*(1), 224–234.

Fourcade, M., Etienne, O., & Yann, A. (2015). The Superiority of Economists. *Journal of Economic Perspectives, 29*(1), 89–114.

Granovetter, M. S. (2002). A Theoretical Agenda for Economic Sociology. In M. F. Guillén, R. Collins, P. England, & M. Meyer (Eds.), *The New Economic Sociology. Developments in an Emerging Field* (pp. 35–60). Russell Sage Foundation.

Greif, A., & Mokyr, J. (2017). Cognitive Rules, Institutions and Economic Growth: Douglass North and Beyond. *Journal of Institutional Economics, 13*(1), 25–52.

Headlee, S. (2010). Economic History. In R. C. Free (Ed.), *21st Century Economics: A Reference Handbook* (pp. 13–22). Sage.

Heilbroner, R. L. (1979). Modern Economics as a Chapter in the History of Economic Thought. *History of Political Economy, 11*(2), 192–198.

Herbst, J. (1965). *The German Historical School in American Scholarship*. Cornell University Press.

Hodgson, G. (2001). *How Economics Forget History*. Routledge.

Hodgson, G. (2007). Evolutionary and Institutional Economics as the New Mainstream? *Evolutionary and Institutional Economics Review, 4*(1), 7–25.

Hodgson, G. (2017). Introduction to the Douglass C. North Memorial Issue. *Journal of Institutional Economics, 13*(1), 1–23.

Hodgson, G. M., Mäki, U., & McCloskey, D. (1992). Plea for a Pluralistic and Rigorous Economics. *American Economic Review, 82*(2), 25.

Kates, S. (2013). *Defending the History of Economic Thought*. Edward Elgar.

Keynes, J. M. (1936). *The General Theory of Employment, Interest and Money*. Macmillan.

Klaess, M. (2003). Historiography. In W. J. Samuels, J. E. Biddle, & J. B. Davis (Eds.), *A Companion to the History of Economic Thought* (pp. 491–505). Blackwell.

Kurz, H. D. (2016). *Economic Thought. A Brief History*. Columbia University Press.

Laidler, D. (2001). *The Role of the History of Economic Thought in Modern Macroeconomics*. Department of Economics Research Reports, 2001–6.

Lazear, E. P. (2000). Economic Imperialism. *The Quarterly Journal of Economics, 115*(1), 99–146.

Louzek, M. (2011). The Battle of Methods in Economics. The Classical Methodenstreit –Menger vs. Schmoller. *The American Journal of Economics and Sociology, 70*(2), 439–463.

Marchionatti, R., & Cedrini, M. (2017). *Economics as Social Science: Economics Imperialism and the Challenge of Interdisciplinary.* Routledge.

Marcuzzo, M. C. (2008). Is History of Economic Thought a Serious Subject? *The Erasmus Journal of Philosophy and Economics, 1*(1), 107–123.

Marcuzzo, M. C., & Zacchia, G. (2016). Is History of Economics What Historians of Economic Thought Do? *History of Economic Ideas, 24*(3), 29–46.

Menger, C. (1883). *Untersuchungen über die Methode der sozialwissenschaften und der Politischen Ökonomie insbesondere.* Duncker and Humblot.

Morgan, M. (2012). *The World in the Model. How Economists Work and Think.* Cambridge University Press.

Richter, R. (2001). '*Bridging Old and New Institutional Economics: Gustav Schmoller, the Leader of the Younger German Historical School, Seen with Neoinstitutionalists' Eyes.* Research Paper, University of Saarland.

Romer, P. M. (2015). Mathiness in the Theory of Economic Growth. *American Economic Review, 105*(5), 89–93.

Roncaglia, A. (2014). Should the History of Economic Thought Be Included in Undergraduate Curricula? *Economic Thought, 3*(1), 1–9.

Samuels, W. (1997). The Work of Historians of Economic Thought. *Research in the History of Economic Thought and Methodology, 15*, 188–198.

Schabas, M. (1992). Breaking Away: History of Economics as History of Science. *History of Political Economy, 24*(1), 187–203.

Schmoller, G. (1883). *Zur Methodologie der Staats-und Sozialwissenschaften, Jahrbuch für Gesetzgebung, Verwaltung und Volkswirtschaft im deutschen Reich* (pp. 239–258). Duncker & Humblot.

Schumpeter, J. A. (1926). *Gustav von Schmoller und die Probleme von heute. Jahrbuch für Gesetzgebung, Verwaltung und Volkswirtschaft im deutschen Reich* (pp. 337–388). Duncker and Humblot.

Schumpeter, J. A. (1954). *History of Economic Analysis.* Oxford University Press.

Shionoya, Y. (Ed.). (2001). *The German Historical School: The Historical and Ethical Approach to Economics.* Routledge.

Shionoya, Y. (2005). *The Soul of the German Historical School: Methodological Essays on Schmoller, Weber and Schumpeter.* Springer.

Sombart, W. (1982). Wirtschaft. In A. Vierkandt (Ed.), *Handwörterbuch der Soziologie* (pp. 209–216). Enke.

Sombart, W. (1987). *Der moderne Kapitalismus.* DTV.

Swedberg, R. (1991). The Battle of Methods: Toward a Paradigm Shift? In A. Etzioni & P. R. Lawrence (Eds.), *Socio-Economics. Toward a New Synthesis* (pp. 13–34). M. E. Sharpe.

Swedberg, R. (2000). *Max Weber and the Idea of Economic Sociology*. Princeton University Press.

Vaughn, K. L. (1993). Why Teach the History of Economics? *Journal of the History of Economic Thought, 15*(2), 174–183.

Viner, J. (1917). Some Problems of Logical Method in Political Economy. *Journal of Political Economy, 25*(3), 236–260.

Weber, M. (1972). *Wirtschaft und Gesellschaft*. J.C.B. Mohr.

Weber, M. (1988a). Wissenschaft als Beruf. In M. Weber (Ed.), *Gesammelte Aufsätze zur Wissenschaftslehre* (pp. 524–555). J.C.B. Mohr.

Weber, M. (1988b). *Gesammelte Aufsätze zur Wissenschaftslehre*. J.C.B. Mohr.

Weintraub, E. R. (2002). *How Economics Became a Mathematical Science*. Duke University Press.

Winch, D. N. (1962). What Price the History of Economic Thought. *Scottish Journal of Political Economy, 9*(3), 193–204.

Wunder, T. A. (2010). Economic Methodology. In R. C. Free (Ed.), *21st Century Economics: A Reference Handbook* (pp. 23–32). Sage.

CHAPTER 9

Schumpeter's Split Between "Pure" Economics and Institutional Economics: Why Methodological Individualism Was Not Fully Considered

Introduction

The chapter deals with Joseph A. Schumpeter and his efforts to treat economics methodologically. Some authors argue that Schumpeter maintained his principal scientific positions over the course of his life.[1] It is said that he came up with his main ideas very early on in his European times and that he worked out those ideas more thoroughly during the following decades without changing his early positions very much. Compared to this view, one may see at least one clear shift in Schumpeter's principal positions between the early and late periods of his career. The chapter discusses this shift, which is centered on Schumpeter's scientific positioning. In *Das Wesen und der Hauptinhalt der theoretischen Nationalökonomie* (1908), Schumpeter developed and pioneered his methodological individualism which is acknowledged. However, a comparison of these early positions with methodological writings in his *History of Economic Analysis* (1954) shows that he did not shift from methodological individualism to an

Bögenhold, Dieter. Schumpeter's Split Between "Pure" Economics and Institutional Economics: Why Methodological Individualism was not Fully Considered, in: *International Advances of Economic Research*, 2018, Vol. 24 (3), 253–264.

D. Bögenhold, *Neglected Links in Economics and Society*,
https://doi.org/10.1007/978-3-030-79193-3_9

institutional perspective that addresses the academic interplay and sees economic action rooted in historical predispositions, paths, and social constraints. Both perspectives are related to each other. In our view, this clearly articulates a perspective of institutional economics that emphasizes social embeddedness of economic behaviour.

Currently Schumpeter is viewed as a truly interdisciplinary theorist. He worked continuously in a perspective which can be characterized as academic cross-fertilization. Therefore, posthumously, Schumpeter's different articles were sorted into books as collected papers, political speeches, articles in socioeconomics, papers on economic policies, essays on daily politics, papers on economic theory, and articles on the history of economic thought (e.g. Schumpeter, 1952, 1953). In a first instance, many contemporaries know primarily Schumpeter's ideas as they were developed in *The Theory of Economic Development* (Schumpeter, 1963), perhaps also his book on *Business Cycles* (Schumpeter, 1939) and, of course, his argumentation in *Capitalism, Socialism, and Democracy* (Schumpeter, 1942), but lesser known is his systematization of academic development and his methodological roadmap.

The discussion focuses on the principles of Schumpeter's academic thought, which led him to create his diverse works and which were reflected systematically in some of his writings, from which Schumpeter emerged as a theorist of science. Besides working on specific substantial topics, throughout his life Schumpeter dealt with methodological issues in different works. He wrote articles on rationality, on positivism in economics, on mathematical methods in economic theorizing (Schumpeter, 1906), "How to Study Social Sciences" (translated title) (Schumpeter, 1915), "Gustav von Schmoller und die Probleme von heute" (Schumpeter, 1926), and many more articles. Referring to books, his book *Epochen der Dogmen- und Methodengeschichte* (Schumpeter, 1914, published in English as *Economic Doctrines and Method* in 1954), was certainly a major contribution to methodology in economics. Despite these many different works, I view Schumpeter's first book *Das Wesen und der Hauptinhalt der theoretischen Nationalökonomie* (Schumpeter, 1908) and his last book *History of Economic Analysis* (Schumpeter, 1954) as those studies that are among his most diverse and show his latest and most up-to-date statements concerning the division of social sciences and the role of economics in relation to sociology, history, and other academic branches.

Das Wesen und der Hauptinhalt der theoretischen Nationalökonomie (Schumpeter, 1908) was published when Schumpeter was only 25 years old. He wrote the book while staying in Cairo, Egypt, before his career started in Vienna. *History of Economic Analysis* (Schumpeter, 1954) was published four years after the death of Schumpeter, which was in 1950. The substantial preface of the *History of Economic Analysis* reads like a manual on how to refer to the different academic branches and how to integrate them into a coherent universal social science, which is far from being a narrow economic science of modern representation (Bögenhold, 2014). Schumpeter must be regarded as someone who stayed on the solid ground of a well-studied history of mainstream economics which led him to argue offensively for an institutional approach integrating economics with different further social sciences by avoiding the formulation of a divisional order or ranking, which was already highlighted by Swedberg (1991).

Of course, Schumpeter's *History of Economic Analysis* has been extensively printed, translated, and reprinted in several editions. However, especially the preface appears somewhat neglected in Schumpeterian discourse and his argumentation needs so much more text marking, because it must be read as a fine synthesis of arguments as developed in the first battles of methods between Carl Menger and Gustav von Schmoller and the second battle of methods between Schmoller and Max Weber and others (Shionoya, 2005; Bögenhold, 2008; Backhaus & Hansen, 2000; Louzek, 2011). In this sense, the old controversies were updated. In *History of Economic Analysis* (Schumpeter, 1954), many questions were addressed in a more elegant and rigorous way. While Schumpeter is mostly regarded as a pioneer of evolutionary economics (Kurz, 2012, 2015), who argued in favour of this perspective in *The Theory of Economic Development* (Schumpeter, 1963), and especially in *Capitalism, Socialism and Democracy* (Schumpeter, 1942), the last one containing the famous formulation of creative destruction (Fagerberg, 2003), one may also view Schumpeter as an institutional economist who was searching for his methodological programme.

Methodological Individualism: An Undecided Term with Different Meanings

There is still a controversial discussion regarding what methodological individualism really is and what it has meant. Udehn (2002) discussed the variety of different meanings of methodological individualism. He distinguished between softer and stricter variants of the programme. Elster

(1982) suggested that Marxism and game theory did not match with methodological individualism for different reasons. Urquhart (2013) discussed methodological individualism historically but always in specific relation to Marxism. Also, Vercelli (2016) discussed methodological individualism for contemporary economics in a negative light. Hodgson (2007) explained methodological individualism and depicted the simple, but generally neglected, point that the meaning of the term has never been precisely stated and the idea is in fact ambiguous as to what it refers to (Davis, 2016, p. 3). There are also further terms, such as micro and macro or agency and structure, which aim at similar problems and which link to the debate on methodological individualism. Somehow similar dichotomies become evident when comparing economics and sociology, since competing paradigms regarding the responsibility of the individual actor exist in both academic domains (Coleman, 1990; Neck, 2015). However, more generally, one may conclude with Granovetter (2017) that the human agent in economics is conceptualized as a figure without any, or at least without many, social influences, while the human agent in sociology appears to be very much an effect of social influences. In consequence, Granovetter (1992) wrote that the actor in economics appears to be under-socialized and in sociology the actor is just the opposite, (s)he is over socialized. Speaking for economics, Arrow (1994) explained the programme of methodological individualism as an intellectual attempt to rationalize the workings of an economy and of economic procedures through the lenses of individual decisions.

> *In the usual versions of economic theory, each individual makes decisions to consume different commodities, to work at one job or another, to choose production methods, to save, and to invest. In one way or another, these decisions interact to produce an outcome which determines the workings of the economy, the allocation of resources in short. It seems commonly to be assumed that the individual decisions then form a complete set of explanatory variables. A name is given to this point of view, that of methodological individualism, that is necessary to base all accounts of economic interaction on individual behaviour.* (Arrow, 1994, p. 1)

In other words, while economists necessarily have to agree that human beings are always in a social environment, they mostly "concentrated on the features of the individual in isolation" (Hodgson, 2015, p. 56). This tradition goes back to Menger, who tried to reduce the complex phenomena to the actions of individual actors. Especially in his *Principles of Economics* (Menger, 1976, originally 1871), Menger tried to bring complicated matters of the economy to their simplest elements, these being the actions of individual human beings. Menger did not make use of the term methodological individualism but wrote about the atomistic method, which was meant to take the individual human agent as the starting point of analysis (Neck, 2014).[2] In some way, the perspective became central to Austrian economics. Hayek raised the issue that it is a marvel (Hayek, 1945, p. 527), that economists take for granted what should be questioned, for example, why do people do what they do. However, Hayek introduced the idea of a spontaneous order, which was characteristic of the price system at an aggregate level, which is an unintended result of individual decisions. "Its misfortune is the double one that it is not the product of human design and that the people guided by it usually do not know why they are made to do what they do" (Hayek, 1945, p. 527). For Hayek, methodological individualism is always in conflict with evolutionary ideas (Lindemans, 2012).

Joseph A. Schumpeter (1908) explicitly took up these questions when he discussed assumptions and consequences of methodological individualism. It was his first book (Schumpeter, 1908) in which he orchestrated a broad discussion on the need to argue atomistically or to think in terms of social determinism. One 10-page chapter entitled "The Methodological Individualism" (1908, part I, chapter 6) explained different concepts of human action. Among these concepts, Schumpeter already used explicitly the term homo oeconomicus (Schumpeter, 1908, p. 85), which was seen as a utility maximizer to be employed in "pure economics" (Schumpeter, 1954). The homo oeconomicus was a semantic construct of hypothetical nature (Schumpeter, 1908, p. 87). Lastly, Schumpeter did a meta-reflection regarding appropriate models to engage in economics.[3]

In order to clarify the semantics, Schumpeter distinguished between political and methodological individualism:

> *Both concepts have nothing in common. The first refers to general statements like the freedom of people to develop themselves and to take part in well-being and to follow practical rules. The second does not include any proposition and does not involve a specific starting point. It just means that one starts from the individual in order to describe certain economic relationships.* (Schumpeter, 1908, pp. 90–91, translated by Heertje, 2004, p. 153)

Later in *History of Economic Analysis* (Schumpeter, 1954, p. 888), Schumpeter also introduced sociological individualism which referred to the self-governing individual that "constitutes the ultimate unit of the social sciences and that all social phenomena resolve themselves into decisions and actions of individuals that need not or cannot be further analyzed in terms of superindividual factors" (Schumpeter, 1954, p. 888). Although Schumpeter already performed many charming advances in the direction of sociology (Schumpeter, 1908, pp. 539–541), he did not go further at the end of his career to spell out forms of possible and reasonable cooperation and practical academic management (also Hodgson, 2012, pp. 31–33).

Schumpeter's discussion on methodological individualism suggests that it was, in contrast to Menger's use of atomism, really undecided. Heertje (2004) was certainly right that methodological individualism

> *conceals a double restriction. First, it is concerned with pure economics. Second, pure economics only refers to the analysis of flows of goods. This fact explains why the concept does not show up in other works by Schumpeter. One would expect the application of methodological individualism to the theory of economic development, innovation, bureaucracy and democracy, but these applications are outside the narrow framework that Schumpeter has chosen for this interpretation of methodological individualism.*(Heertje, 2004, p. 154)

Schumpeter's discussion oscillated permanently between a broad and a narrow interpretation of methodological individualism.

> *While Schumpeter's broad view of economic and social relationships has contributed to insights into the role of entrepreneurs, innovators, bureaucrats, intellectuals and politicians, his narrow interpretation of methodological individualism, in fact, blocked the analysis of the rich pattern of individuals acting in real life.* (Heertje, 2004, p. 154)

This observation has serious consequences since Schumpeter had an undecided split between methodological individualism as a heuristic principle towards pure theory on the one hand and an analysis of the institutional social and regulatory framework on the other hand. It seems that Schumpeter had difficulties deciding between a method, which analyses the economy in abstracto on the one hand and in concreto on the other, in order to employ the semantic differentiation by Sombart (1982).

From Methodological Individualism to Institutional Economics

Already in his very early writings, Schumpeter (1908, part V) discussed the relationship of economics to sociology, biology, psychology, ethnology, and ethics. However, in retrospect, these biographically early discussions seem a bit unsystematic. Schumpeter orchestrated these areas much more broadly in his late work *History of Economic Analysis* (1954) where he reflected carefully about the division of different scientific branches. Schumpeter practiced an offensive dialogue with neighbouring disciplines like sociology, history, political economy and psychology from the perspective of an economist. But even as an economist he discussed economics as practice and a field of professional activity. First of all, Schumpeter voiced a plea for working in the history of science.

Schumpeter argued not only in favour of economic history that renders a service to economic theory, but also in favour of "a sort of generalized or typified or stylized economic history" (Schumpeter, 1954, p. 20), which includes institutions like private property or free contracting or government regulation; a sort of institutional economics which can be found (Kasper et al., 2012). In this way, economic institutionalism is a lens to look at the working of economies in their dependencies on historical paths, culture, and governances (North, 1990; Hodgson, 1998). Of course, the ordo-institutional approach in the context of Austrian economics of earlier years (Kolev, 2015) did not really acknowledge Schumpeter's split in theory concerns but almost referred, if at all, to Schumpeter and his conceptions of entrepreneurship. Thus, this form of institutionalism is not addressed here.

According to Schumpeter, there are four main reasons to study history. First of all, it has pedagogical advantages. He argues that, for the students, it is very difficult to approach a field without knowing how it is related to the specific historical time. For a thorough understanding, an historical background is required. One could affirm that the methods that are presently in use already embody what has been done in the past. What is not part thereof is no longer important and is not worth taking into consideration. However, our present methods and their results are meaningful only with reference to their historical background. "Scientific analysis is not simply a logically consistent process that starts with some primitive notions and then adds to the stock in a straightline fashion. It is not simply progressive discovery of an objective reality" (Schumpeter, 1954, p. 4).

The second reason is that pertaining to the reading of old theories, one may discover other interpretations of them or new ideas. Schumpeter writes, that "our minds are apt to derive new inspirations from the study of the history of science" (Schumpeter, 1954, pp. 4–5). In his discussion, Schumpeter adds an example: "The productivity of this experience may be illustrated by the fact that the fundamental ideas that eventually developed into the theory of (special) relativity occurred first in a book on the history of mechanics" (Schumpeter, 1954, p. 5). The third cause is that history can give us insights into the ways in which the human mind works. Particularly in the history of science, various types of logic are used and scientific performances are self-revelatory by nature, that is, they reveal the mental processes that have taken place in order to arrive at a certain law or theory. "Scientific habits or rules of procedure are not merely to be judged by logical standards that exist independently of them; they contribute something to, and react back upon, the logical standards themselves" (Schumpeter, 1954, p. 5). Finally, the fourth point deals with economics in particular, which is described as a unique historical process. Fundamentally this process does not differ from the analogous processes in other fields of knowledge but

> *much more than in, say, physics is it true in economics that modern problems, methods, and results cannot be fully understood without some knowledge of how economists have come to reason as they do. In addition, much more than in physics has been lost on the way or remained in abeyance for centuries.* (Schumpeter, 1954, p. 6)

Schumpeter discussed several, from today's standpoint, independent scientific disciplines such as economic history, statistics, theory, economic sociology, political economy, and applied fields as techniques of economic analysis. In a subsequent chapter, he turned his attention to specific discussion topics such as the specific relationship between economics and sociology and between logic and psychology. Here, the reasoning is dense and much deeper than is usually assumed when coming across the conventional image of Schumpeter as a theorist of entrepreneurship. Instead, he engaged in a very precise sociology of science in which diverse matching processes between individual scientific areas and traditions of thought are investigated.

In discussing economic history, statistics, theory, economic sociology, political economy, and applied fields as techniques of economic analysis, a clear conceptual ranking in terms of order is missing. Schumpeter understands each of them instrumentally and he regards the different elements taken together as a box of tools. Obviously, economics is a synonym for economic analysis, which operates through different academic configurations provided by the toolbox. The interplay of different branches comes up like an orchestra where different agents have different functions, but even the smallest voices contribute to the success of the common enterprise.

In contrast to the history of science as a history of changing intellectual ideas, Schumpeter referred to economic history, nomen est omen, as a history of economic and social changes. His plea for an integration of economic history in the orchestra of economic analysis reads this way:

> *Nobody can hope to understand economic phenomena of any, including the present, epoch without an adequate command of historical facts and an adequate amount of historical sense, or of what may be described as historical experience. .... The historical report cannot be purely economic but must inevitably reflect also 'institutional' facts that are not purely economic: therefore, it affords the best method for understanding how economic and non-economic facts are related to one another and how various social sciences should be related to one another.* (Schumpeter, 1954, pp. 12–13)

According to Schumpeter, most of the ongoing errors in economic analysis are due to a lack of historical competencies, which leads him to acknowledge also the terrains of anthropology and ethnology:

> *History must of course be understood to include fields that have acquired different names as a consequence of specialization, such as pre-historic reports and ethnology (anthropology).* (Schumpeter, 1954, p. 13)

Regarding statistics, Schumpeter explained that we shall recognize that statistical methods are part of the tools of economic analysis because statistical figures or series of figures are of vital importance for economics (Schumpeter, 1954, pp. 13–14). Consequently, "an adequate command of modern statistical methods is a necessary (but not a sufficient) condition for preventing the modern economist from producing nonsense" (Schumpeter, 1954, p. 14).

When discussing theory, Schumpeter again did what could also be found in his earlier writings (such as Schumpeter, 1926), which is that he writes the word theory with quotation marks. Schumpeter's intention was to explain that we have no precise commonly shared understanding of what we mean when talking about theory. In this respect Schumpeter proves to be a methodologist with profound knowledge of the philosophy of science. His set of questions includes: When does theory achieve the distinction of being "pure theory"? Why do we need studies in the history of economic thought? What about the intersections between theory, statistics, and economic history? Where are the borders and overlaps between economics, philosophy, psychology, political economy, and economic sociology? Which are general principles of scientific processes?

Schumpeter explains that theory has many meanings and it should not simply be interpreted as a semantic counterpart to practice. Schumpeter (1954, pp. 14–20) explains that three of these meanings are of special relevance: First, theory is an explanation of causal connections. Even if more of those causalities exist, one may summarize them taken together as theory. Second, theory is also a methodology at the level of paradigms, approaches, and procedures which must be discussed academically. Here, we do not expect to find empirical results but methods to achieve scientific knowledge. Third, theory is reserved as a semantic of general economics (Schumpeter, 1926, p. 365 ff.). Viewing this discussion, a reader feels that many items remain provokingly up-to-date and finally unsolved. In the end, Schumpeter tries to find bridges between inductive and deductive procedures in order to arrive at a theory, which should provide an advanced holistic perspective. Already the fact that theory is written with quotation marks indicates Schumpeter's strength in perceiving and acknowledging the complexity of the matter. What is currently a topic in recent science theory was already problematized in Schumpeter's writings, namely that one should not take for granted the wording of theory since different types of theory and correspondingly different semantics coexist. The question of when an academic statement receives the status of being theory still remains on the agenda.

It is not only economic history that renders a service to economic theory, as Schumpeter argues, but also economic sociology:

> *Economic analysis deals with the questions how people behave at any time and what the economic effects are they produce by so behaving; economic sociology deals with the question how they came to behave as they do. If we define economic behavior widely enough so that it includes not only actions and motives and propensities but also the social institutions that are relevant to economic behavior such as government, property inheritance, contract, and so on, that phrase really tells us all we need.* (Schumpeter, 1954, p. 21)

There are several statements where Schumpeter speaks with great appreciation about economic sociology and claims that economics has to seek or to keep in closer contact with sociology because "we cannot afford ... to neglect the developments of sociology" and especially not the "fundamental field of economic sociology in which neither economists nor sociologists can get very far without treading on one another's toes" (Schumpeter, 1954, pp. 25–26).

The following discussion of Schumpeter is concerned with logic, philosophy, and psychology, which are not summarized under techniques of economic analysis but rather are discussed as a basic methodological understanding of his conceptual framework. Schumpeter explained in the introduction to that specific chapter that he uses nothing other than a philosophy of economics (Schumpeter, 1954, p. 25) as a basic theoretical scientific reflection.

The most significant statement about economic psychology is contained in the following words: "Economics like other social sciences deals with human behavior. Psychology is really the basis from which any social science must start and in terms of which all fundamental explanation must run" (Schumpeter, 1954, p. 27). Of course, Schumpeter is impressed by the argumentation of Keynes and Keynesianism of his time, which refers to animal spirits and other behavioural foundations. Also, this type of argumentation matches an idea which he presented in different theoretical discussions on methodological individualism much earlier (Schumpeter, 1908).

His theory of science with a focus on economics in relation to different other academic areas, often historically new and emerging ones, must be viewed as a sociology of scientific ideas. Schumpeter explained this in his own words:

> *From time to time, we shall look up from our work in order to view a piece of intellectual scenery. Slightly less perfunctorily, we shall, for every one of our periods, register some contemporaneous developments in other sciences ... that were relevant or might, for one reason or another, be expected to have been Relevant to the development of our own.* (Schumpeter, 1954, p. 25)

Conclusion

The comparatively less cited preface of *History of Economic Analysis* (Schumpeter, 1954) showed Schumpeter much more in light of a reflected institutional economist who treated history, sociology, psychology and further academic fields respectfully as common tools of scientific discovery. His often-quoted discussion of methodological individualism is less pronounced, and in a narrow light is shown to be a meta discussion that Schumpeter did mainly with ideas provided by his predecessor and partly his contemporaries. His own position remains somehow vague in this respect. The oscillation between methodological individualism and institutional economics must be seen as a split that he did not really perceive as a split and with regard to which he did not really choose one side or another. As his late writings indicate, it looks very much like at the end of his academic life, Schumpeter was much more on the side of an interdisciplinary economist who acknowledged the social embeddedness of social behaviour and institutions. When Schumpeter asks about the meaning of economic action, he discusses models of rationality. In general, all his theorizing is against practices of utilitarianism and against basic assumptions of economic theorizing. In other words, Schumpeter systematizes arguments in favour of an economics oriented towards real life as opposed to axiomatic assumptions of the nature of human beings. All his own applied economics in diverse areas reveal that he was not really governed by methodological individualism.

Notes

1. For a discussion of Schumpeter within his times and in relation to his contemporaries, see Cantner and Dopfner (2015), also Michaelides and Milios (2009, 2015).
2. Reading Menger in light of new institutional economics (NIE), it looks as if a more direct line leads from NIE back to Schmoller, as the counterpart of Menger within the first battle of methods rather than to Menger. "Schmoller's critique of classical economics is strikingly similar to that made more recently by Ronald Coase—the 'father' of the New Institutional Economics" (Furubotn & Richter, 2005, p. 41). Schmoller insisted on the importance of comparative institutional analysis which is so central for current new institutional economics. "He considered such topics as evolution, feelings, and norms, as some modem institutional economists do" (Furubotn & Richter, 2005, p. 42). However, reading new institutional economics as a discussion of organizational forms and efficiency (Williamson, 1973, 1985), the recent level of discussion and terminological apparatus has become much more elaborated than the early discussion of Schmoller or Menger could do at their time (Ménard & Shirley, 2008).
3. For a discussion of the Homo sapiens oeconomicus and different taxonomies see Dopfner (2004).

References

Arrow, K. J. (1994). Methodological Individualism and Social Knowledge. *American Economic Review, 84*(2), 1–9.

Backhaus, J., & Hansen, R. (2000). Methodenstreit in der Nationalökonomie. *Journal for General Philosophy of Science, 31*(2), 307–336.

Bögenhold, D. (2008). Economics, Sociology, History: Notes on Their Loss of Unity, Their Need for Re-integration and the Current Relevance of the Controversy Between Carl Menger and Gustav von Schmoller. *Forum for Social Economics, 37*(2), 85–101.

Bögenhold, D. (2014). Schumpeter as a Universal Social Theorist. *Atlantic Economic Journal, 42*(3), 205–215.

Cantner, U., & Dopfner, K. (2015). Schumpeter and His Contemporaries. *Journal of Evolutionary Economics, 25*(1), 1–20.

Coleman, J. S. (1990). *Foundations of social theory*. Belkman Press.

Davis, J. B. (2016). Hodgson, Cumulative Causation, and Reflexive Economic Agents. In F. Gagliardi & D. Gindis (Eds.), *Institutions and the Evolution of Capitalism* (pp. 78–91). Edward Elgar Publishing.

Dopfner, K. (2004). The Economic Agent as Rule Maker and Rule User: Homo Sapiens Oeconomicus. *Journal of Evolutionary Economics, 14*(2), 177–195.

Elster, J. (1982). The Case for Methodological Individualism. *Theory and Society, 11*(4), 453–482.

Fagerberg, J. (2003). Schumpeter and the Revival of Evolutionary Economics: An Appraisal of the Literature. *Journal of Evolutionary Economics, 13*(2), 125–159.

Furubotn, E. G., & Richter, R. (2005). *Institutions and Economic Theory. The Contribution of the New Institutional Economics*. The University of Michigan Press.

Granovetter, M. S. (1992). Economic Institutions as Social Constructions: A Framework for Analysis. *Acta Sociologica, 35*(1), 3–11.

Granovetter, M. S. (2017). *Society and Economy: Framework and Principles*. The Beknap Press of Harvard University Press.

Hayek, F. v. (1945). The Use of Knowledge in Society. *American Economic Review, 39*(4), 19–30.

Heertje, A. (2004). Schumpeter and Methodological Individualism. *Journal of Evolutionary Economics, 14*, 153–156.

Hodgson, G. M. (1998). The Approach of Institutional Economics. *Journal of Economic Literature, 36*(1), 166–192.

Hodgson, G. M. (2007). Meanings of Methodological Individualism. *Journal of Economic Methodology, 14*(2), 211–226.

Hodgson, G. M. (2012). *From Pleasure Machines to Moral Communities. An Evolutionary Economics Without Homo Oeconomicus*. Chicago University Press.

Hodgson, G. M. (2015). *Conceptualizing Capitalism. Institutions, Evolution, Future*. Chicago University Press.
Kasper, W., Streit, M. E., & Boettke, P. J. (2012). *Institutional Economics. Property, Competition, Policies*. Edward Elgar.
Kolev, S. (2015). Ordoliberalism and the Austrian School. In C. J. Coyne & P. J. Boettke (Eds.), *The Oxford Handbook of Austrian Economics* (pp. 419–444). Oxford University Press.
Kurz, H. (2012). Schumpeter's New Combinations: Revisiting His Theorie der wirtschaftlichen Entwicklung on the Occasion of Its Centenary. *Journal of Evolutionary Economics, 22*(5), 871–899.
Kurz, H. (2015). The Beat of the Economic Heart: Joseph Schumpeter and Arthur Spiethoff on Business Cycles. *Journal of Evolutionary Economics, 25*(1), 147–162.
Lindemans, J. W. (2012). Methodological Individualism and Cultural Evolution: Ontogenetic and Phylogenetic Approaches to Social Order. *Quarterly Journal of Economics, 15*(3), 331–369.
Louzek, M. (2011). The Battle of Methods in Economics. The Classical Methodenstreit–Menger vs Schmoller. *The American Journal of Economics and Sociology, 70*(2), 439–463.
Ménard, C., & Shirley, M. M. (Eds.). (2008). *Introduction. Handbook of New Institutional Economics* (pp. 1–20). Springer.
Menger, C. (1976 [1871]). *Principles of Economics*. NY University Press.
Michaelides, P. G., & Milios, J. G. (2009). Joseph Schumpeter and the German historical School. *Cambridge Journal of Economics, 33*(3), 495–516.
Michaelides, P. G., & Milios, J. G. (2015). The Schumpeter-Hilferding Nexus. *Journal of Evolutionary Economics, 25*(1), 133–146.
Neck, R. (2014). On Austrian Economics and the Economics of Carl Menger. *Atlantic Economic Journal, 42*(3), 217–227.
Neck, R. (2015). The Positivist Dispute After 50 Years–An Unrepentant 'Positivist' View. *Journal of Classical Sociology, 15*(2), 185–190.
North, D. C. (1990). *Institutions, Institutional Change and Economic Performance*. Cambridge University Press.
Schumpeter, J. A. (1906). Über die mathematische Methode der theoretischen Ökonomie. *Zeitschrift für Volkswirtschaft, Sozialpolitik und Verwaltung, 15*, 30–49.
Schumpeter, J. A. (1908). *Das Wesen und der Hauptinhalt der theoretischen Nationalökonomie*. Duncker and Humblot.
Schumpeter, J. A. (1914 [Engl. Transl. 1954]). Epochen der Dogmen- und Methodengeschichte. In K. Bücher, J. A. Schumpeter, & F. V. Wieser (Eds.), *Grundriß der der Sozialökonomik, Vol. 1, Grundlagen der Wirtschaft* (pp. 19–124). J.C.B. Mohr.

Schumpeter, J. A. (1915). Wie studiert man Sozialwissenschaft? In *Schriften des Sozialwissenschaftlichen Akademischen Vereins in Czernowitz* (pp. 5–44). Duncker and Humblot.

Schumpeter, J. A. (1926). Gustav von Schmoller und die Probleme von heute. Schmollers Jahrbuch für Gesetzgebung. *Verwaltung und Volkswirtschaft, 50*, 337–388.

Schumpeter, J. A. (1939). *Business Cycles: A Theoretical, Historical and Statistical Analysis of the Capitalist Process* (Vol. 2). McGraw Hill.

Schumpeter, J. A. (1942). *Capitalism, Socialism, and Democracy.* Harper.

Schumpeter, J. A. (1952). *Aufsätze zur ökonomischen Theorie.* J.C.B. Mohr.

Schumpeter, J. A. (1953). *Aufsätze zur Soziologie.* J. C. B. Mohr.

Schumpeter, J. A. (1954). *History of Economic Analysis.* Oxford University Press.

Schumpeter, J. A. (1963 [1912]). *The Theory of Economic Development.* Oxford University Press.

Shionoya, Y. (2005). *The Soul of the German Historical School: Methodological Essays on Schmoller, Weber and Schumpeter.* Springer.

Sombart, W. (1982 [1931]). Wirtschaft. In A. Vierkandt (Ed.), *Handwörterbuch der Soziologie* (pp. 209–216). Enke.

Swedberg, R. (1991). The man and his work. In R. Swedberg (Ed.), *Joseph A. Schumpeter. The economics and sociology of capitalism* (pp. 3–98). Princeton University Press.

Udehn, L. (2002). The Changing Face of Methodological Individualism. *Annual Review of Sociology, 28*, 479–507.

Urquhart, R. (2013). Taking the Modern for Nature: Methodological Individualism as an Interesting Mistake. *European Journal in the History of Economic Thought, 20*(5), 812–844.

Vercelli, A. (2016). Microfoundations, Methodological Individualism and Alternative Economic Visions. *Review of Political Economy, 28*(1), 153–167.

Williamson, O. E. (1973). Markets and Hierarchies: Some Elementary Considerations. *The American Economic Review, 63*(2), 316–325.

Williamson, O. E. (1985). *The Economic Institutions of Capitalism: Firms, Markets, Relational Contracting.* Free Press.

CHAPTER 10

Schumpeter's Idea of a Universal Social Science

How to Read Schumpeter

Reading the diverse works of Schumpeter (1883–1950) shows that his thinking matches very well with ideas aimed at coherent universal social sciences. Schumpeter not only practiced a transdisciplinary "putting together," he also argued theoretically in favour of his practice by mentioning cross-fertilization or the unmixed blessing (Schumpeter, 1954a, p. 27). His aim was far from delivering a "grand unified theory" (Uhlig, 2012, p. 31), but rather, as a sociologist of science, he reflected on the division of academic branches such as economics and sociology into semi-independent sciences (Schumpeter, 1954a, p. 27). Therefore, Schumpeter was representative of an academic procedure which did not fit with, as he said, "primitive economics" (Schumpeter, 1954a, p. 26). "Primitive economics" has no cooperation with other disciplines and is monodisciplinary and autistic. Spiethoff has said that Schumpeter saw himself as a "gourmet" in issues of theory (Spiethoff, 1949, p. 291). In a nutshell, although Schumpeter is mostly known for his discussion of the entrepreneur and his ideas of innovation, he is also a theorist providing a manual for inter- and transdisciplinary thought, which may serve as a starting point for an up-to-date debate on the integration of fragmented social sciences.

Summarizing the central issues of the argument at the beginning, a few points should be acknowledged: From today's point of view, Schumpeter

D. Bögenhold, *Neglected Links in Economics and Society*,
https://doi.org/10.1007/978-3-030-79193-3_10

is a truly interdisciplinary theorist. He worked continuously in a perspective which must be characterized as academic cross-fertilization. Therefore, posthumously, Schumpeter's different articles were sorted into books as *Collected Papers in Sociology* (Schumpeter, 1953), *Political Speeches* (Schumpeter, 1992), *Essays in Socioeconomics* (Schumpeter, 1987), *Papers on Economic Policies* (Schumpeter, 1985), *Essays on Daily Politics* (Schumpeter, 1993), *Papers on Economic Theory* (Schumpeter, 1952) and articles on the history of economic thought (Schumpeter, 1954b). Many contemporaries know Schumpeter's ideas as they were developed in *Theory of Economic Development* (Schumpeter, 1963), perhaps also his book on *Business Cycles* (Schumpeter, 1939), and, of course, his arguments in *Capitalism, Socialism, and Democracy* (1942),[1] but less well known is his systematization of academic development and his methodological roadmap.

The chapter focuses on the principles of Schumpeter's academic thought, which led him to create diverse works and which were reflected systematically in some of his writings, where Schumpeter emerged as a theorist of science. Aside from working on specific substantial topics, throughout his life Schumpeter dealt with methodological issues. He wrote articles on rationality (Schumpeter, 1991), on "Positivism in Economics" (Schumpeter, 1914a), on "Mathematical Methods in Economic Theorizing" (Schumpeter, 1906), "How to Study Social Sciences" (Schumpeter, 1915), "Gustav Schmoller und die Probleme von heute" (Schumpeter, 1926), and many more articles. Referring to books, his 1908 book *Das Wesen und der Hauptinhalt der theoretischen Nationalökonomie* (Schumpeter, 1908) started with methodological reflections, with chapters entitled "methodological individualism," and his book *Epochen der Dogmen- und Methodengeschichte* (Schumpeter, 1914b, published in *English as Economic Doctrines and Method* in 1954) was certainly a major contribution to methodology in economics. Despite these many different works, Schumpeter's *History of Economic Analysis* (Schumpeter, 1954a) must be viewed as the one study among his diverse works which depicts his latest statement concerning the division of social sciences and the role of economics in relation to sociology, history, and other academic branches.

The substantial preface of the *History of Economic Analysis* (1954a) reads as a manual on how to refer to different academic branches and how to integrate them into a coherent universal social science. This is far removed from being an excessively rigid and emotionally detached narrow economic science of modern representation. There is evidence here that Schumpeter must be regarded as someone who is solidly a well-studied historian of mainstream economics. This leads him to argue offensively for an institutional approach to integrating economics with different social sciences and avoiding the formulation of divisional order or ranking.

Schumpeter's *History of Economic Analysis* (1954a) has been extensively printed, translated, and reprinted in several editions. The preface especially appears to be rather neglected in Schumpeterian discourse. His argumentation requires so much more attention because it has to be read as a fine synthesis of arguments developed in the first battle of methods between Carl Menger and Gustav Schmoller and the second battle of methods between Schmoller, Max Weber, and others. Over a time span of fifty years or more between the "old" classic controversies and *History of Economic Analysis*, we see that many questions have emerged in a more elegant and rigorous way. Schumpeter is mostly regarded as a pioneer of evolutionary economics, and author of the seminal books *Theory of Economic Development* (Schumpeter, 1963 [1912]) and especially *Capitalism, Socialism and Democracy* (Schumpeter, 1942), the latter containing the famous formulation of "creative destruction" (see Bögenhold, 2007). However, one may see Schumpeter mostly as a well-reasoned and guided theorist, who proved to be aware of all strands of debate in the battle of methods and beyond, and who synthesized and offered his own elaborate positions which still have much to offer. Furthermore, our argumentation shows that Schumpeter practiced an offensive dialogue with neighbouring disciplines like sociology, history, political economy, and psychology. Recent discussion on the need for transdisciplinary thought can learn a lot from Schumpeter.

History of Science: How Ideas Evolve

Schumpeter argues not only in favour of economic history as rendering a service to economic theory, but also in favour of "a sort of generalized or typified or stylized economic history" (Schumpeter, 1954a, p. 20) which includes institutions like private property, free contracting, or government regulation.

According to Schumpeter, there are four main reasons to study history. First of all, it has pedagogical advantages. He argues that for students it is very difficult to approach a field without knowing how it relates to the specific historical time. For thorough understanding, a historical background is required. One could affirm that methods presently in use already embody what has been done in the past, and what is not a part thereof is no longer important and not worth considering. However, present methods and results are meaningful only with reference to historical background. "Scientific analysis is not simply a logically consistent process that starts with some primitive notions and then adds to the stock in a straight-line fashion. It is not simply progressive discovery of an objective reality" (Schumpeter, 1954a, p. 4).

The second reason is that pertaining to the reading of "old" theories, one may discover other interpretations or new ideas; Schumpeter writes that "our minds are apt to derive new inspirations from the study of the history of science" (Schumpeter, 1954a, pp. 4–5). In his discussion Schumpeter adds an example: The productivity of this experience may be illustrated by the fact that the fundamental ideas that eventually developed into the theory of special relativity occurred first in a book on the history of mechanics (Schumpeter, 1954a, p. 5).

The third cause is that history can give us insights into the manner in which the human mind works. Particularly in the history of science, various types of logic are used. Scientific performances are self-revelatory by nature; that is, they reveal the mental processes that have taken place in order to arrive at a certain law or theory. "Scientific habits or rules of procedure are not merely to be judged by logical standards that exist independently of them; they contribute something to, and react back upon, the logical standards themselves" (Schumpeter, 1954a, p. 5). Finally, the fourth point deals with economics in particular, which is described as a unique historical process. Fundamentally this process does not differ from analogous processes in other fields of knowledge but "much more than in, say, physics is it true in economics that modern problems, methods, and results cannot be fully understood without some knowledge of how economists have come to reason as they do. In addition, much more than in physics have results been lost on the way or remained in abeyance for centuries" (Schumpeter, 1954a, p. 6).

Given these insightful instructions by Schumpeter as a plea for increased, or at least continuous, attempts to invest in history of economics, one also has to consider Schumpeter's writings as good exemplification of what the history of economic writings can highlight. Brilliant ideas are often hidden and neglected for long periods of time. If one wants to analyse a painting hanging on a wall, one must take a few steps back to see the painting as a whole in order to get a sense of the full composition. The same applies to dealing with science and economics specifically. History of economic thought is a neglected academic area of necessary contextualizing of knowledge which provides a more sufficient working compass.

If students embark upon a new academic discipline such as medicine, biology, or economics, they usually want to learn what is the current state of thought. The majority of people do not want to learn about the discussion that was on the agenda fifty or one hundred years ago, but instead about what the predominant portraits of recent debate are. What is uncontested terrain, what are the competing theories, and where can academic profit for future engagement be found? The difficulty is that academic progress and its change must be conceptualized as a series or process of shortcomings which, conversely, appear as a never-ending story of failures or mistakes, to express it starkly. Evolutionary economists take it as their credo to look at the inner dynamics of change to arrive at an understanding of principles, analogous to how theoretical economists should treat their subject. One has to gain a careful understanding of the history of one's own discipline to see the bolder and fainter lines, which have led to the recent discussion and the current state of the art. In this light, recent debate provides colour. Our current knowledge emerges in a historically transcendent way as a snapshot in a series of academic achievements, be they failures or innovations. Economic theory evolves in specific contexts of social life and societal organization.

The Academic Division of Sciences: Towards the Idea of an Orchestra

The substantial preface of *History of Economic Analysis* discusses, in addition, "techniques of economic analysis" in which Joseph A. Schumpeter included economic sociology, economic history, psychology, political economy, statistics, and others. Furthermore, Schumpeter explores the relationship between "pure" economics and sociology, psychology, philosophy, and logic in detail, providing a systematic discussion of the academic landscape and division. In this discussion he proves to be an intellectual master of multidisciplinary reflection by investigating the sociology of economics. His systematic methodological reflections in *History of Economic Analysis* (1954a) provide a key to understanding what Schumpeter achieved throughout his academic life, namely the combining of new elements of different academic strands. Academically, Schumpeter was highly innovative all his life and provided his own methodological script on how to perform social and economic analysis.

Schumpeter discussed several independent scientific disciplines from today's stand point such as economic history, statistics, "theory," economic sociology, political economy, and "applied fields" such as "techniques of economic analysis." In a subsequent chapter, he turned his attention to specific discussion topics such as the specific relationships between economics and sociology and between logic and psychology. Here, the reasoning is dense and much deeper than is usually assumed when coming across the conventional image of Schumpeter as a theorist of entrepreneurship. Instead, he engages in a very precise sociology of science in which diverse matching processes between individual scientific areas and traditions of thought are investigated.

In depicting the fields of economic history, statistics, "theory," economic sociology, and political economy, and applied fields as "techniques of economic analysis," a clear conceptual ranking in terms of order is missing. Schumpeter understands each of them instrumentally and he regards the different elements taken together as a box of tools. Obviously, economics is a synonym for "economic analysis," which is to be utilized through different academic configurations provided by the toolbox. The interplay of different branches comes up like an orchestra where different agents have different functions but even the smallest voices contribute to the success of the common enterprise.

In contrast to the history of science as a history of changing intellectual ideas, Schumpeter refers to economic history—nomen est omen—as a history of economic and social changes. His plea for an integration of economic history in the orchestra of economic analysis reads as follows: "Nobody can hope to understand economic phenomena of any, including the present, epoch without an adequate command of historical facts and an adequate amount of historical sense, or of what may be described as historical experience. … The historical report cannot be purely economic but must inevitably reflect also 'institutional' facts that are not purely economic: therefore it affords the best method for understanding how economic and non-economic facts are related to one another and how various social sciences should be related to one another" (Schumpeter, 1954a, pp. 12–13). According to Schumpeter, most of the ongoing errors in economic analysis are due to a lack of historical competencies, which leads him to acknowledge also the fields of anthropology and ethnology: "History must of course be understood to include fields that have acquired different names as a consequence of specialization, such as pre-historic reports and ethnology (anthropology)" (Schumpeter, 1954a, p. 13).

With respect to statistics, Schumpeter explains that we should recognize that statistical methods are part of the tools of economic analysis because statistical figures or series of figures are of vital importance for economics (Schumpeter, 1954a, pp. 13–14). Consequently, "an adequate command of modern statistical methods is a necessary (but not a sufficient) condition for preventing the modern economist from producing nonsense" (Schumpeter, 1954a, p. 14).

When discussing "theory," Schumpeter again does what could also be found in his earlier writings (e.g. Schumpeter, 1926). He writes the word "theory" with quotation marks. Schumpeter's intention was to explain that we have no precise commonly shared understanding of what we mean when we talk about theory. In this respect, Schumpeter proves to be a methodologist with profound knowledge of the philosophy of science. His set of questions includes: When does theory achieve the distinction of being "pure theory?" Why do we need studies in the history of economic thought? What about the intersections between theory, statistics, and economic history? Where are the boundaries and areas of overlap among economics, philosophy, psychology, political economy, and economic sociology? Which are the general principles of scientific processes?

Schumpeter explains that "theory" has many meanings and it should not simply be interpreted as a semantic counterpart to practice. Schumpeter (1954a, pp. 14–20) explains that three of these meanings are of special relevance: First, theory is an explanation of causal connections. Even if more of those causalities exist, one may summarize them taken together as "theory". Second, "theory" is also a methodology at the level of paradigms, approaches, and procedures which must be discussed academically. Here, we do not expect to find empirical results but methods to achieve scientific knowledge. Third, "theory" is reserved to a semantic of general economics (see already Schumpeter, 1926, p. 365 ff.). Viewing this discussion, a reader feels that many items remain provokingly up-to-date and finally unsolved. In the end, Schumpeter tries to find bridges between inductive and deductive procedures in order to arrive at a theory which should provide an advanced holistic perspective. Already the fact that theory is written with quotation marks indicates Schumpeter's strength in perceiving and acknowledging the complexity of the matter. What is currently a topic in recent science theory was already identified as problematic in Schumpeter's writings, namely that one should not take for granted the wording of theory since different types of theory and correspondingly different semantics coexist (Bunge, 1996). The question of when an academic statement receives the status of being a theory still remains on the agenda.

It is not only economic history that renders a service to economic theory, as Schumpeter argues, but also economic sociology: "Economic analysis deals with the questions of how people behave at any time and what the economic effects are they produce by so behaving; economic sociology deals with the question how they came to behave as they do. If we define economic behavior widely enough so that it includes not only actions and motives and propensities but also the social institutions that are relevant to economic behavior such as government, property inheritance, contract, and so on, that phrase really tells us all we need" (Schumpeter, 1954a, p. 21). There are several statements where Schumpeter speaks with great appreciation about economic sociology and claims that economics has to seek or to keep closer contact with sociology because "we cannot afford [...] to neglect the developments of sociology" and especially not the "fundamental field of economic sociology in which neither economists nor sociologists can get very far without treading on one another's toes" (Schumpeter, 1954a, pp. 25–26).

Concluding the argument, we see Schumpeter as an author clearly addressing the universe of social sciences in order to put into context elements of academic discussion which are conventionally separated from each other. Using more recent wording, Schumpeter shows that not only does empirical data matter and in this understanding that history matters, but that sociology also matters. Of course, the angle of Schumpeter's thought is the question of an appropriate economic analysis from which he inspects and evaluates the potential of neighboring fields of research. Schumpeter states that the academic field of political economy is widely covered by his explanation of the potential of economic sociology. Insofar as sociology deals with social, political, and economic institutions, there is not much to add about what political economy can do further. A fourth field of economic analysis techniques encompasses the applied fields of modern business administration disciplines and of specialized fields of economics, such as financial or agricultural economics.

Schumpeter is also concerned with logic, philosophy, and psychology, which are not summarized under techniques of economic analysis but which are discussed as a basic methodological understanding of his conceptual framework. He explains in the introduction to the relevant chapter that he uses nothing other than a philosophy of economics (Schumpeter, 1954a, p. 25) as a basic theoretical scientific reflection.

The most significant statement about economic psychology is contained in the following words: "Economics like other social sciences deals with human behavior. Psychology is really the basis from which any social science must start and in terms of which all fundamental explanation must run" (Schumpeter, 1954a, p. 27). Of course, Schumpeter is impressed by the arguments of Keynes and Keynesianism of his time, which refers to animal spirits and other behavioural foundations. Also, this type of argument matches an idea which he presented in a different theoretical discussion on methodological individualism much earlier (Schumpeter, 1908).

Most of our pieces of evidence highlighting Schumpeter's approach are taken from the preface of *History of Economic Analysis* (Schumpeter, 1954a), which is a 1200-page book about the development of economics starting with Aristotle, which Schumpeter left incomplete. The book was published four years after Schumpeter passed away. His theory of science with a focus on economics in relation to other academic areas, often historically new and emerging ones, must be viewed as a sociology of scientific ideas. Schumpeter explained in his own words: "From time to time, we shall look up from our work in order to view a piece of intellectual scenery. Slightly less perfunctorily, we shall, for every one of our periods, register some contemporaneous developments in other sciences ... that were relevant or might, for one reason or another, be expected to have been relevant to the development of our own" (Schumpeter, 1954a, p. 25).

How Schumpeter Practiced His Own Economic Analysis

The book *History of Economic Analysis* (1954a) was the last of Schumpeter's writings. The preface provides a manual on how to interpret economics and in this sense it is a kind of meta-economics, in other words a sociology of economics. However, all his life Schumpeter followed his manual without ever having declared it systematically. Only in his preface to *History of Economic Analysis* do we find this systematic kind of reasoning. However, in his early book *Theory of Economic Development* (Schumpeter, 1963, initially in German 1912),[2] Schumpeter practiced a kind of interdisciplinary investigation when he referred to behavioural foundations of the entrepreneur. "We shall finally try to round off our picture of the entrepreneur in the same manner in which we always, in science as well as in practical life, try to understand human behavior, viz. by analyzing the characteristic motives of his conduct" (Schumpeter, 1963, p. 90).

When Schumpeter asks about the meaning of economic action, he discusses models of rationality. All his theorizing is against practices of utilitarianism and against basic assumptions of economic theorizing. In other words, Schumpeter systematizes arguments in favour of an economics that is oriented at "real life" as opposed to axiomatic assumptions of the nature of human beings. Schumpeter discusses different motives behind entrepreneurial activities (Bögenhold, 2003):

1. "First of all, there is the dream and the will to found a private kingdom, usually, though not necessarily, also a dynasty. The modern world really does not know any such positions, but what may be attained by industrial or commercial success is still the nearest approach to medieval lordship possible to modern man. Its fascination is especially strong for people who have no other chance of achieving social distinction."
2. "Then there is the will to conquer: the impulse to fight, to prove oneself superior to others, to succeed for the sake, not for the fruits of success, but of success itself. From this aspect, economic action becomes akin to sport—there are financial races, or rather boxing-matches."
3. "Finally, there is the joy of creating, of getting things done, or simply of exercising one's energy and ingenuity. ... Our type seeks out difficulties, changes in order to change, delights in ventures. This group of motives is the most distinctly anti-hedonist of the three" (Schumpeter, 1963, pp. 93–94).

Schumpeter provides very important elements for a psychology of entrepreneurial activity as well as for the need to invest in research on economic-related behaviour. He clearly insists that motives, such as the need for achievement and success, can also be found within regular professions and that the financial motive is always present but never dominant. Taken together, Schumpeter specifies seemingly non-rational motives as driving forces for entrepreneurism. Economic life and related motives to participate and to compete can be compared to sports: achieving with the goal of success and receiving rewards in terms of recognition and prestige. In some way, Schumpeter portrays an eroticism of business life which serves as the driving force of champions.

Successful people have comparatively high incomes but that is very often an appreciated secondary effect and not the primary or only source of motivation.

Conclusion and Outlook

In recent decades, modern economics has yielded an increasing number of voices referring to a need to deal with human actors and their concrete motivation as driving forces of economic activity. Herbert Simon (1982) coined the (famous) term of "bounded rationality." Much later, Douglass G. North added that economics treats the issue of human motivation like a black box (North, 1990, p. 17). In the meantime, references to psychology have been deployed increasingly. Kahneman (2012) was recognized for his pioneering work in economic psychology. In his function as the outgoing president of the American Economic Association, Akerlof (2007) recently issued a plea to turn academic energy towards issues of motivation and cognitive structures. In their study, *Animal Spirits* (2009) Akerlof and Shiller posited that the functioning of the whole capitalist system is heavily based upon socio-psychological foundations. Simon, North, Kahneman, Akerlof and some further economists in the same line are Nobel laureates and practice methodologically what Schumpeter (1954a) had already suggested earlier. Sociology increasingly claims new ground and indicates the social embeddedness of institutions and economic behaviour (Granovetter, 1985; Mikl-Horke, 2008; Bögenhold, 2008; Haller, 2014), which follows a script already provided by Schumpeter. His position is quite close to an institutionalist perspective, which tries to embed historical, regional and, in that sense, cultural specifics in order to gain a clear sense of empirical material which differs internationally and historically. Reading Schumpeter is an appropriate tool for finding a way back and for shedding light on contemporary questions. Obviously, many open questions remain. One of the issues to be discussed further is the positioning of Schumpeter within the so-called Austrian economics. Is Schumpeter a major actor of the Austrian school, if it exists as a unique body? Is he just a foot soldier, or does he not belong to the Austrian school at all? The answer is certainly indefinite and vague, depending on how Austrian economics is defined. Another question is how the landscape of the academic division and the economic toolbox might be drawn from the viewpoint of members of different disciplines, e.g. the view of a sociologist, an economist, a historian or a psychologist. Do those academic professionals have separate tool boxes? Sixty years after Schumpeter's preface to the *History of Economic Analysis* (1954a), much of the discussion is still very relevant and Schumpeter proves to be a very important representative of a former generation of universal social scientists.

Notes

1. Ongoing publications of books on Schumpeter exist but most of them concentrate on Schumpeter as a theorist of innovation and entrepreneurship, see, for example, Kurz and Sturn (2012), Becker et al. (2011), Andersen (2009), McCraw (2007), Heertje (2006), Shionoya (1997), Kurz (2005), Reisman (2004), Backhaus (2003), Metcalfe (1998), Moss (1996) and Swedberg (1991).
2. Specialists in the history of economic thought are still debating whether the first publication date was 1911 or 1912; the fact is that it was printed in 1911 but was declared as being published in 1912. Much more important is the fact that the first edition is widely unknown and until recently only very few copies were available in European libraries (a new edition was published as Schumpeter, 2006). Current scholars reading the *Theory of Economic Development* in German refer to a reprint of the second edition, while English readers refer to a reprint of the revised English translation first published in 1934. The English version is not identical to the second German edition (1926), while the German first edition differs substantially from the German second edition. For example, the first German edition had a final seventh chapter (title: "The Holistic View on the Economy") which is largely based on sociological thought, where Schumpeter also refers very much to the issue of demographic patterns.

References

Akerlof, G. A. (2007). The Missing Motivation in Macroeconomics. *The American Economic Review, 97*(1), 5–36.

Akerlof, G. A., & Shiller, R. J. (2009). *Animal Spirits. How Human Psychology Drives the Economy, and Why It Matters for Global Capitalism*. Princeton University Press.

Andersen, E. S. (2009). *Schumpeter's Evolutionary Economics: A Theoretical, Historical and Statistical Analysis of the Engine of Capitalism*. Anthem.

Backhaus, J. G. (Ed.). (2003). *Joseph Alois Schumpeter. Entrepreneurship, Style and Vision*. Springer.

Becker, M. C., Knudsen, T., & Swedberg, R. (2011). *The Entrepreneur. Classical Texts by Joseph Schumpeter*. Stanford University Press.

Bögenhold, D. (2003). Wirtschaftliches Handeln als Sport? Zur Rationalität des Unternehmerbildes bei Joseph A. Schumpeter. In K. Walterscheid (Ed.), *Entrepreneurship in Forschung und Lehre. Festschrift für Klaus Anderseck* (pp. 3–18). Peter Lang Publishers.

Bögenhold, D. (2007). Creative Destruction. In R. E. Weir (Ed.), *Class in America. An Encyclopedia* (Vol. 1, pp. 175–176). Greenwood.

Bögenhold, D. (2008). Economics, Sociology, History: Notes on Their Loss of Unity, Their Need for Re-integration and the Current Relevance of the Controversy between Carl Menger and Gustav Schmoller. *Forum for Social Economics, 37*(2), 85–101.

Bunge, M. (1996). *Finding Philosophy in Social Science*. Yale University Press.

Granovetter, M. (1985). Economic Action and Social Structure: The Problem of Embeddedness. *American Journal of Sociology, 91*(3), 481–510.

Haller, M. (2014). Die Ökonomie—Natur- oder Sozialwissenschaft? Wissenschaftstheoretische und wissenssoziologische Überlegungen zu einer alten Kontroverse. In D. Bögenhold (Ed.), *Soziologie des Wirtschaftlichen. Alte und neue Fragen* (pp. 31–66). VS-Publishers.

Heertje, A. (2006). *Schumpeter on the Economics of Innovation and the Development of Capitalism*. Edward Elgar.

Kahneman, D. (2012). *Thinking, Fast and Slow*. Penguin.

Kurz, H. D. (2005). *Joseph Alois Schumpeter—Ein Sozialökonom zwischen Marx und Walras*. Metropolis.

Kurz, H. D., & Sturn, R. (2012). *Schumpeter für jedermann*. Frankfurter Allgemeine Publishers.

McCraw, T. K. (2007). *Prophet of Innovation: Joseph Schumpeter and Creative Destruction*. Harvard University Press.

Metcalfe, J. S. (1998). *Evolutionary Economics and Creative Destruction*. Routledge.

Mikl-Horke, G. (2008). *Sozialwissenschaftliche Perspektiven der Wirtschaft*. Oldenbourg.

Moss, L. S. (1996). *Joseph A. Schumpeter. Historian of Economics*. Routledge.

North, D. C. (1990). *Institutions, Institutional Change and Economic Performance*. CUP.

Reisman, D. (2004). *Schumpeter's Market. Enterprise and Evolution*. Edward Elgar.

Schumpeter, J. A. (1906). Über die mathematische Methode der theoretischen Ökonomie. *Zeitschrift für Volkswirtschaft, Sozialpolitik und Verwaltung, 15*, 30–49.

Schumpeter, J. A. (1914a). Die positive Methode in der Nationalökonomie. *Deutsche Literaturzeitung, 35*, 2101–2108.

Schumpeter, J. A. (1914b). [Engl. transl. 1954]. Epochen der Dogmen- und Methodengeschichte. In K. Bücher, J. A. Schumpeter and F. v. Wieser (Eds.),

Grundriß der Sozialökonomik, Vol. 1, Grundlagen der Wirtschaft (pp. 19–124). J.C.B. Mohr.
Schumpeter, J. A. (1915). Wie studiert man Sozialwissenschaft?. *Schriften des Sozialwissenschaftlichen Vereins in Czernowitz* (pp. 5–44).
Schumpeter, J. A. (1926). Gustav von Schmoller und die Probleme von heute. *Schmollers Jahrbuch für Gesetzgebung, Verwaltung und Volkswirtschaft, 50*, 337–388.
Schumpeter, J. A. (1939). *Business Cycles: A Theoretical, Historical and Statistical Analysis of the Capitalist Process.* 2 Vols. McGraw Hill.
Schumpeter, J. A. (1942). *Capitalism, Socialism, and Democracy.* Harper.
Schumpeter, J. A. (1952). *Aufsätze zur ökonomischen Theorie.* J. C. B. Mohr.
Schumpeter, J. A. (1953). *Aufsätze zur Soziologie.* J. C. B. Mohr.
Schumpeter, J. A. (1908). [Engl. transl. 1954]. *Das Wesen und der Hauptinhalt der theoretischen Nationalökonomie.* Duncker & Humblot.
Schumpeter, J. A. (1954a). *History of Economic Analysis.* Oxford University Press.
Schumpeter, J. A. (1954b). *Dogmenhistorische und biographische Aufsätze.* J. C. B. Mohr.
Schumpeter, J. A. (1963) [German orig. 1912]. *The Theory of Economic Development. An Inquiry into Profits, Capital, Credit, Interest, and the Business Cycle.* Oxford University Press.
Schumpeter, J. A. (1985). Aufsätze zur Wirtschaftspolitik. (W. F. Stolper & C. Seidl, Ed.). Tübingen: J. C. B. Mohr.
Schumpeter, J. A. (1987). *Beiträge zur Sozialökonomik.* Böhlau.
Schumpeter, J. A. (1991). The Meaning of Rationality in the Social Sciences. In R. Swedberg (Ed.), *Joseph A. Schumpeter. The Economics and Sociology of Capitalism* (pp. 316–338). Princeton.
Schumpeter, J. A. (1992). Politische Reden. (C. Seidl & W. F. Stolper, Eds.). Tübingen: J. C. B. Mohr.
Schumpeter, J. A. (1993). Ökonomie und Psychologie des Unternehmers [1929]. In C. Seidl & W. F. Stolper (Eds.), *Aufsätze zur Tagespolitik: Ökonomie und Psychologie des Unternehmers.* J.C.B. Mohr.
Schumpeter, J. A. (2006). *Theorie der wirtschaftlichen Entwicklung. Reprint of the First Edition From 1912.* Duncker and Humblot.
Shionoya, Y. (1997). *Schumpeter and the Idea of Social Science: A Metatheoretical Study.* Cambridge University Press.
Simon, H. A. (1982). *Models of Bounded Rationality.* MIT.
Spiethoff, A. (1949). Joseph Schumpeter in Memoriam. *Kyklos, 3*(4), 289–293.
Swedberg, R. (Ed.). (1991). *Joseph A. Schumpeter. The Economics and Sociology of Capitalism.* Princeton University Press.
Uhlig, H. (2012). Economics and Reality. *Journal of Macroeconomics, 34*(1), 29–41.

CHAPTER 11

Economics, Sociology, History: Notes on Their Loss of Unity, Their Need for Re-Integration, and the Current Relevance of the Controversy between Carl Menger and Gustav Schmoller

Introduction

We are experiencing a situation of increasing criticism on the state in which economics is being represented nowadays. One of the remarks is that economics has become too formalized and too abstract and that the state of the discipline has become increasingly unable to express many phenomena of "real life" in terms of concrete socioeconomic, cultural, regional, and historic specifica. In this sense, criticism has found a way to get cumulated in terms of "heterodox economics," "postautistic economics," socioeconomics or institutionalism which are new platforms to describe alternative approaches. The claim for fostering interdisciplinary research which we also find in recent times reflects the same diagnosis that our islands of shared knowledge have become too fragmented.

Bögenhold, Dieter. Economics, Sociology, History: Notes on Their Loss of Unity, Their Need for Re-Integration and the Current Relevance of the Controversy between Carl Menger and Gustav Schmoller, in: *Forum for Social Economics*, Vol. 37, No. 2, 2008, pp. 85–101.

D. Bögenhold, *Neglected Links in Economics and Society*,
https://doi.org/10.1007/978-3-030-79193-3_11

The development of academic thought during the twentieth century is marked by a rapid and continual process of accumulation of a vast quantity of scientific material. If we narrow down the field and consider merely economics and social sciences, a drastic accumulation of academic output is evident during the course of the twentieth century. The result is that economics and social sciences find themselves in a totally different position at the beginning of the twenty-first century than they occupied at the end of the nineteenth or beginning of the twentieth.

What is the background to this change? The increasing consolidation and delimitation of economics and the social sciences is of prime importance. Economic subjects have become separated from social sciences institutionally and have themselves been divided into national economics, public finance, and business studies in the process. Social sciences for their part have separated into autonomous subjects: history, sociology, political science, pedagogy, media studies, geography, and a few others.

Even at the beginning of the twentieth century, prominent academics held professorships and chairs in the fields of national economics, business studies, and social sciences. National economics existed without competition as a subject, since professorships for the newer subjects, such as sociology, that have now become standard, still did not exist. These academics concerned themselves with themes, which, from the modern standpoint, are the property of history, sociology, business studies, economics, legal, or administrative sciences.

The chapter wants to deal with the topic. The aim of discussion is to underline that some specific reasons exist which are ultimately connected to the historic course in which the scientific development has run during the last hundred years or so. Much of the essence of current criticism is a criticism of formalism in social sciences and of the missing interplay between economics, history, and sociology at least. A remarkable fact is that many contemporaries are not fully aware of the first battle of methods which was carried out by Carl Menger and Gustav Schmoller more than hundred years ago. This, still unsolved, first Methodenstreit contains some very principal arguments which provides a brilliant background to understand up-to-date debates (Richter, 2001a). Although the debate between Menger and Schmoller was rather sketchy and polemic, the confrontation between inductive and deductive ways to generate scientific statements remains to be a classic piece. The proposed chapter tries to embed recent discussion on ontology and the issue of realism versus formalism in the scenario of the history of economic thought since the first battle of methods in order to find out how much of recent thought reflects the situation of a hundred years ago.

Professionalization, Specialization, and Contradictory Developments

The development of scientific disciplines goes hand in hand with a host of other changes. The structure of professions has changed and social and economic structures have developed many new traits. Furthermore, new times bring with them new questions and new discussions. To a great extent the new contours of intellectual debate reflect the process of historical change.

The essentially positive process by which subjects have gained recognition also has its down side. The price was an increasingly specialized knowledge, which, for systematic reasons, lost sight of neighbouring disciplines. Bridges between the islands of knowledge were ever more seldom sought or found so that forms of knowledge disciplines and intra- and interdisciplinarity fell ever more into the background. The paradoxical effect is that the apparently relentless growth of both economics and sociology, which continues to the present day, is by no means combined with a process of academic consolidation. On the contrary, subjects lose out in numerous aspects, since they are scarcely able to communicate with one another any longer. The subjects appear to have become fragmented theoretically, methodically, and practically.

The principal developments in the rise of sociology and the demarcation of different branches of economics have mainly taken place since the Second World War. Today, the subjects are marked by their impressive plurality in terms of the diversity of topics and methods. As a result, these subjects themselves become differentiated further to the extent that it is ever more difficult to conceptualize them as closed, single-type disciplines.

There was clearly no real correlation between the delineation of the system of disciplines and the corresponding increase in their recognition. Auguste Comte was probably the primary influence on the conception of sociology. In his Cours de Philosophie Positive (1830–1842) Comte formulated the necessity and unavoidability of academic specialization and differentiation. At the same time he recognized the danger of isolation and insularity of knowledge.

Thus he wrote, “It is evidently this division of various types of research amongst various groups of scholars that we have to thank for level of development that knowledge has reached in our time.” However, this division means that it is no longer possible for a modern scholar to engage himself with all disciplines at once—a kind of engagement that was easy and quite normal in the past (Comte, 1907, p. 33). Comte argued that the expansion of the knowledge base goes hand in hand with increasing differentiation and division of labour. The onset of this process, so the argument continued, also had a converse effect. “Even recognising the great results that have been achieved because of this division of labour, and accepting that this is now the true foundation of the general organisation of the academic world, it is still impossible, on the other hand, not to be adversely affected by this current division of labour for the reason of over-specialisation of ideas, which each person pursues with great exclusivity We must take care that human intellect does not finally lose its way in a host of details” (Comte, 1907, p. 33).

Comte’s analysis, formulated in the 1830s, has proved to be extremely accurate. In particular, since the beginning of the new millennium, the process of increasing specialization within disciplines has reached a new level. Economics and social sciences have disintegrated into various small and ever new academic territories, which themselves have divided further. In addition, literature and science have increasingly become separated from one another. Boundaries began to develop between them during the process of self-definition (Lepenies, 1988). This development led Max Weber, who like most of the classic scholars known today, was an interdisciplinary generalist, to conclude that a high academic reputation can best be achieved by withdrawing to extremely specialized subject matter. “In our time, the internal situation, in contrast to the organisation of science as a vocation, is first of all conditioned by the fact that science has entered a phase of specialisation previously unknown and that this will forever remain the case. Not only externally, but inwardly, matters stand at a point where the individual can acquire the sure consciousness of achieving something truly perfect in the field of science only in case he is a strict specialist” (Max Weber, originally 1919, here: 1988, p. 588, translation from Gerth, Wright Mills and Turner (eds.) 1991, p. 134).

With this description of the state of sociology in mind, one is compelled to ask whether it is really possible to speak universally about sociology as a single discipline in the present day. Although the classic European sociologists of the late nineteenth and early twentieth centuries, from

Marx via Durkheim, Simmel, Schmoller and Max Weber up to Werner Sombart approached the subject from an interdisciplinary and holistic perspective, research areas became ever narrower and depth of knowledge increased. With this, the system of knowledge proved to be a divisible social system with its own rules. An independent sociology (of sociology) had to distance itself from this and had to systematize the problems arising from specialization in order to create a valid academic discipline.

With his call for "organised scepticism," Robert K. Merton, an important post-war American socialist, had in mind exactly such a necessity of self-reflection (Merton, 1938). Norbert Elias later formalized this when he described social scientists as chasers of myths (Elias, 1981), who attempt to replace non-provable sequences of related occurrences, myths, and hypotheses with observation of facts. They use models of relationships that can be examined, proved, and corrected by factual observation (Elias, 1981, p. 53, 54). In a certain sense this is directed at that which from another perspective would be formulated in terms of "sociological enlightenment." Sociology could be exposed as the science of the second and third observation in that it formulates relationships that are invisible to others. Sceptics should be self-reflexive, however, and take into consideration the system of organized science.

The subject divisions that emerged during the course of the process of differentiation thus led to the destruction of that which was known as national economics, and which created the contextual unity of the social and economic sciences. At the same time, more and more coexistent, separately communicating "universes of discourse" developed, which are themselves bound within their own systems of regulation.

Reciprocal Export and Import of Ideas between Europe and North America

The question is whether the scientific progress that can doubtless be observed in the development outlined above had the same results internationally, or whether there are differences between countries and subjects. The path towards the establishment of individual subjects in different countries depends on a wide range of factors. Of particular importance are the peculiarities of national educational systems and their historicopolitical context. With regard to the development of American and German sociology, it is clear that what is regarded today as classic sociology was widely considered to be the preserve of economics at the turn of the twentieth century.

Thorstein Veblen is a significant representative of early American sociology, although he has gone down in history as an important figure in the teaching of economic theory. His work was principally directed against the tendency in economic research at the time to create abstract and ahistorical models. As a social economist, Veblen was not always considered to be a mainstream economist during his own time, though today he has found a place within the history of "great economists." In his history of economics in America, for example, Joseph Dorfman even wrote that Veblen was "halfway out of society" (Dorfman, 1949, Vol. 3, p. 438).

Veblen's argumentation is directed equally against the assumptions of classic nationalist school and the position of the Marshall School. At the same time, in particular with his work "Theory of the Leisure Class" (1899), Veblen is regarded as a point of reference in sociology to the present day. According to Paul DiMaggio, for example, Veblen is of central importance alongside Bourdieu in modern-day equality and cultural studies. "The starting point of any discussion of life-styles and consumption patterns must be the work of Thorstein Veblen and Pierre Bourdieu" (DiMaggio, 1994, p. 458).

Veblen and authors immediately after him such as Clark, Mitchell, and others followed a programme, which today would be termed early institutionalism. In the present climate of globalized communication, the reception of academic writings is scarcely restricted to national boundaries or continents. It is commonly assumed, however, that much greater barriers to such reception and communication existed at the end of the nineteenth century. It is therefore particularly interesting to observe today how strong the connections were between the classic sociologists in Europe and the USA as early as the turn of the previous century. Max Weber quoted Veblen many times in his "Protestant Ethics" (Protestantische Ethik, 1904). Veblen himself wrote a series of letters in which he described the parallels between the basis of his own research and Schmoller's. For a time Veblen and Werner Sombart were in regular correspondence and reviewed one another's books. In this way, that which was understood as the "new historical school" in Germany around the turn of the last century found a breeding ground in North America and vice versa (Dorfman, 1955).

In other words, there was already a lively discussion between German and American scholars at the beginning of the twentieth century. In Germany, Frederick Winslow Taylor's methods of so-called scholarly book-keeping and all developments connected with the introduction of the conveyer belt in industry were enthusiastically observed and commented upon. Werner Sombart undertook an invitation tour of the USA. He reworked the impressions gathered during this trip systematically in a book entitled *Why is there no socialism in the USA?* (*Warum gibt es in den USA keinen Sozialismus?*, 1906). Sombart's work appeared in translation in America remarkably quickly (Sombart, 1915).[1]

The current of intellectual ideas was stronger from Germany towards North America than in the other direction. Talcott Parsons, for example, who has since been considered the founder of modern American sociology, went to Germany to study social sciences and economics. Particularly during his doctoral studies at Heidelberg University in 1925–1926 under the supervision of the popular national economist of the day Edgar Salin, Parsons developed a differentiated view of the state of German discussions at the time. Thus he became familiar with the German Historical School, finally completing his studies with research on the subject of economic styles in the works of Max Weber and Werner Sombart. Extracts from this work were published in the *Journal of Political Economy* (Vol. 36, see Parsons, 1928).

Parsons' experience was much the same as many of his contemporaries who are today regarded as sociologists. He too—at least at first—belonged to the subject area of economics. When Parsons returned to the USA from Germany he taught within the Faculty of Economics at Harvard. It was only in 1931 that he moved to the newly founded Faculty of Sociology. In his early years at Harvard, Parsons remained closely associated with the German position. He was responsible for the first English translation of Max Weber's *The Protestant Ethics and the Spirit of Capitalism*.[2] Appearing in 1930, this was the first of Weber's works to be published in English. Later Parsons translated several chapters from Max Weber's *Wirtschaft und Gesellschaft* (see Smelser & Swedberg, 1994, p. 15).

The reality, however, is very much more differentiated than reconstructive categorization has demonstrated. Leaving out a series of individual developments and portraying only the principal trends of the intellectual development of sociological discussion in and between the USA and European countries—Germany in particular—we must theoretically assume that early twentieth century was a time during which American sociology experienced much slower development and became differentiated. Furthermore, it was one in which sociology was characterized by the importation of German classics and their theoretical positions.

Since around the middle of the twentieth century, the pendulum has swung slowly but decisively in the opposite direction. American sociology became increasingly rich and innovative. German scholars had more often to look to North America for interesting themes and methods. Since the 1960s, they have become ever more aware of the sub-disciplines of North American sociology through German translations. With perhaps a little too much simplification, it can now more or less be claimed that, whilst at the beginning of the twentieth century American sociology students had to look towards Germany for the 'State of the Art' in the discipline, the relationship is now completely the opposite.

The emigration of a large number of highly qualified economists and sociologists escaping the holocaust was of particular importance. Numerous famous and lesser-known names were compelled to leave Germany, Austria, and other European countries during the 1930s. Many found their way to North America, often with an intermediate stay in another country, especially Great Britain (many examples with details are given in Hagemann (ed.) 1997 and Hagemann and Krohn (ed.) 1999). This export of ideas and research capacity naturally resulted in a flowering of American sociology, which had become markedly emancipated from Europe in the meantime. The same was also true for economics, for example, from the middle of the century "Austrian Economics" became livelier in the USA than in Austria.

Empiricism versus Theory

The question of the degree of abstraction, that is respective empirical closeness or distance, is to be addressed together with the degree of restriction of scientific theorems with empirical data. This circumstance can further be formulated around the question of the relationship between theory and empiricism in social studies and economics. The aim of theorizing is to explain and describe the connections between different variables of functions in society where classification difficulties arise when the number of variables is high and their sphere of reference is complicated. The clarity of the arguments has been expressed repeatedly, namely the questions of empiricism versus theory and the presentation of data versus generalization, and historical reconstruction versus formal theorizing.

This relatively schematic opposition has existed since the first conflict between Gustav Schmoller and Carl Menger, which is still unresolved (Schumpeter, 1926; Swedberg, 1991).[3] It can be reduced to the principal question of inductive versus deductive working strategies. Whilst Menger, who contemporaneously with the French Leon Walras designed marginal utility theory (Grenznutzentheorie), was a supporter of abstraction and modelling (see Menger, 1883, critically here Veblen, 1909), Schmoller's belief (Schmoller, 1883) was that empirical research must be carried out first and that economic relationships can only be understood with a knowledge of the historical realities of economies (on the historicist school see Schmölders, 1984).

The confrontation between Schmoller and Menger and their differences in terms of content and polemic characterized the first conflict in the social and economic sciences. It is interesting that there was a trace of a principle of argumentation in this conflict, the actuality of which, in my opinion, persists and remains undecided today. Casually formulated, it can be said that we are dealing with the question of the relationship between empiricism and theory. At what point do empirical statements achieve the status of theoretical formulations and—vice versa—to what extent must theoretical constructions be loaded with empirical references? In terms of academic theory, two principally different and competing paths can be discerned here, which can be reduced to an inductive and a deductive method. In introductory teaching materials in economics and social studies this confrontation is addressed in terms of real versus ideal knowledge (see Haller, 1999). In sociology it exists as empirically based research on the one hand, which does not make any greater claim than that it offers "theories of the middle range" (Merton, 1968). On the other hand, it takes the form of abstract theories, which at most make use of the empirical world to illustrate theories that have been constructed deductively (Albert 1964). The fact that the question is actually much older and was dealt with by English empiricists in the eighteenth century is overlooked. Schmoller, who among other things left behind a plurality of works on widely differing topics. He was a most influential and important person in academic life in Germany at the zenith of his life. After his death in 1917, however, Schmoller's influence seemed to have declined considerably.

From this point of view, a parallel can be observed between developments in economics and sociology. In economics there are econometric modellers, whose work is mathematically biased, and there are others, who, on the basis of theorems, collect and evaluate empirical data. Harald Winkel suggested in his *Einführung in die Wirtschaftswissenschaften* (1980) that these two methods cannot necessarily be reconciled, but that each at least has its own specific advantages for certain applications. A similar situation can be observed in sociology. There are scholars who are closer to empirical social research and scholars who are theoreticians and generally far from the empirical.

The connection between empirical research and theoretical formulation is a difficult one, since both often run parallel (Nowak, 1989; Esser, 1989; Mayer, 1989) and there is no adequate shared understanding as to what actually constitutes "theory." Jonathan Turner's critical comment about this was as follows: "Theoretical sociology is often not scientific theory but merely abstract statements that are ideological pronouncements, that cannot be tested, and that are loose frameworks for interpreting social events. Theory is now the label that encompasses many diverse kinds of intellectual activity, from the history of ideas through biographies of major thinkers, from philosophical discourses to analyses of the great works of masters, from critiques of modern society to lambasting the prospects for a science of society. Only a portion of theoretical activity in sociology is devoted to the production of scientific theory" (J. H. Turner, 1998, p. 4). Precisely because there is clearly no single best method it is also important to accept the plurality of approaches. "We suffer from the limitations of our cognitive capacity, and this cognitive overload reinforces the structurally based tendencies in the intellectual world to simplify one's own research speciality, theoretical camp, or political fraction, and to focus solely on the latest research data or technique" (Collins, 1989, p. 137).

In other words, in both social studies and economics there is no single best method of recognition and application. Rather, there is a plurality of competing approaches to and treatment of data with specific advantages and disadvantages. Whatever is quantitatively in the majority in any particular subject is always considered to be "mainstream." The formation of a discipline therefore does not always follow rational criteria. It does not always follow the rules of an ordered discourse, but has its own sphere of regulation, which is itself a subject of the theory of knowledge.

Empirically focused traditional socioeconomics can be connected with many prominent German authors up to the beginning of the Second World War, who continually found ways to overcome the barriers between history, nationalist economics, and sociology. There was no corresponding continuation of the subject during the second half of the twentieth century during the course of the process of specialization described earlier. The differences between North American and European sociology lie in their treatment of the historical foundation of the subject, and above all in the degree of engagement with the subjects of history and economics.

It can be argued on many grounds that the subject-content of sociology, history, business administration, and economics must be more strongly re-integrated. Their subjects are elements within a complex of layers both thematically and in terms of content. The concept of the embedding of social behaviour as we know it and of organizations as "social embeddedness" (Granovetter, 1985) is in a certain sense a label for empirical and theoretical starting-points in economic and organizational sociology. It also attempts to conceptualize dynamic and reciprocal processes of complex relationships in historical sociology, the theory of industrial organization, and management and industrial economics. The impetus implicit or even explicit in such topics is that modern economics can be constructively integrated into economic institutions and that on this basis the division of labour between sociology and economics can be defined more easily.

With regard to the consciousness in comparison with other disciplines, modern-day German sociology appears to be extremely defensive. This defensiveness is difficult to understand especially considering the strength of socioeconomics in German in the past (amongst others, Marx, Schmoller, Weber, Simmel, Tönnies, Schumpeter). It is also surprising taking into account the comparative strength of North American sociology, which lies precisely where connection and competition with other disciplines are sought.

Just three of many areas may be explained in which this is evident: (1) historical and comparative sociology, (2) socioeconomics and business sociology and (3) network research.

To me all three areas appear to be innovative and are leaders in direct competition with other disciplines. They have no definite counterpart in present-day German sociology. The main characteristic of these three thematic areas, in which North American sociology shows marked advantages over German sociology, is its firm anchorage in empirical reference, whilst German contributions more often depend on a philosophical foundation. It is thus very difficult and sometimes even impossible to determine the boundaries between these three areas because they overlap and, at the very least, have a great deal in common.

Sociology, Economics, History

In *Economy and Society* (1956, a book that has since become a classic), Parsons and Smelser commented that they could find observation of a clear division of labour between economics and sociology and that both areas now had only a limited knowledge of the activities and literature of the other. "Few persons competent in sociological theory", they wrote, "have any working knowledge of economics, and conversely … few economists have much knowledge of sociology" (Parsons & Smelser, 1956, p. xviii). During the course of recent convergence of the disciplines, the trend observed by Parsons and Smelser appears to have reversed in parts of North American sociology (for details see Swedberg, 1997). In the first section of the *Handbook of Economic Sociology* (Smelser & Swedberg, 1994), entitled "Principle Topics," at least half of the famous authors included were chiefly known as economists (the work of Brinton and Nee, eds. 1998, is a similar case). In addition, there are further abstracts from the works of established historians and business economists.

Under the label of new institutionalism there is an increasing number of contributions in which sociologists enter constructive discussions with economists without the need for any translation between the disciplines (Hodgson, 1988). Often such debates are even led by sociologists and address sociological issues. The same is true of diverse new organizations within the overall territory encompassed by economics, sociology and historical disciplines. An example is the 'International Society for New Institutional Economics' (ISNIE), founded only a few years ago, and at the head of which have been Nobel Prize winners such as Douglass C. North and Ronald Coase or organizational theorists such as Oliver Williamson. Sociology is expressly included in such research networks even when it does not play a leading part.

In economics altogether it appears that there is a definite reversal of trends away from Platonist abstract modelling. The awarding of the Nobel Prize for Economics to the Americans Gary S. Becker, Robert Fogel and Douglass C. North or to Amartya Sen in the 1990s is representative of a trend in which socioeconomic elements are of greater importance. Fogel, in fact, is more of a historian than a genuine economist and North discusses authors like Polanyi meticulously and quotes sociologists such as Berger and Luckmann (1966). In his writings, A. Sen stands out precisely because of the failure of a coherent theoretical model to materialize in the abstract. Altogether, with regard to North American developments, this points to a turning point, which, in the words of Ernst Helmstedt could be described as "circular progress" (1984, p. 2). Out of academic necessity, this transposition of the "mainstream" in North American economics will also take place in Europe in all probability. Without a doubt sociology has great prospects in that its competencies are clear and are brought into discussions. Also significant is the fact that it does not retreat sulkily into its self-selected shell, but on the contrary, actively seeks to demonstrate its strengths. Sociology is in a position to claim that matters of commercial style, cultural attitude, ethnic specificity, and social factors such as networks and other forms of "human relations" are its prime subjects.

The 'Commission on Behavioral Social Sciences and Education', initiated by the 'National Research Council' in the USA during the 1980s (Gerstein et al., 1988), made it clear that there is a range of important research topics and emphases that involve sociology in some kind of interdisciplinary co-operation. The context of sociology within spatially and temporally related disciplines (i.e. geography and history) is especially relevant with regard to theories with a moderate range of application and in the co-operation of metatheoretical and substantial questions and not in historical formulation of models and abstraction.

Particularly in North American discussions the broad spectrum of authors on historical and comparative sociology is representative of such a programme. The British sociologist Philip Abrams in *Historical Sociology* (1982) described this programme in the following way: "History and Sociology are and always have been the same thing" (Abrams, 1982, p. 5).

Immanuel Wallerstein (1984, 1991), Charles Tilly (1981, 1984), and Michael Mann (1990, 1993) are amongst the most popular representatives of the genre in North America. To the German-speaking reader the flame of American historical sociology implies the "history repeating itself" (Mikl-Horke, 1999). From the American point of view, this might be much more the norm, considering the many traditional sociologists.

The contrary arguments here have long been known. Historians worked ideographically on the description of the singular, universal phenomenon. In contrast, sociologists were nomothetic and attempted to generalize, to formulate theories appropriate to certain categories and phenomena. In recent times this appears to be a somewhat incorrect ideal-typical construction. There are systematic reasons why the structure of knowledge developed in the way it did, namely following the continual process of subject division—and this more radically in Germany than in North America. It appears, however, that there were many more passable bridges between sociology, history, and economics in North America than in Europe. It is likely that the process of academic development has come up against boundaries recently and greater attempt at interdisciplinarity and the re-integration of disciplines will become evident.[4]

Immanuel Wallerstein and colleagues in many countries vehemently argued for an opening-up and reintegration of disciplines in their report for the Gulbenkian Commission on the Restructuring of the Social Sciences entitled *Open the Social Sciences* (1996). It would be best if students were to study within two departments and achieve two separate doctorates. The observer of this development must bear in mind the historical context, however (Wallerstein, 1991). Only when the historical development of sociology is transparent do the potential, the necessities, and the circularity of the process become apparent. One of the founders of sociology, Emile Durkheim, wrote in the preface to the first edition of *Année Sociologique* (1898) that it is wise and productive to draw some other disciplines closer in to sociology that had long been separate from it. What Durkheim had in mind above all was the discipline of history. It was the predestined fate of both disciplines to melt into one another at some point. Around a hundred years later, the historian Douglass C. North stated that our total knowledge of economic or social transformation can only be advanced if the complete laboratory that is available is put to use, that is, the past and knowledge about the past (North, 1997, p. 1). North's research programme brings together such a statement and reads like an explicit "extension" of some of Durkheim's ideas and the treatment of knowledge as it existed in the "New Historical School" around the beginning of the last century.

D. C. North makes it clear that historical research is necessary for the understanding of current social and economic structures. If we are unfamiliar with the path that has already been trodden, at least in broad terms, then we are not in a position to understand the here and now. The same is true of the programme of historical sociology and institutionalism in general. Already in the mid-1960s Berger and Luckmann made this unmistakably clear in *The Social Construction of Reality*, when they wrote that "it is impossible to understand an institution adequately without an understanding of the historical process in which it was produced" (Berger & Luckmann, 1966, pp. 54–55). In my opinion, the correspondence between economy and society will be much more lively if we attempt to integrate economic and social phenomena and their dynamics of change with the question of culturally inflected trade patterns (Granovetter, 1993). One of the elements in which North American sociology leads and is particularly sophisticated is network analysis. Networks can function as a kind of hinge between micro- and macro-dimensions. They integrate trade and communication levels with questions of structural selection and social transformation. Networks function as "sets" of preferences and social contacts between individuals, groups, and institutions. The life-blood of society flows through them.

Modern American sociological network research relies heavily on the tradition of classic German sociology as represented by George Simmel or Max Weber, for example. Recently a branch of research has become established, which, through its vast quantity of empirical themes and methodical applications, is increasingly taken up in economics and the theories of industrial organization and management (Richter, 2001b).

If we had a better memory for the history of knowledge—and the reasons why this is necessary are already to be found in the preface of Joseph Schumpeter's *History of Economic Analysis* (1954)—then we would recognize that much of what has been brought into the wider debates in social and economic discourse since the first conflict of method persists even today and also appears to fall into the cracks at times. To avoid the danger of continually reinventing the wheel, we must ensure that this background is not forgotten. The differentiation process of the division of subjects completed during the twentieth century has reached a point at which there is the danger of a kind of disciplinary autism. A key to the way out of the situation is synergy through communication and interdisciplinarity.

Interdisciplinarity: The Need for a Programme

To summarize the observations made earlier, there is a series of systematic and rational reasons why the system of knowledge has reached the point at which we find it today. From the point of view of the relationship of individual subjects to one another, but also the situation within the subjects themselves, in which the status of empiricism to theory and from the production of foundations and practical applications has not been systematically resolved, it appears that the support for increasing interdisciplinarity is often treated as a key concept. It can also be justified in terms of system and content, however. After all, one of the most serious deficiencies of the current educational system is not that too little is studied, but that the wrong things are learned. The claim for fostering interdisciplinary research which we find in recent times reflects the diagnosis that our islands of shared knowledge have become too fragmented and that we need a reintegration of different academic disciplines, at least of economics, sociology, and history.

The *Crossing Boundaries* route (Hirschman, 1999) seems to have been followed more in North America. Altogether one has the impression that at the beginning of the twenty-first century North American sociology is less concerned with theoretical sociology than it appeared to be around two decades ago. There are still some exceptional theoretical sociologists in North America, but in quantitative terms, the majority are engaged in specialist sociologies. These specialist sociologies are characterized by a defensive and competitive attitude towards neighbouring disciplines. They are impressive in their empirical orientation and their distance from socio-philosophical models and socio-normative components. The great European theories represented by such names as Foucault, Lyotard, Bourdieu, Giddens, Luhmann, and Habermas remain enormously attractive in North America. They are "imported" to North America, whilst the subject develops its own profile there through "professionalisation". An additional problem is that it becomes ever more difficult to identify the boundaries of the discipline of sociology. The British sociologist Jennifer Platt has remarked of American sociology that "There is serious difficulty in treating some developments as specifically sociological, either because ideas initiated in other disciplines have been directly imported (for example path analysis, semiotics) or because the moving front is cross-disciplinary" (Platt, 1998, p. 4). In the evaluation of the achievements in the history of sociology during the past hundred years we must attempt to discover how innovative and circular elements have been combined.[5]

When talking about interdisciplinarity, of course, we are also talking about the design of academic statements and theories. How elegant and how universal shall a matter be treated? Much of neo-classic advancement in economics and much of theoretical sociology tries to foster universal laws as general laws of economies and societies. Sterility is just the aim of such efforts. However, sterile approaches suffer the lack of concrete historical and spatial and cultural coordination or specification. They are missing the institutional framework, and, among other things, they lost history (Hodgson, 2002). Much of recent debate in neoinstitutional thought is based on thought which was already discussed within the framework of—so called—old institutionalism and the (younger) historical school. When talking about the problem of abstraction in social sciences we are—by nature—forced to think about inductive versus deductive methods which was principally already the basic confrontation between Carl Menger and Gustav Schmoller.[6] We have the idea that much of the development of the twentieth century was in the sense of Carl Menger: tendencies to elaborate theoretical statements in order to arrive at more general and universal laws. However, the price of abstraction is that we lack the atmosphere of the "real world." When we observe, in some respects, a revival of interest in Schmoller's work nowadays, this revival has to be interpreted in combination with a general revival of instititutionalism, especially in economics (Richter, 2001a).

The dynamic force within working and professional worlds points to the increased necessity to acknowledge the complex interplay of different social and economic institutions for an adequate understanding of diverse processes in economy and society. In the history of economic thought we commonly find the so-called "battle of methods" between the Austrian Carl Menger and the German Gustav Schmoller. However, one can find similar arguments later between Koopman and his "Measurement without Theory" attack against the National Bureau of Economic Research (NBER) under the auspices of Mitchell (see Mirowski, 1989).

In so far, we are always acknowledged to deal with unsolved questions on formalism versus empiricism or on deductive versus inductive methods. If we follow the historian David Landes when he says "Culture makes almost all the difference" (Landes, 2000), we must conclude what already Werner Sombart expressed at the beginning of the 1930s: Sombart said that "economy in abstracto" never exists, as no religion, no arts, no language, no state exists "in abstracto", but only as a specific one (Sombart, 1982, p. 210). The design of our academic landscape and its contents must be structured in combination with the question where our current state of academic development has come from historically, and where we want to go in the future and to which questions academic debate shall contribute to. Economics has lost sociology and history more and more, and the economic discipline feels a bit as the superstar among the disciplines in recent times. The chapter has tried to call for some attention to reintegrate academic areas which belonged together a century ago but have separated more and more. A global economy with fast-changing societies and technologies has an impact for an adequate organization of scientific knowledge. Fostering interdisciplinary exchange is one of these needs.

Notes

1. For reasons that cannot be discussed in detail here, Max Weber became much more widely known during the second half of the twentieth century than Werner Sombart. Even today there are still rich discussions about Max Weber's work and aspects of his biography (for a small selection, see Collins (1986), Kalberg (1994), Käsler (1995) and Swedberg (1998)). Secondary literature on Sombart has also grown in recent years (Backhaus 1996), but there is still no English translation of his principal work, "Der moderne Kapitalismus" in spite of Dorfman's reasoned complaints about this (1959). "The lack of an English translation and the tremendous length of the work (three thousand pages) no doubt prevented a widespread knowledge of the work except at secondhand. Sombart attempted, as the subtitle suggests, 'an historical and systematic exposition of Europe's economic life from its beginning to the present day'. His approach was similar to that of Max Weber but with far less emphasis on the role of religious institutions. It was theoretical, nor in the sense of classical economics, but in the effort to supply detailed facts and documentation in support of his preconceived notions of evolutionary economic behavior. ... Despite sharp criticisms of Sombart's work, particularly as to the validity of its detailed facts and the twisting of these facts to fit the author's preconceptions, many of his conclusions were thought to be the result of brilliant insight. His analysis of a mature capitalist economy was notable. More than any other thinker, Sombart was responsible for the general option of the term 'capitalism' as a description of the modern individual or corporate business economy. As a result of his work the stigma that had attached to the term from radical literature was largely wiped out" (Dorfman, Vol. IV, 1959, p. 182, 183).
2. (New York: Charles Scribner's Sons, 1930). Talcott Parsons added a short preface to it. The article was then republished in the Weber volume edited by Hans Heinrich Gerth and Charles Wright Mills (1993). Recently *Protestant Ethics* has been newly published with a substantial introduction by Randall Collins (1998).
3. The fact that the question is actually much older and was dealt with by English empiricists in the eighteenth century is overlooked. Schmoller, who among other things left behind a plurality of works on widely differing topics, was a most influential and important person in academic life in Germany at the zenith of his life. After his death in 1917, however, Schmoller's influence seemed to have declined considerably.
4. A number of similar developments is outlined in the UNESCO "World Social Science Report" (1999).

5. Albert (2004) shows some principles of academic competition and progress which illustrate that scientific progress has never one final and exclusive ultima ratio.
6. Even the concept of socioeconomics, which has become popular again recently, has its origins in German scholarship. As far as I am aware, it was first put forward by Dietzel (1883, 1895).

References

Abrams, P. (1982). *Historical Sociology*. Sommerset: Open Books.

Albert, H. (1964). Probleme der Theoriebildung. In H. Albert (Ed.), *Theorie und Realität* (pp. 3–70). Mohr.

Albert, M. (2004). Methodologie und die Verfassug der Wissenschaft—Eine institutionalistische Perspektive. In M. Held, G. Kubon-Gilke, & R. Sturn (Eds.), *Ökonomik des Wissens. Jahrbuch Normative und institutionelle Grundlagen der Ökonomik 3* (pp. 127–150). Metropolis.

Backhaus, J. (Ed.). (1996). *Werner Sombart (1863–1941). Social Scientist* (Vol. Volume I-III). Metropolis.

Berger, P. L., & Luckmann, T. (1966). *The Social Construction of Reality: A Treatise in the Sociology of Knowledge*. Anchor Books.

Brinton, M. C., & Nee, V. (Eds.). (1998). *The New Institutionalism in Sociology*. Russell Sage Foundation.

Collins, R. (1986). *Max Weber: A Skeleton Key*. Sage.

Collins, R. (1989). Sociology: Proscience or Antiscience? *American Sociological Review, 54*(1), 124–139.

Collins, R. (1998). *Introduction, to: Max Weber: The Protestant Ethik and the Spirit of Capitalism* [orig. translated by Talcott Parsons]. Roxbury.

Comte, A. (1907). Cours de Philosophie Positive, Vol. I [orig. 1830], Paris.

Dietzel, H. (1883). Der Ausgangspunkt der Sozialwirtschaftslehre und ihr Grundbegriff. *Zeitschrift für die gesamte Staatswissenschaft, 39*(1), 1–80.

Dietzel, H. (1895). *Theoretische Sozialökonomik*. C. F. Wintersche Verlagsbuchhandlung.

DiMaggio, P. (1994). Social Stratification, Life-Style, and Social Cognition. In D. B. Grusky (Ed.), *Social Stratification in Sociological Perspective* (pp. 458–468). Westview Press.

Dorfman, J. (1955). The Role of the German Historical School in American Economic Thought. *American Economic Review, 45*(2), 17–28.

Dorfman, J. (1946–59). *The economic mind in American civilization*, 5 Vols. New York: Viking Press.

Elias, N. (1981). *Was ist Soziologie?* [orig. 1970]. Juvent.

Esser, H. (1989). Verfällt die “soziologische Methode”? *Soziale Welt, 40*(1–2), 57–75.

Gerth, H. H., & Mills, C. W. (1993). *From Max Weber: Essays in sociology* (orig. 1946). London: Routledge.
Gerstein, D. R., Luce, R. D., Smelser, N. J., Sperlich, S., & National Research Council; Division of Behavioral and Social Sciences and Education; Commission on Behavioral and Social Sciences and Education; Committee on Basic Research in the Behavioral and Social Sciences (Eds.). (1988). *Committee on Basic Research in the Behavioral and Social Sciences and Education: The Behavioral and Social Sciences: Achievements and Opportunities.* National Academy Press.
Granovetter, M. (1985). Economic Action and Social Structure: The Problem of Embeddedness. *The American Journal of Sociology, 91*(3), 481–510.
Granovetter, M. (1993). The Nature of Economic Relationships'. In R. Swedberg (Ed.), *Explorations in Economic Sociology* (pp. 3–41). Russell Sage Foundation.
Hagemann, H. (Ed.). (1997). *Die deutschsprachige wirtschaftswissenschaftliche Emigration nach 1933.* Marburg.
Hagemann, H., & Krohn, C.-D. (Eds.). (1999). *Biographisches Handbuch der deutschsprachigen wirtschaftswissenschaftlichen Emigration nach 1933.* K. G. Saur.
Haller, M. (1999). *Soziologische Theorie im systematisch-kritischen Vergleich.* UTB.
Helmstädter, E. (1984). Die Geschichte der Nationalökonomie als Geschichte ihres Fortschritts. In O. Issing (Ed.), *Geschichte der Nationalökonomie* (pp. 1–14). Franz Vahlen.
Hirschman, A. O. (1999). *Crossing Boundaries.* MIT Press.
Hodgson, G. M. (1988). *Economics and Institutionalism. A Manifesto for a Modern Institutional Economics.* Polity Press.
Hodgson, G. M. (2002). *How Economics forgot History: The Problem of Historical Specifity in Social Sciences.* Routledge.
Kalberg, S. (1994). *Max Weber's Comparative-Historical Sociology.* University of Chicago Press.
Käsler, D. (1995). *Max Weber: Eine Einführung in Leben, Werk und Wirkung.* Campus.
Landes, D. (2000). Culture malies almost all the difference. In L. Harrison, & S. P. Huntington (Eds.). *Culture matters. How values shape human progress.* New York: Basic Books, 2–13.
Lepenies, W. (1988). *Between Literature and Science: The Rise of Sociology.* Cambridge University Press.
Mann, M. (1990). *The rise and decline of the nation state.* Oxford: Blackwell.
Mann, M. (1993). *The sources of social power.* Cambridge: Cambridge University Press.
Mayer, K. U. (1989). Empirische Sozialstrukturanalyse und Theorien gesellschaftlicher Entwicklung. *Soziale Welt, 40*(1–2), 297–308.
Menger, C. (1883). *Untersuchungen über die Methode der Sozialwissenschaften und der politischen Ökonomie insbesondere.* Duncker & Humblot.

Merton, R. K. (1938). Science and the Social Order. *Philosophy of Science, 5*(3), 321–337.
Merton, R. K. (1968). *Social Theory and Social Structure* [orig.1957]. The Free Press.
Mikl-Horke, G. (1999). *Historische Soziologie der Wirtschaft. Wirtschaft und Wirtschaftsdenken in Geschichte und Gegenwart.* Oldenbourg.
Mirowski, P. (1989). The Measurement Without Theory Controversy: Defeating Rival Research Programs by Accusing them of Naive Empirism. *Economies et Societés, 23*, 65–87.
North, D. C. (1997). Where Have We Been and Where Are We Going?. *Economic History* 9612001. https://ideas.repec.org/p/wpa/wuwpeh/9612001.html
Nowak, S. (1989). Comparative Studies and Social Theory. In M. L. Kohn (Ed.), *Cross-National Research in Sociology* (pp. 34–56). Sage.
Parsons, T. (1928). "Capitalism" in Recent German Literature: Sombart and Weber. *The Journal of Political Economy, 37*(1), 641–661.
Parsons, T. (Ed.). (1930). *Max Weber: The Protestant Ethics and the Spirit of Capitalism.* Charles Scribner's Sons.
Parsons, T., & Smelser, N. (1956). *Economy and Society: A Study in the Integration of Economic and Social Theory.* The Free Press.
Platt, J. (1998). *The Methodological Heritage of American Sociology.* Paper presented at the XIV World Congress of Sociology, Montreal.
Richter, R. (2001a). *Bridging Old and New Institutional Economics: Gustav Schmoller, the Leader of the Younger German Historical School, Seen with Neoinstitutionalists' Eyes.* Research Paper: University of Saarland.
Richter, R. (2001b). *New Economic Sociology and New Institutional Economics.* Paper presented at the Conference of the International Society for New Institutional Economics (ISNIE), Berkeley.
Schmoller, G. (1883). *Zur Methodologie der Staats- und Sozialwissenschaften.* Jahrbuch für Gesetzgebung, Verwaltung und Volkswirtschaft im deutschen Reich (pp. 239–258). Leipzig: Duncker & Humblot.
Schmölders, G. (1984). Historische Schule. In O. Issing (Ed.), *Geschichte der Nationalökonomie* (pp. 107–120). Franz Vahlen.
Schumpeter, J. A. (1926). *Gustav von Schmoller und die Probleme von heute.* In Jahrbuch für Gesetzgebung, Verwaltung und Volkswirtschaft im deutschen Reich (pp. 337–388). Duncker & Humblot.
Schumpeter, J. A. (1954). *History of Economic Analysis.* Oxford University Press.
Smelser, N. J., & Swedberg, R. (1994). The Sociological Perspective on the Economy. In N. J. Smelser & R. Swedberg (Eds.), *The Handbook of Economic Sociology* (pp. 3–26). Princeton University Press und Russell Sage Foundation.
Sombart, W. (1906). *Warum gibt es in den Vereinigten Staaten keinen Sozialismus?* J.C.B. Mohr.
Sombart, W. (1915). *The Quintessence of Capitalism.* Dutton.

Sombart, W. (1982). Wirtschaft. In A. Vierkandt (Ed.), *Handwörterbuch der Soziologie* (pp. 209–216). Enke.
Swedberg, R. (1991). "The Battle of Methods": Toward a Paradigm Shift? In A. Etzioni & P. R. Lawrence (Eds.), *Socio-Economics. Toward a New Synthesis* (pp. 13–34). M. E. Sharpe.
Swedberg, R. (1997). New Economic Sociology: What Has Been Accomplished, What is Ahead? *Acta Sociologica, 40*(2), 161–182.
Swedberg, R. (1998). *Max Weber and the Idea of Economic Sociology.* Princeton University Press.
Tilly, C. (1981). As Sociology Meets History. *Theory and Society, 12*(3), 437–451.
Tilly, C. (1984). *Big Structures, Large Processes, Huge Comparisons.* Russell Sage Foundation.
Turner, J. H. (1998). *The Structure of Sociological Theory.* Wadsworth Publishing Company.
UNESCO (Ed.). (1999). *World Social Science Report.* UNESCO.
Veblen, T. (1899). *Theory of the Leisure Class.* The Macmillan Company.
Veblen, T. (1909). The Limitations of Marginal Utility. *The Jornal of Political Economy, 17*(9), 620–636.
Wallerstein, I. (1984). *The Politics of the World Economy.* Cambridge University Press.
Wallerstein, I. (1991). *The Capitalist World Economy.* Cambridge University Press.
Wallerstein, I. (1996). *Open the Social Sciences. Report of the Gulbenkian-Commission on the Restructuring of Social Sciences.* Stanford University Press.
Weber, M. (1988). Wissenschaft als Beruf [orig. 1919]. In M. Weber (Ed.), *Gesammelte Aufsätze zur Wissenschaftslehre* (pp. 582–613). J.C.B. Mohr.
Winkel, H. (1980). *Einführung in die Wirtschaftswissenschaften.* Ferdinand Schöningh.

CHAPTER 12

Schumpeter, Veblen, and Bourdieu on Institutions and the Formation of Habits

Dieter Bögenhold, Panayotis G. Michaelides, and Theofanis Papageorgiou

Introduction

There is no doubt that Joseph Alois Schumpeter, Thorstein Veblen, and Pierre Bourdieu are among the most influential academics that have merged classical political economy with sociology and are considered as pioneers of institutional and evolutionary thinking (Bögenhold, 2007a, 2007b, 2007c). Unfortunately, so far, some aspects of their works remain less widely discussed, or even unexplored, and as a result, possible linkages such as theoretical and methodological parallels between their works remain inadequately acknowledged, with the exception of a number of contributions, such as O'Donnell (1973), Zingler (1974), Cramer and Leathers

The chapter is coauthored by Panayotis G. Michaelides, & Theofanis Papageorgiou, previously published as: Bögenhold, D., Panayotis G. Michaelides, & Theofanis Papageorgiou (2016). Schumpeter, Veblen and Bourdieu on Institutions and the Formation of Habits, Munich REPEC Working Paper: Munich. https://mpra.ub.uni-muenchen.de/74585/8/MPRA_paper_74585.pdf

D. Bögenhold, *Neglected Links in Economics and Society*,
https://doi.org/10.1007/978-3-030-79193-3_12

(1977), Ferrarotti (1999), Gurkan (2005), Papageorgiou et al. (2013), Valiati and Fonseca (2014), and Papageorgiou and Michaelides (2016).

In this framework, the principal similarity in the works of the three theoreticians is to be found in the fact that the economy is not conceived of as an independent mechanism, where subjects act rationally according to expectations or utility maximization; instead, their writings incorporate economic, sociological, and political perspectives with regard to the functioning of the economic system and the behaviour of "economic agents." Given that Economics, as a science, tends to systematically ignore the theoretical interaction between academics (Bögenhold, 2010a), it is not surprising that so little attention has been paid to their similar theoretical frameworks.

This chapter aims at bridging the gap in the literature, comparing Schumpeter, Veblen, and Bourdieu with respect to the role of institutions, the formation of individual action, and the role of habits and instincts in social and economic life where they are formed and cover diverse fields and notions, such as Consumption, Preferences, Art, Knowledge, Banking, and even Capitalism. In this context, the connection of the three great scholars is substantive as well as methodological in nature. The theories of Schumpeter, Veblen, and Bourdieu are of a rather complex nature, and as such, it is quite difficult to situate them in a clear-cut intellectual tradition.[1]

Historical and Methodological Framework

Joseph Schumpeter was born in 1883 and his writings covered a very broad range of topics, including the dynamics of economic development, the integration of economic, sociological, and political perspectives with regard to the feasibility of capitalism and, of course, the history of economic thought (Papageorgiou & Michaelides, 2016, p. 2; Bögenhold, 2016), while opting for economic sociology and economics as a universal social science (Shionoya, 2004). As put by Harris et al. (1951, p. 89): "the experience of those early years in Vienna never really left him." Veblen, born in 1857, lived in the Gilded Age of American capitalism, and was undoubtedly influenced by the general economic environment. The world of the young Veblen bore a great resemblance to a self-sufficient household economy very much in contrast with nineteenth-century American capitalism (O'Donnell, 1973, pp. 200–201), and the deeper roots for his radical thought could be traced there.

Schumpeter and Veblen were inspired by their similar academic milieus, since they lived in almost the same period of modern capitalism. In contrast, Pierre Bourdieu, born in 1930, lived in an era when political economy and sociology were already separated in epistemological and scientific terms, distanced from the "real coherent" and the simplified abstraction, into a scientific discourse adequately "matured," giving way to "parcelled out" questions, specific for each scientific field. Bourdieu's vocation in philosophy shifted abruptly to the social sciences after he was drafted into the French army and sent to Algeria at the height of its Liberation War (1956–1962). His theoretical project began as an attempt to formulate a method of sociological and anthropological analysis that mediates between simply reproducing the perceptions of the culture studied and a scientific codification of those perceptions that gives them objective shape, but not a shape that corresponds to anything in the workings of that culture (Loesberg, 1993, p. 1033).

Even though Veblen, Bourdieu, and Schumpeter may not be strictly classified into a single "school of thought," they all tried to link political economy with sociology, giving way to a preferential foundation of institutional, evolutionary, and structuralist thought.[2]

Of course, this methodological tradition gives specific space to the analysis of human behaviour, institutions, and a holistic view of the capitalist way of production through their complex and contradictory relation. In this spirit, certain aspects of standard neoclassical economics, with reference to equilibrium theorizing, modelling and rationality, were criticized from a methodological point of view.

The economists of the Classical School tried to derive general laws regarding the economic process in the same way that neo-classical and monetary economics do. The marginal revolution shifted attention to individual choices, seeking to unravel laws that condition both the individual and the economy, placing political economy onto a strict scientific level and based on "exact" laws similar to those of the natural sciences: "Pure theory in economics is a science which resembles the physio-mathematical sciences" (Walras, 1954 [1874], p. 81). Or to put it into wording of Jevons at the same time: "It is clear that Economics, if it is to be a science at all, must be a mathematical science" (Jevons, 1871, introduction). That was the time in which economics, sociology, and history started with a process of decoupling (Bögenhold, 2008). Furthermore, the issues of teleology and determinism in political economy are crucial, since all theoretical traditions have adopted different versions thereof. Needless to say, all three theoreticians' works have in common the same kind of determinism, different from the Classical one, where phenomena cannot be separated from their context, and as a result clear causal relationships may not be derived.

Veblen is well known for his critique towards classical and neo-classical economics on the basis that they were built upon outmoded preconceptions and were "animistic"[3] and "teleological,"[4] and the resulting science was "taxonomic" and subjective in its method (Veblen, 1990 [1919], pp. 68–73, 82, 146). It was Veblen who wrote his dissertation on Kant's Critique of Judgement and recognized that this amounted to a reversion of teleological thinking, ignoring the general tide moving against teleology in science (Turner, 2003, p. 35). Thus, he identified two distinct classes of scientific endeavour,[5] which he termed teleological and evolutionary methods of thought (Argyrous & Sethi, 1996, p. 476). By teleology, Veblen referred to the tendency to view the laws of nature as purposively oriented towards a final end or consummation (Coats, 1954, p. 529).

Through the rejection of the notion of (Walrasian) equilibrium, Schumpeter wanted to give economic substance to certain theories of his time (Santarelli & Pesciarelli, 1990; März, 1991, Arena, 1992; Heilbroner, 2000). According to Schumpeter: "Development is the distinct phenomenon entirely foreign to what may be observed in the circular flow or in the tendency towards equilibrium." "It is spontaneous and discontinuous change in the channels of the flow, disturbance of equilibrium which forever alters and displaces the equilibrium previously existing" (Schumpeter, 1983 [1934], p. 64).[6] Thus for Schumpeter, teleology is "the attempt to explain institutions and forms of behaviour causally by the social need or purpose they are supposed to serve; which is not always erroneous" (Schumpeter, 1954, p. 58).

For Bourdieu, the mathematical formalization of economics cannot be criticized in itself. However, the main problem is that it allows neo-classical economists to separate economic intuition even further from the social and historical conditions in which it is embedded[7] (Lebaron, 2003, p. 558). In the same spirit, modelling and hypothesis testing tend to systematically neglect the historical and contextual ground. The simplified models of economics are mostly removed from the ethnographic or sociological observations of the underlying realities (Lebaron, 2003, p. 558). According to Benjaminsen (2003, p. 8), Bourdieu rarely makes use of the concept of causality, mainly because of his criticism towards positivism and also towards the middle range tradition, which relies on a unidimensional social ontology based on a naive realism (Bourdieu, 1984; Bourdieu & Wacquant, 1992).

Furthermore, Pierre Bourdieu opposed rational choice theory as grounded in a misunderstanding of how social agents operate. Instead, taking the opposite view, he argued against the continuous calculation of action according to explicit rational and economic criteria. In fact, social agents operate according to an implicit practical logic—a practical sense—and bodily dispositions, their "feel for the game" the habitus, and field. The habitus, being a structure that reflects the structure of the individual's environment in the past, reflects Bourdieu's perception of holistic or institutionalist individualism. The subject becomes the dominant pole in perception, but "carries the world within." This apparatus combines traditionally subjective (teleology, construction) and traditionally objective (structure) aspects (Weik, 2010, p. 495). Action is not inherently teleological, let alone, pace Bourdieu, oriented toward a single overall type of end: Affectivity can determine what people do independently from and in the absence of teleology (Schatzki, 1997, p. 305). The habitus is Bourdieu's major concept to portray how institutions, conventions, and other practices influence and shape the individual human being with regard to her/his body, preferences, attitudes, etc. (Weik, 2010, p. 487).

Schumpeter's inherent nature of the cyclical motion in economic change infuses economic life with a deterministic element. Trends in the short term may exist, evolution follows regularities and thus a short-term determination may exist in the fluctuations, although no general predetermined result in the long-term future of capitalist development is in force and regularities are too weak to allow prediction, a meaning that shares similarities with path dependence (Papageorgiou & Michaelides, 2016, p. 8). According to Frank (1998), predicting and forecasting future economic development is not possible within Schumpeter's dynamic theory of economic development, precisely because the creative response of the entrepreneur brings into the theoretical model an element of indeterminateness. Innovation, being at the core of capitalist change in the Schumpeterian system, leads to different results depending on the capitalist phase and the social context. The "routinisation" of innovation, the institutional framework in which it takes place and the hostility that is produced in the capitalist strata seem to remove the elements of technological determinism from the Schumpeterian schema and seem to establish what we might call multiple equilibria (Papageorgiou & Michaelides, 2016, p. 9).

Veblen regarded capitalist development as a "cumulative causation," having "no trend," "no final term," and "no consummation." In his own words "It is a scheme of blindly cumulative causation, in which there is no trend, no final term, no consummation. The sequence is controlled by nothing but the vis a tergo of brute causation, and is essentially mechanical" (Veblen, 1907, p. 304). However, Veblen has taken some highly deterministic positions, arguing that technical change, and its associated institutional structure, revolutionizes capitalism in favour of engineers and the industrial workers and against the pecuniary motives of the business class, while society is divided in a war of two ideologies, somehow forming a war of capitalism and socialism, and the question as to which will dominate remains open (Papageorgiou & Michaelides, 2016, p. 9).

Social position, in Bourdieu's framework, is "what gives the best prediction of practices and representations; but, to avoid conferring what used to be called 'estate' on social identity (which is nowadays more and more completely identified with occupational identity), the place that 'being' had in the old metaphysics, i.e. the function of an essence from which all aspects of historical existence are seen as deriving (in accordance with the formula operatio sequitur esse), it must never be forgotten that this status, and the habitus that is generated within it, are products of history that can be changed, with more or less difficulty, by history" (Bourdieu, 1985, p. 739).

Thus, Bourdieu's apparatus turns to a historical determination open to evolution, with an aleatory, largely unpredictable outcome, being in that way partially nondeterministic. It is worth mentioning, this apparatus bears resemblance to the Veblenian and Schumpeterian schema, where determinism exists in terms of a path-dependent process (Papageorgiou & Michaelides, 2016, p. 8). According to Schumpeter, there is a correspondence, sometimes weak, between the economic and social functions and individuals' conflicting ends. This correspondence is effective as soon as the individuals reveal some aptitudes to perform their economic and social functions. Human motives are always embedded in a social and historical context under which they have emerged (Festre & Garrouste, 2008, p. 379). Routines are part of the institutional settings, "which compel individuals and groups to behave in certain ways whatever they may wish to do—not indeed by destroying their freedom of choice but by shaping the choosing mentalities and by narrowing the list of possibilities from which to choose" (Schumpeter [1942] 1975, pp. 129–130). The performance of individual actors depends on the institutional and social contexts. Institutional change embodied in economic change takes place only when individuals overcome previously existing collective routines (Papageorgiou et al., 2013, p. 1245).

On Individualism and the Formation of Habits

Veblen accused neo-classical economics on the basis of the purely individualistic foundation of their theory: "An adequate theory of economic conduct, even for social purposes, cannot be drawn in terms of the individual simply—as is the case in the marginal-utility economics—because it cannot be drawn in terms of the underlying traits of human nature simply" (Veblen 1909, p. 629). Meanwhile, "the human material with which the inquiry is concerned is conceived in hedonistic terms; that is to say, in terms of a passive and substantially inert and immutably given human nature. The psychological and anthropological preconceptions of the economists have been those which were accepted by social sciences some generations ago" (Veblen, 1898a, p. 389).

In fact, Schumpeter praised Pareto for getting rid of the concept of "utility" and suggested that maximizing rationality was not a realist feature (Freeman & Louçã, 2001). Also, for Schumpeter, there is no rationality on hedonism of the entrepreneur; the entrepreneur is in no sense rational in his "characteristic motivation of the hedonist kind"; "hedonistically the entrepreneur would be irrational" (Schumpeter, 1983 [1934], p. 92). Finally, Schumpeter seems to have been opposed to Austrian psychologism—the essence of economic behaviour is in the satisfaction of wants along with the maximization principle and the law of the diminishing marginal utility. He argued that "as saturation increases the demand for further food would decline and, as a result, the saturated individual is only willing to pay a decreasing price for every additional quantity ... Why is such an explanation given?" (Schumpeter, 1908, p. 68).

Bourdieu rejects both methodological individualism and holism, as the expression of mistaken conception of the relation between individual and society (Bourdieu & Wacquant, 1992, p. 126). Individual and society are not two distinct realities in Bourdieu's framework, but only social individuals related to one another (Udehn, 2001, p. 164). Even though the original theoretical development of the concept focused on the individual as the unit of Bourdieu's analysis, the concept of social capital was later extended to a group level where it became an attribute of communities and nations (Coleman, 1988; Portes, 2000) but social capital was always addressing the micro-macro link (Bögenhold, 2013). A general science of the economy of practices that does not artificially limit itself to those practices that are socially recognised as economic must endeavour to grasp capital, that "energy of social physics"… in all of its different forms … I have shown that capital presents itself under three fundamental species (each with its own subtypes), namely, economic capital, cultural capital, and social capital (Bourdieu & Wacquant, 1992, pp. 118–119). Bourdieu's conception of human behaviour is communicated through the ideas of habitus and social field.

The habitus, the durably installed generative principle of regulated improvisations, produces practices which tend to reproduce the regularities immanent in the objective conditions of the production of their generative principle, while adjusting to the demands inscribed as objective potentialities in the situation, as defined by the cognitive and motivating structures making up the habitus (Bourdieu, 1977, p. 78). In Bourdieu's hands habitus, however, remains a black box, yet one that is nonetheless essential to thinking about the effects of mobility between fields, both on the individual and on the transformation of fields themselves (Burawoy, 2011, p. 6). In Bourdieu's words, "this means that our object becomes the production of the habitus, that system of dispositions which acts as mediation between structures and practice; more specifically, it becomes necessary to study the laws that determine the tendency of structures to reproduce themselves by producing agents endowed with the system of predispositions which is capable of engendering practices adapted to the structures and thereby contributing to the reproduction of the structures" (Bourdieu, 1977, p. 487).

The concept of habitus generates practices that, like moves in a game, are governed by the regularities of the social structure and in so doing reproduce those structures. But practices and knowledge are bound together by the body whose importance the intellectualist vision misses (Burawoy, 2011, p. 4). The social order inscribes itself in bodies, that is to say, we learn bodily, and express our knowledge bodily—all under the organizing power of the habitus, itself largely unconscious (Burawoy, 2011, p. 4).

Schumpeter focuses on the individual as the initiator of economic change, "the bearer of innovation," reflecting his adherence to "the Schumpeterian version of" methodological individualism. It should be noted that Schumpeter's methodological individualism is not the methodological individualism[8] of the marginalists, since he was the first to coin the term. By this term, Schumpeter considers methodological individualism to mean "just that one starts from the individual in order to describe certain economic relationships" (Schumpeter, 1908). In other words, the individual may be conceived of as the unit of evolution. In Schumpeterian terms, methodological individualism is "the approach in which determination of economic phenomena, for instance, values and prices, surplus value and profits can be traced to individual decisions and choices" (Schumpeter, 1954, pp. 888–889). The individual is not seen as homo economicus that aims at satisfying his/her needs through utility maximization, but as a human being who has social and psychological needs, as well (Bögenhold, 2014). Generalization of the individual behaviour to the whole society is, thus, not possible. The social character of the motives along with the existence of society and social classes that influence individual behaviour is the final reason for the substantially different character of Schumpeter's individualism. Finally, the process of routinization of innovation underlines that entrepreneurship and thus individuals' actions are heavily dependent on the social context and the institutional framework.

Thus, a relevant question of great interest is the following: "Who is the bearer of change in the capitalist process?" On the one hand, Schumpeter's innovations are introduced by entrepreneurs, moved by the entrepreneurial habits: the "dream and will to found a private kingdom," the "joy of creating," and the "will to conquer," giving to the argument an anthropomorphic and animistic character. Entrepreneurship becomes the "ultimate cause" of capitalist development, since "the mechanisms of economic change in capitalist society pivot on entrepreneurial activity" (Schumpeter 1951 [1927], p. 150), as opposed to the manager, the capitalist or industrialist "who merely may operate an established business" (Schumpeter, 1983 [1934], p. 74). The entrepreneur is "rational" when he carries out the new plans, though he is in no sense rational in his "characteristic motivation of the hedonist kind"; "hedonistically the entrepreneur would be irrational" (Schumpeter, 1983 [1934], p. 92). The motives are both social and psychological: the "will to found a private kingdom," a "dynasty" inspired by the ideal of the medieval lordship, including "from spiritual ambition down to mere snobbery," the "will to conquer," the will to prove superior to others, to succeed for the sake of success itself and finally the intrinsic motive of getting things done, "the joy of creativity." Schumpeter argued that entrepreneurship is not a "vocation," since "everyone is an entrepreneur only when he carries out new combinations" (Schumpeter, 1983 [1934], pp. 77–78). It is the "spiritual constitution" that differentiates entrepreneurs from common people (Schumpeter,

1911, p. 163 cf., pp. 142–143). The entrepreneur meets considerable resistance from his surroundings; people are set in their ways as a "railway embankment in the earth" (Schumpeter, 1983 [1934], p. 84). He is a "man of action" ready to get into "energetic action" (Schumpeter, 1911, p. 132). The entrepreneur "appears out of nowhere"; he comes from outside the existing economic reality (see Bögenhold, 2010b).

Veblen's approach may be classified in what is often called the "impersonal and nonanimistic" evolution of capitalism. According to Veblen, human evolution is impersonal. In his system the evolutionary process escapes the individual, and takes place through the habits of thought, conventions, and institutions, and this is what is often called the "elimination of personality" that dominated the Veblenian thought and that goes hand in hand with his anti-teleological spirit. In fact, "It is on individuals that the system of institutions imposes those conventional standards, ideals and cannons of conduct that make up the community's scheme of life" (Veblen, 1909, p. 627).

Veblen identified three basic drives or instincts that govern human behaviour: the instinct of workmanship or the impulse to work in order to "turn things to human use," closely connected to the habits of thought (Veblen, 1898b, p. 190); the instinct of idle curiosity, referring to the propensity to understand and explain the external world through the use of imagination; and the instinct of parental bent, stressing human interest in the welfare of others (Veblen, 1898b, 1919 [1906], 1964 [1914]). Under the impact of technology and its associated institutional structure, the balance and realization of the basic human instincts changes drastically. He argued: "In the modern culture, industry, industrial processes, and industrial products have progressively gained upon humanity, until these creations of man's ingenuity have latterly come to take the dominant place in the cultural scheme; and it is not too much to say that they have become the chief force shaping men's daily life, and therefore the chief factors shaping men's habits of thought. Hence men have learned to think in the terms in which the technological processes act" (Veblen, 1990 [1919], p. 17). He, thus, concluded that economic change is always in the last resort a change in the habits of thought, a fact that is true even for changes in the mechanical process of industry (Veblen, 1898b, p. 189).

According to Bourdieu (1985, p. 724), the social field can be described as a multidimensional space of positions such that every actual position can be defined in terms of a multi-dimensional system of co-ordinates whose values correspond to the values of the different pertinent variables.

Bourdieu's framework revolves around power, provoking power relations imposed upon all who enter the social field, irreducible to the intentions and will of the individual and incapable to be unveiled through the direct interactions among the agents. As with the capitalist mode of production so with the notion of field, individuals necessarily enter into relations of competition in order to accumulate capital, according to the rules of the market. Bourdieu's fields have the same character, each having their own distinctive "capital" that agents seek to accumulate, bound by rules of competition that give the field a certain functional integrity and relative autonomous dynamics.

Bourdieu also recognizes a conflict between the two fractions, but casts that conflict in terms of struggles over categories of representation, the so-called classification struggles. Recognizing that intellectuals are the source of ruling ideology, "the illusion of the class about itself," Bourdieu also sees the possibility of their generating a symbolic revolution that can shape the "deepest structures of the social order." Symbolic violence is the coercion, which is set up only through the consent that the dominated cannot fail to give to the dominator (and therefore to the domination) when their understanding of the situation and relation can only use instruments of knowledge that they have in common with the dominator, which, being merely the incorporated form of the structure of the relation of domination, make this relation appear as natural. Or, in other words, when the schemes they implement in order to perceive and evaluate themselves or to perceive and evaluate the dominators (high/low, male/female, white/black, etc.) are the product of the incorporation of the (thus neutralized) classifications of which their social being is the product (Bourdieu, 2000 [1998], p. 170). It is not clear whether this "shaking up" will actually undermine the domination of the dominant class. There is not even a hint that it will create opportunities for the dominated to challenge their subjugation. One has to ask, therefore: What are the interests that lie behind any such "symbolic revolution?"

What differentiates Veblen from determinism is his view, expressed in his later works, that the machine-induced habits of thought may not win out against the existing pecuniary habits of thought (Papageorgiou & Michaelides, 2016, p. 12). Habituation, being perhaps the "most important contribution" of Veblen in the field of social change, "occurs through the relentless inculcation of a habit of thought as man makes a living through a particular mode of production" and thus is "behaviouristic in nature" (Dugger, 1979, p. 428). Also, Raines and Leathers (1993, p. 250) emphasized the unremitting character of the process of habituation such that institutional structure is "insensibly but incessantly changing as it runs" (Veblen, 1990 [1914], p. 17).

The unintentional nature of habituation is further elaborated by Rutherford (1998, p. 469) as follows: "the unintentional nature of the process" is preserved as the adaptation takes place not as a result of purposeful change or rational assessment, but as a result of the habituation that occurs through the conditioning influence of the new material circumstances, what Veblen calls the "discipline of a new order of experience" (Veblen, 1919, p. 9). The evolutionary process takes place not through the individual, but through the habits of thought, conventions, and institutions. Habits both endure and adapt in line with "changes in material facts." The material means of life take the form of "prevalent habits of thought, and it is as such that they enter into the process of industrial development" (Veblen, 1898a, p. 375).

In parallel to the Veblenian term of habituation, Bourdieu uses the term "legitimation."[9] In Bourdieu's framework, the arts and literature can no doubt offer the dominant agents some very powerful instruments of legitimation, either directly, through the celebration they confer, or indirectly, especially through the cult they enjoy, which also consecrates its celebrants. But it can also happen that artists or writers are, directly or indirectly, at the origin of large-scale symbolic revolutions (like the bohemian lifestyle in the nineteenth century, or, nowadays, the subversive provocations of the feminist or homosexual movements), capable of shaking the deepest structures of the social order, such as family structures, through transformation of the fundamental principles of division of the vision of the world (such as male/female opposition) and the corresponding challenges to the self-evidences of common sense (Bourdieu, 2000 [1997], p. 105).

On Institutions

Undoubtedly, the role of institutions is of great importance in all three theoreticians' works. Schumpeter, in his *Theory of Economic Development*, stated that "economic sociology deals with institutions," which is contrasted to economic theory dealing with purely economic phenomena and mechanisms (Schumpeter, 1983 [1934], pp. 60–61). Institutional development is intended to achieve the synthesis of theory and history (Shionoya, 2008, p. 7). Although Schumpeter referred to himself as the "arch-enemy of Institutionalism," Festre and Garrouste (2008, p. 372) argued that the connection between conflicting ends and Schumpeter's contribution to economic sociology favours an "institutionalist" interpretation of Schumpeter's theory, in which conflicts between self-interest and class-interest play an important role.

Institutions as such are introduced in the Schumpeterian schema only in *Socialism, Capitalism and Democracy* where they play a central role, closely related to the future of capitalism. Institutional and non-institutional factors enter into complex forms of interaction (Swedberg, 2002, p. 247). In Schumpeter's work, the capitalist civilization consists of institutions as well as of items such as "motivation," "lifestyle," "atmosphere," "rationalism," art, science, and so on (Swedberg, 2002, p. 249) that are prerequisites for capitalism to exist. The more fundamental institutions are property and contract and these are getting weaker in capitalist strata, along with the "recent" emergence of the third key institution, "the big enterprise." Property is hollowed out: Shareholders and managers have substituted the traditional owner of the business and the latter has disappeared. While the old type of owner knew his factory inside-out, managers and shareholders only have an abstract concept of property, symbolized by the share (Swedberg, 2002, p. 246): "The big enterprise" is transformed to the engine of capitalist development and social transformation takes the entrepreneurs' place.

However, even though institutional changes are predominantly seen in a collective social context, Schumpeter's analysis is not based on class analysis in the Marxian sense of the term. In fact, there is no class struggle, no impoverishment of the masses and thus no social classes as bearers of a cause, but rather social functions that take place in economic evolution, such as social leadership (see Rahim, 2009, p. 70). Furthermore, social classes are not "our making" or a "creation of the researcher," but "social entities that we observe," or "social organisms, living, acting and suffering as such" (Schumpeter, 1951 [1927], p. 137). Schumpeter (1951 [1927], p. 165) asserted that the contents of classes are changing like "a hotel or an omnibus, always full, but always of different people," Also, for Schumpeter, "groups or social classes are not in general to be explained by reference to a particular purpose; mostly, sociological location and history are necessary to understand their nature and behavior"; which, however, does not mean that there are "no class interests and thus a distinction between individual interests and class interests" (Festre & Garrouste, 2008, pp. 374–5).

For Schumpeter, social classes are not independent from social functions; rather they are mutually dependent. Social classes are related to Zeitgeist and social values (social leadership). Each social area has a social function and social functions are attributed to social classes. In other words, the rank of a social class depends on the ability of innovation (leadership) and in that way class structure is determined by diverse factors other than economic ones (Papageorgiou & Michaelides, 2016, p. 19). The institutional individualistic stance is further analysed by acknowledging that: "Class is something more than an aggregation of class members. It is something else, and this something cannot be recognized in the behavior of the individual class member. A class is aware of its identity as a whole, sublimates itself as such, has its own peculiar life and characteristic 'spirit'" (Schumpeter, 1951 [1927], p. 140). In that way, it is impossible to conceive social classes in a solely holistic or individualistic context. Schumpeter himself seems to argue against his overall individualistic stance in stressing the importance of the social milieu on individual action: "We know that every individual is fashioned by the social influences in which he grows up. In this sense he is the produce of the social entity or class and therefore not a free agent" (Schumpeter, 1951, p. 286).

Institutional change is one of the most complex issues of Veblen's theory (Brette, 2003). Veblen identified institutions in his *Theory of Leisure Class* as follows: "products of the past process, are adapted to the past circumstances, and therefore never in full accord with the requirements of the present. At the same time, men's present habits of thought tend to persist indefinitely, except as circumstances enforce a change. These institutions which so have been handed down, these habits of thought, points of view, mental attitudes and aptitudes, or what not, are therefore a conservative factor". Or, alternatively, institutions are seen as principles of action, which underlie the current scheme of economic life, and as such, they are not to be called into question without questioning the existing law and order (Veblen, 1990 [1919], pp. 239–240). Often, institutions are considered as habits, probably because of Veblen's famous phrase: "Institutions are settled habits of thought common to the generality of men" (Veblen, 1909, p. 626). Elsewhere, institutions are referred to as "habits of thought, points of view, mental attitudes and aptitudes" (Veblen, 1994 [1899], p. 133), in the sense that "every situation is a variation of what has gone before it and embodies as causal factors all that has been effected by what went before." Following Coats (1954, p. 533), "every institutional situation is a product of everything that has proceeded it."

For Veblen, class antagonism is engendered by conflicting habits that arise from the discipline of ownership, on the one hand, and from that of workmanship, on the other, rather than by differential conditions of income and production (Harris, 1934, p. 45). On the importance of class consciousness in forming class interest, Veblen (1967 [1923], p. 6) argued that "the effectual division of interest and sentiment is beginning visibly to run on class lines, between the absentee owners and the underlying."

It has already been argued that society is formed on the basis of the conflict of two opposing ideologies. Veblen identifies the struggle in terms of a class struggle, which tends to divide society. But as soon as private property is firmly implanted, rather well-defined class distinctions begin to crystallize. Institutional change takes place through dialectical processes; the dialectical processes—habituation being one of them—do not depend on class interests but on prevalent habits of thought. Institutional change in that sense is the response in the altered discipline of life under changing cultural conditions (Veblen, 1990, p. 18). The interest on class and its habituation does not exclude the possibility of individual interests and thus individual habituation.

According to Jenkins (1992, p. 123), Bourdieu does not have an adequate theory of institutions; on the contrary, he constructs them sociologically on the basis of data of the individuals that form part of them. For Bourdieu, the whole history of the social field is present, at each moment, both in a materialized form—in institutions such as the permanent machinery of parties or unions—and in an embodied form—in the dispositions of the agents who operate these institutions or fight against them. Perception of the social world is the product of a double social structuration: On the "objective" side, it is socially structured because the properties attached to agents or institutions do not offer themselves independently to perception, but in combinations that are very unequally probable (and, just as animals with feathers are more likely to have wings than are animals with fur, so the possessors of a substantial cultural capital are more likely to be museum-goers than those who lack such capital); on the "subjective" side, it is structured because the schemes of perception and appreciation available for use at the moment in question, especially those that are deposited in language, are the product of previous symbolic struggles and express the state of the symbolic power relations, in a more or less transformed form (Bourdieu, 1985, pp. 727–728). If Bourdieu's mode of argumentation is web-like and ramifying, if his key concepts are relational (habitus, field, and capital are all constituted of "bundles" of social ties in different states, embodied, objectified, institutionalized, and they all work most powerfully in relation to each other), it is because the social universe is made that way, according to him (Wacquant, 2002, p. 182).

It has already been argued that Bourdieu's framework revolves around power, provoking power relations imposed to all who enter the social field, irreducible to the intentions and will of the individual and incapable to be unveiled through the direct interactions among the agents, sketching a struggle in the way Veblen did. These social fields are as wide to shape and appear in the form of habits of thought and as material to be conceived in the formation of institutions. In the same vein, the crystallization of legitimation with hysteresis, in Bourdieu's work, seems to give lead not to the dominant but to the existence of power relations sketching preferential ties to the works of Michel Foucault. Of course, Bourdieu's schema shares in parallel a distinct process of change in the habits of thought with Veblen, the first being more substantivist and the second more relativist. The parallels between Veblen and Bourdieu are also to be found in the confusion between habits of thought and institutions, probably because they shared theoretical traditions closer to Marxism. It was Veblen who argued that institutions refer to previous circumstances in the same way but with a time lag and that institutions are sums of what has happened before, just as Bourdieu argues.

Furthermore, ownership of the different types of capital, namely, economic capital, cultural capital, and social capital, bears resemblance to the moral and ethical psychology of the Schumpeterian entrepreneur in terms of their irrationality and nobility, when seen as social capital or cultural capital and, at the same time, it bears resemblance to the Veblenian notion of ownership of capital, if the notion is reduced to mere economic terms and economic capital. However, we are not sure that Bourdieu would agree with this point of convergence, since the three different types of capital are tied into a "distinct whole," an institutionalizing process, the parts of which cannot be separated. In any case, the process of institutionalization of capital merges the Veblenian with the Schumpeterian thought.

On the basis of knowledge of the space of positions, one can separate out classes, in the logical sense of the word, that is, sets of agents who occupy similar positions and who, being placed in similar conditions and subjected to similar conditionings, have every likelihood of having similar dispositions and interests and therefore of producing similar practices and adopting similar stances. Thus, contrary to the nominalist relativism that cancels out social differences by reducing them to pure theoretical artefacts, one must therefore assert the existence of an objective space determining compatibilities and incompatibilities, proximities and distances (Bourdieu, 1985, p. 725). A class exists insofar—and only insofar—as mandated representatives endowed with plena potestas agendi can be and feel authorized to speak in its name. In accordance with the equation "the Party is the working class," or "the working class is the Party," it is a sort of existence in thought, an existence in the thinking of a large proportion of those whom the taxonomies designate as workers, but also in the thinking of the occupants of the positions remotest from the workers in the social space (Bourdieu, 1985, p. 741). This working class "as will and representation" (in the words of Schopenhauer's famous title) is not the self-enacting class, a real group really mobilized, that is evoked in the Marxist tradition, while no less real, with the magical reality that (as Durkheim maintained) defines institutions as social fictions. It is a "mystical body," created through an immense historical labour of theoretical and practical invention, starting with that of Marx himself, and endlessly re-created through the countless, constantly renewed, efforts and energies that are needed to produce and reproduce belief and the institution designed to ensure the reproduction of belief (Bourdieu, 1985, p. 742).

Bourdieu, Veblen, and Schumpeter seem to have similar views on institutions. First, they are part of the social milieu. The underlying framework, much wider than merely economic and social, is common in the analysis of all theoreticians. The capitalist civilization is a key notion to understanding the way in which institutions work and evolution takes place. The role of the capitalist civilization and their relation with institutions is a common point for Veblen and Schumpeter. In the words of Veblen: "The material framework of modern civilization is the industrial system, and the directing force which animates this framework is business enterprise [...] This economic organization is the 'Capitalist System' or 'Modern Industrial System" (Veblen, 1975 [1904], p. 7).

Second, institutions have a causal role in the shaping of human behaviour and in the evolution of capitalism. Their role is complex, in the sense that they are part of the contradictory powers that shape instincts, behaviours, and habits of thought. This schema has both causal power and at the same time is being shaped by institutions: "The wants and desires, the end and aim, the ways and means, the amplitude and drift of the individual's conduct are functions of an institutional variable that is of a highly complex and wholly unstable character" (Veblen, 1909, p. 629) and "the response that goes to make up human conduct takes place under institutional norms and only under stimuli that have an institutional bearing; for the situation that provokes and inhibits actions in any given case is itself in great part of institutional cultural derivation" (Veblen, 1909, p. 629).

For Bourdieu, the status of a "regulatory idea," which is capable of suggesting principles of action, would be to forget that there are universes in which it becomes a "constitutive" immanent principle of regulation—such as the scientific field and to a lesser extent the bureaucratic field and the judicial field, and that as soon as the principles claiming universal validity—those of democracy, for example—are stated and officially professed, there is no longer any social situation in which they cannot serve, at least, as symbolic weapons in struggles of interests or as instruments of critique for those who have a self-interest in truth and virtue (Bourdieu, 2000 [1997], p. 127).

Finally, if we are interested in introducing into the analysis powers that resist evolution, we will find again striking similarities between Bourdieu, Veblen, and Schumpeter. The powers that resist evolution may be found, broadly speaking, in the contradicting factors, for example, in the agents that resist innovation and economic change, and the resistance of the business class with its pecuniary ends to the "intrusion of new technology" and to "industrial serviceability." Some trends are clear, especially in the short-run. In Bourdieu's schema, what this "countertraining" might look like is never elaborated. Whether class struggle might be a form of "countertraining" is especially unclear, because Bourdieu never entertains the idea of class struggle or even allows for "collective resistance" to the dominant culture. The working classes are driven by the exigencies of material necessity, leading them to make a virtue out of a necessity. They embrace their functional lifestyle rather than reject the dominant culture. An alternative culture remains beyond their grasp because they have neither the tools nor the leisure to create it (Bourdieu, 1984 [1979], chapter 7). As the dominated fraction of the dominant class, intellectuals are in a contradictory position. Certain parts may identify with the dominated classes and indeed try to represent the latter's interests. As such, they may even pursue an agenda hostile to the dominant class as a whole. However, it is an intellectualist illusion that they share interests with the dominated. Finally, all three seem to share a kind of institutional individualism.

Conclusions

Bourdieu, Schumpeter, and Veblen shared the opposition to certain aspects of standard neoclassical economics. Their critique consisted of two main arguments. First, a central point in the theoretical constructions of Bourdieu, Schumpeter, and Veblen is their antiteleological view of capitalist evolution and the resulting critique of the teleological view of equilibrium and standard neoclassical modelling. Second, all three academics rejected rationality and methodological individualism, in terms of utility maximization. Veblen and Bourdieu rejected methodological individualism, while Schumpeter gave a substantially different meaning to the term from the meaning bestowed by the neoclassical school, and the notion of utilitarianism and hedonism based on a passive and substantially inert and immutably given human nature. The focus on the individual in the works of Bourdieu, Schumpeter, and Veblen may endorse an institutionalist individualist view of phenomena. Also, even though they all reject determinism, they all seem to accept the approach that allows for multiple equilibria.

Additionally, the notion of evolution of the capitalist process as a unique transformation of various powers in the economic system is common in Bourdieu, Veblen, and Schumpeter. In a holistic framework, any given agent shapes and is simultaneously shaped by the "whole,"that is, the power of capital in the former and capitalist evolution in Veblen and Schumpeter. The role of the individual in the capitalist process is significant. Even though, based on some of Schumpeter's writings, we may consider the entrepreneur as a mere unit in the economic process and thus the economic process as "depersonalized and automatized," the greater part of Schumpeter's work refers to the entrepreneur as the bearer of technological change and thus of economic evolution, motivated by values and ethics (Bögenhold, 2010b). For Schumpeter, entrepreneurship is a social function and thus technology is an affair of the individual. Technological change is an affair of the community and thus a social function in Veblen. Habitus, field, and capital are all constituted of "bundles" of social ties in different states, embodied, objectified, institutionalized, and they all work most powerfully in relation to each other. All appear in the form of the individuals in Bourdieu's works, pushing Jenkins to conclude that Bourdieu does not have an adequate theory of institutions; on the contrary, he constructs them sociologically on the basis of data of the individuals that form part of them.

In the same vein, in his *Capitalism, Socialism and Democracy*, Schumpeter (1975, pp. 129–30) wrote that: "mankind is not free to choose ... things economic and social move by their own momentum and the ensuing situations compel individuals and groups to behave in certain ways whatever they may wish to do." In this framework, we believe that his late writings seem to recognize the limits that the social capital imposes on the individual and, in this vein, Schumpeter (1951, p. 153) argued that the choices open to individuals are by no means unlimited. In the same spirit, Bourdieu defined provoking power relations imposed upon all who enter the social field, irreducible to the intentions and will of the individual and incapable to be unveiled through the direct interactions among the agents.

For Veblen, institutional change, in that sense, is the response to changing cultural conditions in the same way that for Bourdieu there is always a time lag in the legitimation of the dominated from the struggle. The notion of struggle is common to all three theoreticians, either in the form of a struggle in the traditional Marxist sense between opposite classes as in Veblen, or in the form of a struggle in terms of power in the Foucauldian sense in Bourdieu, or in a more Darwinistic sense between entrepreneurs and their conservative surroundings in Schumpeter.

It should be noted that Schumpeter began to write in a social, political, theoretical, and ideological environment at a time when evolutionary ideas dominated social thought, whereas Veblen was inspired by a Marxist view of the Gilded Age of American capitalism; and Bourdieu was writing in an era dominated by new-classical economics and structuralist and post-structuralist sociology and philosophy. After all, in sociological terms, the "social capital" is always more than the sum of the individual capitals. In conclusion, the connection between Bourdieu, Veblen, and Schumpeter may be very useful for analysing the various readings of their works and for understanding other economic issues.

Notes

1. Of course, the theoretical threads that tie evolutionary and institutional thinking together may be said to have been drawn from Marxism. For instance, in relation to Veblen and Marx, there has been a longstanding controversy regarding the relationship between their theories. Walling (1905), for instance, emphasized the Marxian character of Veblen's thought, even though the majority of writers may seem to conclude that "Veblen was

not an American Marxist" (Corey, 1937, p. 168). On the other hand, Schumpeter too was called a "bourgeois Marx" by his famous teacher Eugene von Boehm-Bawerk. Of course, Bourdieu was a prominent structuralist Marxist, pronouncing that "the historical success of Marxist theory, the first social theory to claim scientific status that has so completely realized its potential in the social world" (Bourdieu, 1985, p. 742).

2. It is clear that Schumpeter was an institutional economist in scope and content but, possibly for reasons of ideology, world view and career, was loathe to admit it. Rather, he was avid in his desire to examine all points of view and to absorb everything that was good in them (Shionoya, 2008, p. 5). According to Shionoya (1997), his ambition was to create a "universal social science". Veblen understood the evolutionary sciences as being concerned with non-teleological processes of cumulative change and causation. Thus, he succeeded to study the competition of the units as a dynamic process and not as a stationary process (Liagouras, 2009, p. 1048). According to Swedberg (2011, p. 67), Bourdieu's analysis of the economy was developed over such a long time period, is so rich and goes in so many interesting directions, that we are justified in speaking of Bourdieu's economic sociologies in plural; while most sociologists know about Bourdieu's study Distinction (1986) and its analysis of consumption, there is less awareness of the fact that Bourdieu himself, towards the end of his life, said that he had produced three major studies of economic topics. These are: his work in Algeria on "the economy of honour and 'good faith'" (1950s and 1960s); his study of credit (Bourdieu, 1963); and his study of the economy of singlefamily houses (Bourdieu, 1999).
3. The "substantially animistic" attitude to the nature and direction of temporal sequences reduces economic theory to economic taxonomy: "a body of logically consistent propositions concerning the normal relation of things" (Veblen, 1898a, pp. 383–384).
4. Veblen blamed neo-classical and Austrian economics for their static and teleological methodology postulating equilibrium as the legitimated end of all economic phenomena (Veblen, 1898a, p. 382).
5. Veblen argued that socio-economic evolution must be regarded as a substantial unfolding of life (Veblen, 1897, p. 137), where "It is primarily the social system that would preserve or develop the capacity for change, not significantly the human genotype" (Veblen, 1990 [1914], p. 18). His understanding of the nature of capitalism is perhaps best expressed in the following quotations: "The economic life history of the individual is a cumulative process of adaptation of means to ends that cumulatively change as the process goes on, both the agent and his environment being at any point the outcome of the last process" (Veblen, 1898a, p. 391), emphasizing that "An evolutionary economics must be a theory of cumulative

sequence of economic institutions stated in terms of the process itself" (Veblen, 1898a, p. 393).

6. Schumpeter attributed the internal dynamics of capitalism to "a vision of the economic evolution as a distinct process generated by the economic system itself" (Schumpeter, 1911, p. 166). The idea of evolution is not only linked to economic development in isolation, but also to political, social and institutional changes, since the most characteristic purpose of his work was to analyse the evolution of capitalism as a civilization (Shionoya, 2008, p. 1). In fact, "the term evolution comprises all the phenomena that make an evolutionary process non-stationary" (Schumpeter, 1954, p. 965).
7. The use of economic analogies by Bourdieu has often been the object of criticism. For some scholars, it reveals an "economistic" vision of the social world, too much inspired by neoclassical economics. For other scholars, the economic analogy is a kind of mechanical metaphor, inspired by a holistic vision of society. His notions of interest, capital, and so on, are defined by objective class conditions, that is to say, by structural (or global) determinist dimensions. Individuals, especially artists and creators, are denied any singular capacity of creation and rational action corresponding to cognitive autonomous strategies or representations (Lebaron, 2003, p. 552).
8. This is the methodological position that aims to explain all economic phenomena in terms of the characteristics and the behaviour of individuals. We must reduce all collective phenomena to the actions, interactions, aims, hopes and thoughts of the individual (Popper, 1957, p. 88). The individualist contends that only individuals are responsible actors on the social and historical stage (Agassi, 1960, p. 244). In this context, Schumpeter considered it necessary to make a sharp distinction between political and methodological individualism, as the two concepts have nothing in common. The first refers to the freedom of people to develop themselves and to take part in well-being and to follow practical rules. The second just means that "one starts from the individual in order to describe certain economic relationships" (Schumpeter, 1908, pp. 90–91).
9. Legitimation is not instant and passive, it is the result of a struggle, determining for the dominated, seen a posteriori as hysteresis, for which Bourdieu's favourite example is the devaluation of educational credentials that, in his view, explain the student protest of May 1968. The result was a divergence between class habitus and the labour market simultaneously in a number of fields, so that their normally disparate temporal rhythms were synchronized, merging into a general crisis, conducted in a singular public time, producing an historical event that suspended common sense. Instead, we have a field of domination governing the struggle between the consecrated incumbents and the new challengers, the avant-garde (Burawoy, 2011, p. 5). The position of a given agent, within the social space, can thus

be defined by the positions he occupies in the different fields, that is, in the distribution of the powers that are active within each of them. These are, principally, economic capital (in its different kinds), cultural capital and social capital, as well as symbolic capital, commonly called prestige, reputation, renown, and so on, which is the form in which the different forms of capital are perceived and recognized as legitimate. The categories of perception of the social world are: the product of the internalization and the incorporation of the objective structures of social space. Consequently, they incline agents to accept the social world as it is, to take it for granted, rather than to rebel against it (Bourdieu, 1985, p. 728).

References

Agassi, J. (1960). Methodological Individualism. *British Journal of Sociology, 11*(3), 244–270.

Arena, R. (1992). Schumpeter after Walras: 'Economie pure' or 'stylised facts'? In T. Lowry (Ed.), *Perspectives on the History of Economic Thought* (Vol. VIII). Edward Elgar.

Argyrous, G., & Sethi, R. (1996). The Theory of Evolution and the Evolution of Theory: Veblen's Methodology in Contemporary Perspective. *Cambridge Journal of Economics, 20*(4), 475–495.

Benjaminsen, L. (2003). *Causality and Social Ontology—On Relational Structures and Cognitive Rationality.* 6th ESA Conference, Murcia 2003, Research Networks No. 21 Social Theory.

Bögenhold, D. (2007a). Bourdieu. In R. E. Weir (Ed.), *Encyclopedia of American Social Class* (Vol. I, pp. 91–92). Greenwood Press.

Bögenhold, D. (2007b). Creative Destruction. In R. E. Weir (Ed.), *Encyclopedia of American Class* (pp. 175–176). Greenwood Press.

Bögenhold, D. (2007c). Veblen. In R. E. Weir (Ed.), *Encyclopedia of American Social Class* (pp. 898–900). Greenwood Press.

Bögenhold, D. (2008). Economics, Sociology, History: Notes on Their Loss of Unity, Their Need for Re-integration and the Current Relevance of the Controversy between Carl Menger and Gustav Schmoller. *Forum for Social Economics, 37*(2), 85–101.

Bögenhold, D. (2010a). From Heterodoxy to Orthodoxy and Vice Versa: Economics and Social Sciences in the Division of Academic Work. *American Journal of Economics and Sociology, 69*(5), 1566–1590.

Bögenhold, D. (2010b). What Drives the Process of Creative Destruction?. In P. G. Michaelides (Ed.), Special Issue on: Technology and Economic Analysis. *Bulletin of Political Economy, 4*(2), 85–107.

Bögenhold, D. (2013). Social Network Analysis and the Sociology of Economics: Filling a Blind Spot with the Idea of Social Embeddedness. *American Journal of Economics and Sociology, 72*(2), 293–318.
Bögenhold, D. (2014). Schumpeter as a Universal Social Theorist. *Atlantic Economic Journal, 42*(3), 205–215.
Bögenhold, D. (2016). Joseph. A. Schumpeter (1883–1950). In G. Ritzer (Ed.), *Encyclopedia of Sociology* [2nd extended ed.]. Blackwell. https://doi.org/10.1002/9781405165518.wbeoss034.pub2
Bourdieu, P. (1963). Travail et travailleurs en Algérie. Mouton.
Bourdieu, P. (1977). *Outline of a Theory of Practice.* Cambridge.
Bourdieu, P. (1984). *Homo Academicus.* Polity Press.
Bourdieu, P. (1985). The Social Space and the Genesis of Groups. *Theory and Society, 14*(6), 723–744.
Bourdieu, P. (1999). *The Weight of the World: Social Suffering in Contemporary Societies.* Stanford University Press.
Bourdieu, P. (1997) [2000]. Pascalian Meditations. Polity Press.
Bourdieu, P. (1998) [2000]. Acts of Resistance: Against the Tyranny of the Market. Polity Press.
Bourdieu, P., & Wacquant, L. (1992). *An Invitation to Reflexive Sociology.* The University of Chicago Press.
Brette, O. (2003). Thorstein Veblen's Theory of Institutional Change: Beyond Technological Determinism. *European Journal of the History of Economic Thought, 10*(3), 455–477.
Burawoy, M. (2011). *Theory and Practice: Marx Meets Bourdieu.* http://burawoy.berkeley.edu/Bourdieu/3.Marx.pdf
Coats, A. W. (1954). The Influence of Veblen's Methodology. *Journal of Political Economy, 62*(6), 529–537.
Coleman, J. (1988). Social Capital in the Creation of Human Capital. *American Journal of Sociology, 94*, 95–120.
Corey, L. (1937). Veblen and Marxism. *Marxist Quarterly, 1*, 62–68.
Cramer, D., & Leathers, C. (1977). Veblen and Schumpeter on Imperialism. *History of Political Economy, 9*(2), 237–255.
Dugger, W. (1979). The Reform Method of John R. Commons. *Journal of Economic Issues, 13*(2), 369–381.
Ferrarotti, F. (1999). The Businessman as Protagonist in Veblen and Schumpeter. *International Journal of Politics, Culture and Society, 13*(2), 241–248.
Festre, A., & Garrouste, P. (2008). Rationality, Behavior, Institutional, and Economic Change in Schumpeter. *Journal of Economic Methodology, 15*(4), 365–390.
Frank, M. (1998). Schumpeter on Entrepreneurs and Innovation: A Reappraisal. *Journal of the History of Economic Thought, 20*(4), 505–516.

Freeman, C., & Louçã, A. (2001). *As Time Goes by: From the Industrial Revolution to the Information Revolution*. Oxford University Press.

Gurkan, C. (2005). *A Comparison of Veblen and Schumpeter on Technology*. STPS Working Papers No. 509. Ankara: Middle East Technical University.

Harris, A. (1934). Economic Evolution: Dialectical and Darwinian. *Journal of Political Economy, 42*(1), 34–79.

Harris, S. E., Haberler, G., Leontief, G. W., & Mason, E. S. (1951). Professor Joseph A. Schumpeter. *The Review of Economics and Statistics, 33*(2), 89–90.

Heilbroner, R. (2000). *The Worldly Philosophers: The Lives, Times and Ideas of the Great Economic Thinkers* (7th ed.). Penguin.

Jenkins, R. (1992). *Pierre Bourdieu*. Routledge.

Jevons, W. S. (1871). *Theory of Political Economy*. Macmillan.

Lebaron, F. (2003). Pierre Bourdieu: Economic Models against Economism. *Theory and Society, 32*(5–6), 551–565.

Liagouras, G. (2009). Socio-economic Evolution and Darwinism in Thorstein Veblen: A Critical Appraisal. *Cambridge Journal of Economics, 33*(6), 1047–1064.

Loesberg, J. (1993). Bourdieu and the Sociology of Aesthetics. *English Literary History, 60*(4), 1033–1056.

März, E. (1991). *Joseph Schumpeter: scholar, teacher and politician*. New Haven: Yale University Press.

O'Donnell, L. A. (1973). Rationalism, Capitalism, and the Entrepreneur: The Views of Veblen and Schumpeter. *History of Political Economy, 5*(1), 199–214.

Papageorgiou, T., Katselidis, I., & Michaelides, P. G. (2013). Schumpeter, Commons, and Veblen on Institutions. *The American Journal of Economics and Sociology, 72*(5), 1232–1254.

Papageorgiou, T., & Michaelides, P. G. (2016). Joseph Schumpeter and Thorstein Veblen on Technological Determinism, Individualism and Institutions. *The European Journal of the History of Economic Thought, 23*(1), 1–30.

Popper, K. R. (1957). *The Poverty of Historicism*. The Beacon Press.

Portes, A. (2000). The Two Meanings of Social Capital. *Sociological Forum, 15*(1), 1–12.

Rahim, E. (2009). Marx and Schumpeter: A Comparison of Their Theories of Economic Development. *Review of Political Development, 21*(1), 51–83.

Raines, P., & Leathers, C. (1993). Evolving Financial Institutions in Veblen's Business Enterprise System. *Journal of the History of Economic Thought, 15*(2), 249–264.

Rutherford, M. (1998). Veblen's Evolutionary Programme: A Promise Unfulfilled. *Cambridge Journal of Economics, 22*(4), 463–477.

Santarelli, E., & Pesciarelli, E. (1990). The Emergence of a Vision: The Development of Schumpeter's Theory of Entrepreneurship. *History of Political Economy, 22*(4), 677–696.

Schatzki, T. R. (1997). Practices and Actions: A Wittgensteinian Critique of Bourdieu and Giddens. *Philosophy of the Social Sciences, 27*(3), 283–308.
Schumpeter, J. (1908). *Das Wesen und der Hauptinhalt der theoretischen Nationalökonomie*. Duncker and Humblot.
Schumpeter, J. (1911). *Theorie der wirtschaftlichen Entwicklung*. Dunker Humbolt.
Schumpeter, J. (1951 [1927]). Die sozialen Klassen im ethnisch homogen Milieu. Archiv fur Sozialwissenschaft und Sozialpolitik, 57, 1–67.
Schumpeter, J. (1954). *History of Economic Analysis*. Oxford University Press.
Schumpeter, J. (1975 [1942]). *Capitalism, Socialism and Democracy*. Harper and Brothers.
Schumpeter, J. (1983 [1934]). The Theory of Economic Development. Harvard University Press.
Shionoya, Y. (1997). *Schumpeter and the Idea of Social Science: A Meta Theoretical Study*. Cambridge University Press.
Shionoya, Y. (2004). Scope and Method of Schumpeter's Universal Social Science: Economic Sociology, Instrumentalism, and Rhetoric. *Journal of the History of Economic Thought, 26*(3), 331–347.
Shionoya, Y. (2008). Schumpeter and Evolution: An Ontological Exploration. In Y. Shionoya & T. Nishizawa (Eds.), *Marshall and Schumpeter on Evolution: Economic Sociology of Capitalist Development*. Edward Elgar.
Swedberg, R. (2002). The Economic Sociology of Capitalism: Weber and Schumpeter. *Journal of Classical Sociology, 2*(3), 227–255.
Swedberg, R. (2011). The Economic Sociologies of Pierre Bourdieu. *Cultural Sociology, 5*(1), 67–82.
Turner, S. (2003). *The Cambridge History of Science: The Modern Social Science* (Vol. 7). Cambridge University Press.
Udehn, L. (2001). *Methodological Individualism: Background, History and Meaning*. Routledge.
Valiati, L., & Fonseca, P. C. (2014). Institutions and Culture: Thorstein Veblen's and Pierre Bourdieu's Economic Thought in Dialogue. *Iberian Journal of the History of Economic Thought, 1*(1), 1–17.
Veblen, T. (1897). Review of Max Lorenz. *Journal of Political Economy, 6*(1), 136–137.
Veblen, T. (1898a). Why Is Economics Not an Evolutionary Science? *Quarterly Journal of Economics, 12*(3), 373–397.
Veblen, T. (1898b). The Instinct of Workmanship and the Irksomeness of Labor. *American Journal of Sociology, 4*(2), 187–201.
Veblen, Thorstein. (1975). *The Theory of Business Enterprise* [orig. 1904]. New York: Augustus Kelley.
Veblen, T. (1906). The Socialist Economics of Karl Marx and His Followers I: The Theories of Karl Marx. *Quarterly Journal of Economics, 20*(3), 578–595.

Veblen, T. (1907). The Socialist Economics of Karl Marx and His Followers II: The Later Marxism. *Quarterly Journal of Economics, 21*(1), 299–322.

Veblen, T. (1909). The Limitations of Marginal Utility. *Journal of Political Economy, 17*(9), 620–636.

Veblen, T. (1967 [1923]). Absentee Ownership and Business Enterprise in Recent Times: The Case of America. Beacon.

Veblen, T. (1990 [1914]). *The Instinct of Workmanship, and the State of the Industrial Arts.* Transaction Books.

Veblen, T. (1990 [1919]). *The Place of Science in Modern Civilisation and Other Essays.* Transaction Books.

Veblen, T. (1994 [1899]). The Theory of the Leisure Class: An Economic Study in the Evolution of Institution. Macmillan.

Wacquant, L. (2002). Taking Bourdieu in the Field. *Berkeley Journal of Sociology, 46*, 180–186.

Walling, W. (1905). An American Socialism. *International Socialist Review, 5*, 577–578.

Walras, L. (1954 [1874]). Elements of Pure Economics or the Theory of Social Wealth. Routledge Library Editions.

Weik, E. (2010). Research Note: Bourdieu and Leibniz: Mediated Dualisms. *The Sociological Review, 58*(3), 486–496.

Zingler, E. (1974). Veblen vs Commons: A Comparative Evaluation. *Kyklos, 27*(3), 322–344.

Author Index[1]

[1] Note: Page numbers followed by 'n' refer to notes.

D. Bögenhold, *Neglected Links in Economics and Society*,
https://doi.org/10.1007/978-3-030-79193-3

Subject Index[1]

[1] Note: Page numbers followed by 'n' refer to notes.

D. Bögenhold, *Neglected Links in Economics and Society*,
https://doi.org/10.1007/978-3-030-79193-3

The manufacturer's authorised representative in the EU is Springer Nature Customer Service Centre GmbH, Europaplatz 3, 69115 Heidelberg, Germany. If you have any concerns regarding our products, please contact ProductSafety@springernature.com

Printed and bound by CPI Group (UK) Ltd, Croydon, CR0 4YY

30/09/2026

02225456-0006